THE LEAGUE OF WIVES

Also by Heath Hardage Lee

Winnie Davis:
Daughter of the Lost Cause

THE LEAGUE OF WIVES

The UNTOLD STORY *of the* WOMEN

WHO TOOK ON *the* U.S. GOVERNMENT

to BRING THEIR HUSBANDS HOME

HEATH HARDAGE LEE

CONSTABLE

CONSTABLE

First published in the US in 2019 by St Martin's Press

This edition published in Great Britain in 2019 by Constable

Copyright © Heath Hardage Lee, 2019

1 3 5 7 9 10 8 6 4 2

The moral right of the author has been asserted.

A CIP catalogue record for this book
is available from the British Library.

ISBN: 978-1-47213-178-2 (hardback)
ISBN: 978-1-47213-179-9 (trade paperback)

Designed by Donna Sinisgalli Noetzel

Printed and bound in Great Britain by Clays Ltd, Elcograf S.p.A

Papers used by Constable are from well-managed forests
and other responsible sources.

Constable
An imprint of
Little, Brown Book Group
Carmelite House
50 Victoria Embankment
London EC4Y 0DZ

An Hachette UK Company
www.hachette.co.uk

www.littlebrown.co.uk

*To the courageous wives of American prisoners
and missing in action of the Vietnam War:
"The First Ladies of America."*

CONTENTS

THE LEAGUE OF WIVES

PROLOGUE

PRESIDENT FRANKLIN DELANO ROOSEVELT surveyed the flat, sandy fields of North Island, on the Coronado peninsula, with an acquisitive eye. FDR, a former assistant secretary of the Navy, saw enormous potential in these jackrabbit-infested plains. Within a few weeks of his visit, the president issued an executive order clearing Coronado of its longtime Army presence and claiming the entire area for a new naval base. With war in the Pacific raging, the island would become a recognized cog in the military's success during World War II."[1]

Naval Amphibious Base Coronado was constructed on this barren spot in 1944, and Coronado was now the Navy's training base, its social center, and its incubator for outstanding pilots and their families. They flocked to the peninsula like migrating swallows, seeking out nesting grounds.

With its Spanish-themed architecture, swaying palm trees, and beautiful stretches of beach, Coronado must have seemed like an exotic Shangri-la to its new inhabitants. As the Navy's dominance grew, so did the tight-knit Navy community, which had its own unique rules and regulations. These rules created a military caste system whereby an officer's rank translated directly to his wife and family's status in this community. The commanding officer and his wife were at the top of the military heap. The men and women knew their place within the system and obeyed orders, both at work and at play. The crisp military element soon formed an essential part of the peninsula's cultural fabric.

In contrast to the rigid Navy presence, well-heeled jet-setters seeking Coronado's restorative climate made the town a destination for them: movie stars, politicians, even European royalty. Hollywood icons Jimmy Stewart, Clark Gable, and Katharine Hepburn flocked to the luxurious, red-turreted Hotel del Coronado to see and be seen. Or not . . . "Black eyes became all the rage there" when the hotel became the retreat of choice for Hollywood actresses recovering from face-lifts.[2] The classic comedy *Some Like It Hot*, starring Marilyn Monroe, Tony Curtis, and Jack Lemmon, was filmed at the hotel in 1958, enhancing the establishment's already glamorous reputation.[3]

"The Del," as the hotel came to be known to locals, boasted its own resident ghost, as well as gigantic crown-shaped light fixtures designed by *Wizard of Oz* author L. Frank Baum, a frequent visitor to Coronado and the hotel in the 1920s.[4] The formerly sleepy oceanfront town became a sun-drenched version of the Emerald City, with the Del as its palace and naval aviators crossing its skies in their F-8 fighter jets.

By the early 1960s, Coronado had plenty of Munchkins, too. Children ran rampant day and night all over A Avenue, where naval commander James Bond Stockdale, his wife, Sybil, and their four sons—Jim Jr., Sid, Stanford, and Taylor—lived. There were at least fifty-six kids living on the Stockdales' block when the boys were small. One family that lived close by had twelve children. Their mother made daily grocery store runs to feed her brood and had a drinking fountain installed in their home.[5]

The bridge across San Diego Bay that would connect the peninsula of Coronado to the city of San Diego in 1969 was not yet built.[6] Consequently, there was almost no traffic for mothers to worry about. The children were out day and night skateboarding, popping "wheelies" on their bikes, playing Frisbee, and happily avoiding adult supervision. The older kids surfed at Coronado Beach, where the Navy SEALs began doing training exercises in 1962.[7] Coronado in this era was straight out of a Beach Boys song: a small, idyllic Southern California town that looked like a Hollywood film set.

No one yet knew that the biggest drama the island peninsula would see would not be of the cinematic variety. Instead it would be born of the unexpected consequences of the Vietnam War—a conflict that would bring death to the island and wreak havoc on the lives of the town's high-flying Coronado Navy pilots, their wives, and their children.

During the lengthy Vietnam conflict (1965–1973) and even earlier, the Communist North Vietnamese would capture hundreds of American military pilots from Coronado and from all across the country. These men would become prisoners of war (POWs) for years or, even worse, would disappear forever as missing in action (MIA). Their wives, who worked tirelessly to save them, were told by their own government to "keep quiet" and to stay in the shadows, out of the media spotlight, until their government could bring the men home.

After years of silence, the ladies decided this approach simply would not do.

Over time, these military wives would take matters into their own hands, forever changing the course of their husbands' fates and American military culture. The story of these largely unknown heroines begins here in Coronado, with a reluctant sorority of women who would become more powerful and influential than they could ever have imagined.

One

THE RIGHT WIFE

IN THE 1960s, NAVY fighter pilots had a 23 percent likelihood of dying in an aircraft accident over a twenty-year career—not including combat deaths.[1] In order to survive in this line of work, a man had to possess an enormous ego—one that rivaled those of heads of state or Hollywood film stars. Confidence, a steady hand, and the idea that you could never, ever be shot down were requirements for anyone in this dangerous business. If you thought for more than two seconds about what you were doing, you would most likely end up dead—and kill everyone else on the plane with you.

A 1975 study in *Aviation, Space, and Environmental Medicine* on "the outstanding jet pilot" found that many successful pilots were first-born children with a close relationship with their father, "reinforcing 'positive male identification.'" Another finding from the same study noted that "21 of the first 23 astronauts who went on space flights were first born. The pilots were self-confident, showed a great desire for challenge and success and were non-introspective."[2] In author Tom Wolfe's famous words, these men were made of "the right stuff."

The right stuff extended beyond the professional into the personal; a pilot had to enjoy parties, since his time on earth might be short. He had to be able to hold his liquor (lots of it) at night, and then get up at the crack of dawn and climb into the cockpit before his morning coffee.

Finally, a pilot needed the right wife: attractive, kind, a model mother, and an excellent cook. Her job was to be sure he could do *his* job. The military cranked out training manuals for her that were every bit as rigorous as his. Each branch of the service put officers' wives through their own kind of basic training, advising the young women who married into the military on everything from their wedding-night lingerie to "Conversational Taboos at Social Gatherings." Women were judged on their abilities in the domestic sphere above all, and were given advice from senior wives, such as "The food you serve and the way you serve it are just as revealing as the kind of person you are as the house which is your background and the clothes you wear. It is fun to dream up new color combinations in both decorations and in foods."[3]

The Navy Wife was a government-approved guide to the rules of naval etiquette and hierarchy. A wife's status mirrored her husband's rank. Everything she did or said would reflect on him and could affect his career. More than one social faux pas in their byzantine world of calling cards, shrimp forks, and proper thank-you notes might result in a young officer getting "passed over" for a promotion. More serious offenses could even end in exile at some desolate military outpost. Most military wives realized that their "best interest (promotion, advancement, success in any form) was accomplished by playing within the rules." In this way, the wives were empowered to play a significant role in their husbands' careers, and thus in their own lives and those of their families.[4]

Customs from Victorian times still prevailed in the Navy and other service branches. The tradition of formal calls upon senior servicemen by junior officers and their wives was standard. Both the officer and his wife had their own calling cards, which had to be presented during "calling hours" at the home of the senior officer. Cards were typically left on a silver tray placed in the household just for this purpose. "A man leaves a card for each adult in the house . . . a woman never calls on a man, you leave cards only for the adult women of the household."[5]

Young Navy wives were cautioned, "Wives influence their husbands in many ways, and the excellence of a man's performance of duty has a direct relationship to the happiness and stability of his home life."[6] Army wives were cautioned, in their own *The Army Wife* protocol manual, not to be "a stone around his neck."[7]

The Air Force Wife manual laid out perhaps the most potent psychological message to young military wives: without a tranquil home life, disaster was just around the corner. A pilot's blood—and the blood of his colleagues—might just end up on his wife's hands. "It is said that domestic troubles have killed more aviators than motor failures, high-tension wires and low ceilings, so as an Air Force wife your responsibility is great and your job is of big proportions if you live up to the finest traditions of this Service."[8]

These military messages of exacting protocol created a powerful bond among the pilots' wives. While their husbands risked death in distant lands, their wives developed a code of support of their own that was reinforced in a positive manner by the military. These women were encouraged to cultivate "a kind of empathy unknown to civilian wives—an identification, a pride . . . in your husband's role."[9] Until the Vietnam War, however, many of these wives would have no idea how critical this support for one another would become.

If the Navy could have selected two people to represent the Ideal Fighter Pilot and the Ideal Fighter Pilot's Wife, Jim and Sybil Stockdale would have won the titles.

Commander James Bond Stockdale was born on December 23, 1923, in Abingdon, Illinois. He was the product of a solid midwestern upbringing, featuring football and the family farm. But from childhood on, Jim hungered for life beyond his small town. The tales that his father, Vernon, told about his life as a naval chief petty officer inspired his son to follow in his footsteps and soar even higher.

When Jim was seven, Vernon, who later became an executive in a china company, took him cross-country to the Naval Academy to see the midshipmen on parade. The pageantry made a deep impression on the boy, and from then on he dreamed of attending the academy. As an adult, Jim remembered, "From the time of my first memories, there had been no question about it: I would be going to Annapolis to make a career in the navy dad loved so much."[10]

After an illustrious high school career both on and off the football field, Jim was accepted into the Naval Academy class of 1947. There he would meet his lifelong friend, Alabama native Jeremiah Denton. Years later, Jim and Jerry would work together under incredible circumstances.[11]

Like her husband, Sybil Bailey had been raised in a rural setting, growing up in a white clapboard house on her family's prosperous dairy farm in New Haven, Connecticut. But Sybil's parents valued culture and the finer things, too. As a young girl, Sybil was obsessed with dance and adored her tap and ballet lessons. "If I'd had long legs and a liberated mother, I think I might have become a Rockette."[12] The Baileys made enough money to acquire a Victorian cottage in nearby Sunset Beach, where Sybil spent many summers fishing, sailing, and daydreaming about boys.

"My favorite fantasy was that I was really a royal princess, and that a handsome prince had already been chosen as my future husband." Although Sybil was privileged enough that she assumed she would always have help in her married home, her mother insisted that she needed to learn to cook—just in case. Sybil just laughed. *Leave that to the servants,* she thought.[13]

Very much against her will, Sybil was sent off to boarding school for her junior year in high school. To her mother's delight, she was accepted the next year into exclusive Mount Holyoke College, in South Hadley, Massachusetts, one of the "Seven Sisters" schools, the female counterparts to the Ivy League. While attending Mount Holyoke, Sybil would have often heard founder Mary Lyon's admonition to students: "Go where no one else will go, do what no one else will do." One day she would become one of the school's distinguished alumnae, but as a student, she majored in Cute Boys 101. Even so, she did well in her classes, pursuing a double major in history and religion.[14]

During her sophomore year, Sybil met the perfect roommate. Tall, blond, and stunning, Bebe Woolfolk was a native of Richmond, Virginia. She and Sybil found that they had many interests in common. Bebe recalled Sybil as a very determined person who "liked to run the show," and they would share many road trips in Sybil's beat-up convertible—as well as double dates—in college and beyond. After graduating from Mount Holyoke in January of 1946, the two young women shared an apartment in Richmond.

The former Southern Civil War capital was now awash with good-looking single men coming home from World War II. The fuel shortages that had put an end to road trips to male colleges during the war were gone, and the lack of eligible young men had now turned into a deluge of them. *So many men, so little time,* Bebe laughed as she recalled the era years later.[15]

They became teachers at the all-female St. Catherine's School, in West End, Richmond. Founded by notable educator Virginia Randolph Ellett in 1890, the school boasted Colonial Revival architecture, ivy-covered walls, and graceful brick arcades: an appropriate setting for the two recent Mount Holyoke graduates. Sybil taught modern dance and medieval history while Bebe taught typing. They also drove day students to and from school, monitored study hall, and chaperoned boarding students.

Jobs did not keep Sybil and Bebe from their primary objective: having fun while pursuing their respective "Mrs." degrees. "None of this slowed down my social life in the least," Sybil recalled. "Richmond is a social city, and Bebe introduced me to most of the young men returning home from World War II."[16]

The handsome prince Sybil had dreamed about during her girlhood was about to arrive, right on time.

On Easter weekend 1946, Sybil and Bebe went to Annapolis at the invitation of their teacher friend Anne Rogers. Anne was engaged to a student at the Naval Academy. She arranged blind dates for Sybil and Bebe, and the young women were giddy over the prospect of meeting dashing naval midshipmen.

In Sybil's version of the story, she and Bebe paired off by height with two young midshipmen: the taller, blond-headed Marvin Scoggins and the shorter, dark-haired Jim Stockdale. Bebe was very tall, and she towered over Jim, necessitating the pairing with Sybil. Bebe's tale is slightly different: "Sybil stepped right up to Jim! She knew!"[17] The newly minted couple found much to admire in each other—both were practical, driven, and organized.

It was a whirlwind courtship, and by March of 1947 Sybil and Jim were engaged, effectively putting an end to Sybil's teaching career. "I forgot not only classes, but chapel services I was supposed to conduct, and faculty meetings I was required to attend." Now, instead of preparing assignments for her students, Sybil had her nose in *The Navy Wife*.[18] Little did she know how much her life would deviate from this military protocol playbook as the years passed.

For now, she was just a romantic-minded young woman swept off her feet by blue-eyed James Bond Stockdale, an officer and a gentleman in a starched white Navy dress uniform. The couple married in Sybil's hometown, at the North Branford Congregational Church, on June 28, 1947.[19] The next day, the newlyweds flew to Key West so Jim could attend sonar school. Sybil's career as a Navy wife began with military precision—and no delays for a honeymoon.

Over the course of the 1950s, life in the Navy meant moves to Pensacola, Florida; Norfolk, Virginia; Patuxent, Maryland; and Los Altos, California (in what is now Silicon Valley). Sybil slid right into her new role as a wife, mother, and hostess. The relatively peaceful and prosperous fifties made for a fortunate time to gain her footing as a Navy wife.[20]

It was an era when filling that role still had a sepia-toned glow. "The world of a 1950s' officer's military wife was, outwardly seen, one of relative privilege: lovely brunches, civilized teas, over-the-top parties, proper hats, white gloves, silver tea services."[21] Women like Sybil and her peers also had the luxury of helping their husbands build their military careers without the life-and-death worries of wartime. Midcentury wives tended to have a heightened devotion to protocol and the rituals of military life, and this fixation would both help and hinder the way they dealt with what came their way.

For now, there was no reason to question this system and the Navy life that had been so good to her, Jim, and what would soon be the couple's four boys: Jim Jr. was born in 1950, Sid in 1954, Stanford in 1959, and baby Taylor in 1962. By the early sixties, Jim was the Navy commander, air group (CAG) of Screaming Eagles Fighter Squadron 51, and Sybil reigned in Coronado as the highest-ranking officer's wife. She was almost forty and had grown proficient at the military game. She knew from experience that "sociability was a professional requirement and practical necessity, as every officer's wife understood. It not only ameliorated the hardships of frequent moves, extended deployments, and imminent dangers that went with military life, it was essential to the business of advancing careers."[22]

Despite casting everything aside to become Mrs. CAG Stockdale, Sybil's sharp intelligence and natural love for education compelled her to do more. After she earned a master's degree from Stanford University in 1959, Jim followed suit, earning his own master's from Stanford in 1962. He became intensely interested in the Greek Stoics and their philosophy, studies that would later sustain him and even perhaps save his life.

In 1962, the couple moved to Coronado, where Jim was assigned to a fighter squadron in San Diego. While he was deployed in April of 1964, Sybil bought a charming Tudor cottage at 547 A Avenue that reminded her of her childhood home. Family life was heaven. The beach, the sunny and temperate weather, and the warm camaraderie among the Navy families made for smooth sailing.

Jim and Sybil had arrived. She liked to imagine that Peter Pan was watching their happy family life through the English windows of their snug new home. She felt protected, safe, and content.[23]

Inevitably, Jim's next deployment arrived. To his chagrin, he had just missed action in the Korean War. This time, he was determined not to miss out on the action bubbling up in Southeast Asia. He was a fighter pilot, and warfare was what he was trained for.

In the weeks prior to his 1964 departure for Vietnam, Jim headed to the San Diego mountains for Survival, Evasion, Resistance, and Escape (SERE) school. All officers assigned to combat zones went through this program, created in 1962 by American prisoners from the Korean War.[24] The tenets of the course were based on the U.S. military's Code of Conduct, especially Article 3, which provided the SERE acronym and applied especially to prisoners of war: "If I am captured I will continue to resist by all means available. I will make every effort to escape. I will accept neither parole nor special favors from the enemy." The men were all trained to live—and die if necessary—by this Code.[25]

The men were sent deep into the mountains northeast of San Diego to play a 1960s military version of *The Hunger Games*. The lessons were top secret. SERE was known to provide "a grim crash course in what to expect as a downed pilot in hostile territory."[26]

In the unlikely scenario that any of them were captured (most pilots found this idea laughable; a good aviator would *never* get shot down), the course taught the trainees coping strategies. They learned how to outsmart, outwit, and outlast the enemy. Korean War vets serving as trainers advised the SERE newbies that if the men could resist their jailers for just a few months, they would be home free. The enemy would eventually give up when they saw how tough American military men were.

Jim returned home, dusty and physically and mentally worn out from his SERE training. Despite his exhaustion, he may have secretly chuckled to himself at the thought that, compared with what Sybil was doing at home, managing four active, rambunctious boys, SERE school might have been the easier assignment.[27]

As CAG of the VF-51 Screaming Eagles, based out of Naval Air Station Miramar, north of San Diego, Jim decided the time had come for a "traditional (a little wild) old time aviator" party.[28] He and Sybil planned the be-all, end-all bash for his men at 547 A Avenue in December of 1964, celebrating their return from a Gulf of Tonkin deployment on the USS *Ticonderoga*. Their next deployment, on the USS *Oriskany* (dubbed by Navy men "the Big Risk"), was not far off: they would leave for Asia again in April of 1965.

The Stockdales rolled up the rugs, hired a local rock band, threw their French doors open to the outside, and set up a well-stocked bar for their guests. G&Ts (a Sybil favorite), manhattans, sidecars, and Harvey Wallbangers flowed freely.

That evening, the Screaming Eagle pilots drove up in Corvettes, sporting trim flight suits and accompanied by their pedal-pusher-clad wives and girlfriends. Here on the West Coast, things were much more casual than on the stuffy East Coast, even in military circles. The band played surf music and hits from 1964: Jan and Dean and the Beach Boys.[29] A Beatle wig made the rounds, passing from one pilot's head to another as the party gained momentum. Sybil ended up in the middle of the crowd, dancing with a six-foot-three pilot named Bud Collicott, who sported the Beatle wig.

Bud later carried Sid, the second Stockdale son, on his shoulders, giving the boy a bird's-eye view of the scene. Sid remembered the night vividly, recalling a roomful of "pilots at the top of their game having a good party before they deployed."[30] His older brother, Jim, said, "I think they were all completely sure they were invincible . . . It was as close as Mom and Dad ever came to hosting a blowout."[31]

These pilots were surfing the wave of military life with ease, riding high thanks to frequent parties, copious amounts of alcohol, and their own naturally high levels of testosterone. They tended to overlook any clouds on the horizon and considered themselves immune from mortal ills like the death and destruction of war.

Later, however, they would find themselves feeling like a squadron of Icaruses flying too close to the sun.

Two

IT CAN'T HAPPEN TO US . . .

ON THE NIGHT OF Saturday, July 17, 1965, thirty-nine-year-old military wife and mother Jane Denton sat in the darkness with her three youngest children, Mike, Madeleine, and Mary Beth, at the Virginia Beach Drive-In Theater. The family had just arrived to see *Mary Poppins*, the Disney blockbuster that was sweeping the nation. The 1950s-era drive-in was just a few miles from the beach, attracting moviegoers from many Navy families who lived and worked around Naval Air Station Oceana as well as the summer tourist crowd.[1] Jane's job description was essentially the same as that of her fictional counterpart on the screen that night: like Mary Poppins, she was on duty twenty-four hours a day while her Navy pilot husband, Commander Jeremiah "Jerry" Denton, was away on a nine-month deployment to Vietnam.

The young members of the "M Society" (composed of Mike, Madeleine, and Mary Beth, with "Mom" Jane being the "founding" member) were thrilled to have some time alone with their busy mother who was consumed with the household duties of managing her small army of seven children. The four older children, Jerry III, Don, Jim, and Billy, were constantly busy with sports and school activities. Jane was a pretty brunette with milky skin and luminous brown eyes. But she often felt older than her years trying to manage her boisterous brood alone.

Jane kept telling herself that the war in Southeast Asia would soon be over and that Jerry would be back home with the family by Christmas. But something deep within her was fearful for their future. Tonight, in the darkness of the theater, her inner radar picked up signals that something was wrong. She went from feeling unsettled one minute to experiencing a gut punch of panic the next. A terrible sense of foreboding engulfed her. She remembered that "a strange feeling of dread and fear came over me and I lost my composure and confidence for the first time since Jerry left. I panicked and wept in the dark there. Was this a premonition? It was between 10 and 11 PM when this took place and the feeling persisted after the tears stopped."[2]

Jane was a seasoned military wife used to being alone for months at a time while her husband was deployed. She was not prone to hysterics and had proven her mettle, making numerous moves at home and abroad for her husband's career. She was now happily settled in the big white house at 3125 Watergate Lane in Virginia Beach. But her instinct told her that her settled Navy family home life was about to change drastically.

The next day, her intuition proved to be spot-on.

Jane had woken up early that Sunday morning, written Jerry a letter, and taken all seven children to Mass. She was a fervent Catholic, and her religion gave her solace, comfort, and a place where (*thank you, God*) the children had to be quiet, if only for that one hour on Sundays. The family had just returned home when the doorbell rang.

"Mom! Someone's here to see you!" yelled her son Billy. Jane's heart stopped. She took a deep breath and rushed down the stairs. Standing before her were Captain Stuart "Stu" Nelson and his pretty blond wife, Barbara. What Nelson told her next was the news she had been dreading: Jerry had been shot down during the bombing of the port facility of Thanh Hóa, in North Vietnam. The "good" news was that he had been spotted ejecting from his plane with his parachute and had made it safely to shore. Now the search was on, but a rescue scenario did not seem likely.[3] Jane was in shock upon receiving the news. As the hours passed, she began to tap into her deep Catholic faith to keep herself calm.[4]

After falling from the humid tropical skies over Vietnam, forty-one-year-old Navy pilot Jeremiah "Jerry" Denton was enraged.

Jerry and his bombardier and friend Lieutenant William "Bill" Tschudy were shot down by enemy fire, ejecting successfully from their A-6 Intruder aircraft. Jerry emerged, wet and dripping, on a riverbank to find himself surrounded by North Vietnamese soldiers who gestured at him menacingly with rifles and machetes. His fighter pilot mentality kicked in instantly: "Dazed and bleeding as I was, my principal emotion was fury. I was mad as hell at being shot down, and even angrier at being captured."[5]

Bill had parachuted down perfectly from the aircraft. He remembered it being "very quiet on the way down; I didn't hear a thing for a good while. The noise increased the closer I got to the ground." The American pilot landed on his feet in a village hamlet, surrounded by palm trees. He was rushed by villagers, who immediately stripped him of all of his clothes but his underwear. They forced Bill to walk barefoot for about a mile, to a small enclosure. Inside, he was shocked to see Jerry Denton sitting in a motorcycle sidecar. His leg was injured and propped up.

Bill recalled Jerry saying, "How are you?" Bill blurted out the first thing that came into his mind: "I'm sore!" He hoped later that Jerry did not think he was angry—he just didn't know what else to say.

That night, both men were taken in separate trucks to Hanoi. Jerry later said he heard Bill making noises that night. Bill could not see or hear Jerry. They would not meet again until 1973.[6]

Back in Virginia Beach, Jane's support crew quickly appeared. Her dear friend from college, Kitty Clark, flew down immediately. Local Navy wives and neighbors mobilized to help with childcare and meals. Both Jane's and Jerry's families in Mobile, Alabama, were notified. As after a funeral, a whirl of casseroles, phone calls, letters, and telegrams overwhelmed the newly minted MIA wife. Perhaps due to her proximity to Oceana naval base, everyone seemed to know the situation—and Jane's predicament. Jerry was one of the early shoot-downs, and the protocol for handling these situations quietly didn't seem to be in place—yet—in Virginia Beach.

On Monday, July 19, the scenario became even more surreal when two letters that Jerry had posted before he was shot down arrived. Jane wrote in her diary: "Had two letters from Jerry today—wonderful, comforting ones. During last night I realized in my heart that Jerry was not going to be picked up and prepared myself for the news that the search had been cancelled. Tonight Captain Nelson brought that news and details of the flight. God helps me to bear what seemed unbearable. My sister arrived tonight. Our children are wonderful and strong. The younger ones (Mal & Mike) are with friends (Carvers)."

The next day, July 20, would have been Jerry's change-of-command day. Another letter from the lost pilot arrived at the Dentons' Watergate Lane home. Jane remembered the phone ringing constantly and insistently, demanding her attention. Casseroles continued to flood the household until there was no more room in her refrigerator to hold them all. Jane fervently wished she could send Jerry that food—food she and her children neither needed nor wanted. Instead she arranged a special Mass for Jerry. And they all continued to pray. The next few days passed in a blur, in the same manner. Jane recalled, "I went through the motions. God helped me maintain calm for the most part."

An official telegram arrived, special delivery, on July 23, confirming the news. Though Jerry had been sighted landing in a small village area, he had been declared missing in action. "It is with utmost regret I must inform you that the report further states that the extensive search by the Navy and Air Force has failed to locate any trace of your husband since 18 July 1965."[7]

The same day she received the telegram, Jane also saw the first photo of Jerry in captivity. She already saw evidence in the picture of how he was being treated by his captors. She wrote again in her diary: "Jerry's picture was released by Com. in Tokyo. It was dreadful and I fear that he is being inhumanely treated. God help him. I saw the picture on TV at noon. Later I went to 7–11, bought a paper, kept it folded until I got to church where I sat in the back pew and opened it to see my love's poor face on the first page. I prayed. I then went by Fr. Summer's rectory and sought comfort. Then back home to my wonderful family."[8]

Though Jerry and Bill had been assigned to work together in Vietnam, their wives had not yet met. There had been a squadron party at the Oceana Officers' Club before the two men deployed. Both couples had attended the party, but somehow Jane and Janie had missed meeting each other there.

A chic, friendly young woman with a pixie haircut and sparkling blue eyes, Janie Tschudy had been in Northern Michigan visiting her family when the news of the shoot-down hit. She and her son, Michael, had gone to the beach that day with Janie's niece Casey. It was a windy, overcast day, and Janie had an unsettling feeling that something was off. Nothing she could put her finger on, but she felt her composure slipping, and the three arrived home early from their outing.

"Janie, you need to eat!" her mother exclaimed.

"Mother, I'm not really hungry," Janie insisted.

"No, you have to eat. I made a pot roast!"

So Janie and Michael dutifully ate. After they finished, Janie's parents told her the news. Debbie Snead, the wife of Bill's CO (commanding officer), had called Janie's father earlier that day to tell him that Bill and Jerry had been shot down and were missing. "That was it. There was no more to go on," Janie remembered.

A few days later, Janie was on her way back to Virginia Beach with Michael. Her whole world had just fallen completely to pieces. Her instinct had told her something was wrong that day at the beach, but she had no idea of the impact this would have on her life from this day forward. She spent several days with Michael at a friend's house in Virginia Beach. Then Debbie Snead took her to meet her fellow MIA wife Jane Denton.

There was no awkwardness. The two women talked for hours about their husbands and their mutual predicament. Jane had seven children, Janie just one. Jane was thirty-nine, and Janie was twenty-seven. Jane was a seasoned Navy wife, Janie just a newbie. But these differences, their husbands' ranks, their places in the military wife hierarchy—it all fell away. Such things were usually a barrier to communication— younger wives were often afraid to talk to higher-ranking officers' wives—but none of that mattered now. The women became instant friends and confidantes.[9]

On Friday, an ominous broadcast hit the airwaves from the Communist capital of Hanoi, announcing that two American pilots had been "sent by McNamara [President Lyndon B. Johnson's secretary of defense] personally, and would be treated as imperialist criminals."[10] Jane and Janie both heard the pronouncement. The two women were so stunned at this point that neither knew quite how to react.

Jane and Janie continued to observe the social graces prescribed during emergencies. They graciously hosted hordes of company and sent thank-you notes for the Jell-O fruit salads, tomato aspic (the children all gagged when confronted with this dish), and Bundt cakes drizzled with frosting.

Southern women like Jane were exceptionally well trained in the exhausting custom of entertaining others during times of mourning. It was just what you did—there were (and still are) whole cookbooks devoted to recipes for the bereaved. Jane and Janie's situation was like a living death—no one (including their own government) knew exactly what had happened to their men. Everyone assumed the worst. Well-meaning friends continued to flow in. Jane wished everyone would go away and leave her to her own private grief.[11]

After almost four months apart, Sybil arrived in Tokyo's Haneda Airport on July 24, 1965, ecstatic to see her husband. Jim was on a nine-month deployment to Japan on the USS *Oriskany*. Stanford, Sid, Taylor, and Jim Jr. were deposited with their grandparents so the couple could enjoy a romantic reunion. Sybil could not wait to see her husband. This vacation would be a welcome respite from her four rambunctious boys. Sybil adored them, but she had to manage them like a drill sergeant to keep the peace. Being a military wife meant being a single parent for long stretches. Sybil could not imagine being able to maintain her sanity without her work tutoring elementary school children and her local friends.

Within a few days of Sybil's arrival in Japan, the Stockdales attended a champagne reception at the Atsugi Officers' Club. A huge ice sculpture of a Navy plane rose above the crowd as the centerpiece. Life on base and within the naval community there seemed idyllic. The couple enjoyed sunset cocktail parties in lovely Japanese gardens, shopping in the upscale Ginza district, massages, and Japanese hot baths together.[12] It was truly paradise.

A side trip to the seaside town of Atami provided an unexpected window into Japan and its history. Sybil and Jim's cook during their stay told them in halting English that her husband had been killed by American bombs in World War II. She mentioned this offhandedly, and seemingly without animosity. The next day, Jim looked out their hotel window and pointed to the hills. "You know, that fellow who speaks English told me there was a Japanese prison camp right there in those hills during the war." A hotel worker who spoke English had mentioned this to him the previous day. "Kind of gives you an eerie feeling, doesn't it?"[13] Sybil didn't give this history lesson a second thought. World War II was ages ago. The past was over, and Japan now seemed to embrace the American military men—and their wives. They seemed to welcome their presence and their business on the island.

After their seaside visit to Atami, they decided to journey to the mountains near Hakone. They lodged at the famous Fujiya Hotel. Sybil remembered Jim holding her "with extra gentleness and closeness as we danced to the haunting strains of 'Beyond the Reef.' If life could stand still forever, I thought, I'd have it do so now." All too soon, the Stockdales found their leave together coming to an end.

A few days later, Jim checked in with his fellow officers at the officers' club. After a few beers with his buddies, they revealed that his Naval Academy classmate Jerry Denton had been shot down and captured just a few days earlier. A melancholy mood descended over the club and the revelry quickly subsided. Denton was an experienced, highly skilled naval aviator. Clearly, it was not just the young, hotshot pilots who were getting shot down.

Before Sybil flew home, Jim bought her a beautiful strand of pale blue baroque pearls as a Christmas gift. The couple agreed that he would bring them home to her at Christmas, when his deployment ended. As Sybil departed for her flight home, the couple said one final "I love you" and walked away from each other. They had mutually agreed not to look back.[14]

In Virginia Beach, Jane continued to deal with the news of Jerry's shoot-down. She didn't wait long—only eight days—to head to Washington to see what else she could learn from the top. Jane was one of the first POW wives to use her D.C. connections to obtain additional information. Her college friend Kitty Clark, who worked at the State Department as a congressional liaison, provided a conduit for Jane to find out more about her missing husband.[15] At this point, only a small number of aviators had been shot down, but the numbers would continue to steadily increase as the American bombing campaigns in Vietnam intensified.[16]

Despite her visit to Washington, Jane was the last person on earth who wanted to "rock the boat" or make any kind of waves in her Navy community. She was a southern lady from a genteel family in Mobile, Alabama, who avoided attention. Jane had been raised with the adage that a lady's name should appear in print three times only: at birth, marriage, and death.

Jane and Jerry were very much a couple of their era in 1965. They each played their assigned roles just as society expected them to. She had left Mary Washington College, in Fredericksburg, Virginia, two years early to marry Jerry at the U.S. Naval Academy. From this time on, Jane was a devoted, dutiful Navy wife. Her husband gave her high marks for her positive attitude: "From the day I married her," Jerry once said, "she was an ideal Navy Wife, and was later elected President of many Officers' Wives Clubs. She put up with many common Navy Wife hardships with a smile and was a tremendous boost to my morale."[17] Jane had played the role of traditional, conservative wife well, pleasing her more dominant husband. But the thought of losing Jerry was enough to set a fire under Jane. She couldn't just sit there and accept the role of the helpless military wife—she was capable and resourceful. She had to find out what else she could do to get him back home.

On Monday, July 26, Jane drove to Washington with her old friend Doris Beatty. She and Jerry had met Doris and her husband, Navy doctor Ralph Beatty, when the couples were stationed together at Villefranche-sur-Mer, in the South of France. In 1956, Jerry and Ralph joined forces to create the "Haystack concept," which made aircraft carriers more difficult to find during times of combat. Thanks to Haystack, Jerry and Ralph achieved a measure of fame and respect among their peers. This experience together had created a bond between the men and subsequently between their wives. As a fellow Navy wife, Doris knew better than most the dangers Jerry faced and the fallout Jane was dealing with on the home front.[18]

Despite the seriousness of the situation, Jane made sure to get her hair done before her meetings at the State Department. Appearances were crucial. Her hairdo was lacquered firmly in place when she arrived for her meetings. More important, she made and organized pages of her notes, preparing her questions in advance.

On Wednesday morning, Jane went to work with Kitty, who had facilitated numerous introductions on her friend's behalf. Jane was pleased that Ambassador Leonard Unger, the ambassador to Laos, was most considerate and interested in Jerry. She wrote her questions and his answers down in her notebook. She also saw Walter Jenkins at the State Department, an old U.S. Naval War College friend of her husband's.

The next day, Jane was escorted by Captain Julian Lake to the Pentagon, where she met with Admiral Hare, second in command in the Judge Advocate General's office. This meeting led to a visit to the Bureau of Naval Personnel (BuPers), where Captain Bob Baldwin had scheduled appointments for Jane. She met with Captain Higgins, Commander Jenkins, and Mr. Miller in the Casualty Assistance office. The men showed her more releases of information concerning Jerry and Bill, answered her questions, and discussed the situation further with Jane. They day was capped off with a short but sympathetic meeting with Vice Admiral Benedict "B. J." Semmes Jr., the chief of BuPers.

After this exhausting round of interviews at the Pentagon, Jane retreated to the Beattys' home in Washington. Chaplain Leon S. Darkowski came to the Beattys' that night to visit with Jane. Coincidentally, that very week, he was escorting a priest from South Vietnam around D.C. "I wonder if we could help your husband through my contact?" suggested Darkowski. Jane's heart leapt—this might be an additional way to gather information, she thought. However, the Navy quickly discouraged this plan. As Jane later reported in her diary, "The chaplain checked on this idea, and it was decided that such a move might do more harm than good."[19]

Jane was determined to follow the U.S. government rules to the letter. She was terrified of deviating from protocol in any way. The priest from South Vietnam represented a tempting opportunity for information gathering, but it was too far off the beaten path for her to risk it.

Jane returned on August 10 for another series of meetings, beginning with one at the American Red Cross headquarters. In foreign wars, the International Red Cross was (and still is) authorized to act as a conduit for communications between prisoners of war and their families back home. The Geneva Conventions of 1949 also defined the rights and privileges of prisoners of war. Jane expected the men's North Vietnamese jailers to abide by these rules.[20] But as Bill Tschudy would explain years later, "the Red Cross was forbidden to set foot in North Vietnam" by the Communists.[21] The signs were there, even at this point, that the Red Cross was not making any inroads on behalf of captured Americans.

When Jane met with Samuel Krakow, director of the Office of International Services for the American Red Cross, and Winston Henry, adviser to the vice president on Red Cross matters, she was immediately struck by how ill at ease the two men seemed. She later wrote, "We sat on a sofa, they seemed uncomfortable—for all their impressive titles, they were pretty helpless." They showed her letters that had been written on behalf of Jerry and Bill to the International Red Cross: predictably, there had been no response from the North Vietnamese.

Jane next met with Henry Hall Wilson, LBJ's liaison to the House. He was no more helpful than the Red Cross reps and less sympathetic. Wilson warned her, in his condescending manner, "If you try pushing too many buttons, you can mess up the switchboard." Jane wrote later that he had instructed her to go home to her family and "stop trying to punch buttons myself because the best qualified people would be doing it for me."[22] This bitter pill, meant to tranquilize Jane, only fired her up more. Still, she took Wilson's dubious advice and left. Jane wasn't yet sure what rules to follow, and she still felt that Jerry would want her to follow Navy guidelines to the letter. She decided that for now, adhering to military protocol was all she could do to help her captured husband, but she wasn't going to wait forever.

In 1965, Vietnam was still seen by most Americans as a faraway war in a small country that could not possibly pose a significant threat to the U.S. military. At this point, many pilots going into the conflict saw a Vietnam deployment as an opportunity to try out state-of-the-art F-4 Phantom jets and A-6 Intruders. Some U.S. Navy and Air Force pilots considered their Vietnam tours to be joyrides from which they would emerge triumphant. This assumption would prove tragically incorrect.

By 1966 the number of POWs was increasing due to LBJ's intensified bombing campaign, Operation Rolling Thunder, which involved constant airstrikes. That year saw 105 officers shot down, and their numbers continued to grow. They joined 102 of their fellow servicemen in captivity, some of whom had been held since 1961 in the filthy Vietnamese prison system.[23]

Despite this scenario, both Jim Stockdale and Jerry Denton deployed to Vietnam never suspecting the extent to which the country would turn out to be a black hole for pilots, an endless war, and a political quagmire for the United States. Stockdale and many other pilots flew dozens of bombing missions over Vietnam unscathed. Like soldiers in the American Civil War, most American pilots believed this war would be short and over in a matter of months.

Why were American military men sent to this Southeast Asian hinterland to begin with?

This war in Vietnam between the Vietnamese and outside powers wasn't the first. The French had fought unsuccessfully against a colonial rebellion by the North Vietnamese in what was known as the First Indochina War, losing spectacularly at the Battle of Dien Bien Phu in 1954.

When the French were not able to reestablish control of Vietnam, U.S. president and former general Dwight Eisenhower warned Americans that if North Vietnamese Communist leader Ho Chi Minh and his new regime were allowed to grow unchecked, and if one Southeast Asian country fell to Communism, so might other countries surrounding it. This "domino theory" became the foreign policy base from which the U.S. government would operate for decades to come.[24]

Despite their awareness of the bloody French defeat in Vietnam, Americans unhesitatingly plunged into the Vietnam abyss for round two. The Vietnam War would prove to be the longest war in American history until the U.S. conflict in Afghanistan began in 2001.[25] In September of 1954, the United States and its allies (France, Great Britain, New Zealand, Australia, the Philippines, Thailand, and Pakistan) created SEATO (the Southeast Asia Treaty Organization), joining forces with the Republic of Vietnam (i.e., South Vietnam) against the Communist forces of the North Vietnamese Army (NVA), controlled by Ho Chi Minh, and those of the Viet Cong (VC), based in the South.

U.S. involvement in the region escalated in the 1960s during President John F. Kennedy's administration. Though the United States had strongly supported South Vietnam's first president, Ngo Dinh Diem, since his 1955 inauguration, the American government began to recoil from the regime as the political situation in South Vietnam deteriorated. On May 8, 1963, Diem's soldiers fired on Buddhist protesters at

Hue, killing eight people, six of them women. Buddhist monks burned themselves to death in protest. Diem's minority Catholic regime brutally repressed and openly discriminated against those from the Buddhist majority. After repeated warnings from the U.S. government, JFK, his ambassador Henry Cabot Lodge Jr., and others in the JFK cabinet decided Diem was on his way out. In early November of 1963, the United States facilitated his demise by handing him over to the South Vietnamese military.[26]

According to historian Luke Nichter, "What we did was to provide important signals to the South Vietnamese, who did want Diem toppled and gone—and some thought killing him was the only way to make sure he stayed gone—as well as different types of logistical support . . . We effectively provided the gun, but they pulled the trigger. We were an accomplice to murder, but not the murderers."[27]

Consequently, it was found that JFK himself had "engineered a cover-up [of the Diem coup] and ordered incriminating cables at the State Department, the CIA, and the Defense Department destroyed."[28] When JFK was assassinated that November, his vice president, Lyndon B. Johnson, not only inherited the presidency—he also inherited the problematic Vietnam conflict, with all its bloody, complex diplomatic history.

Former U.S. national security adviser, U.S. Army lieutenant general, and military historian H. R. McMaster claims that LBJ inherited a dysfunctional military structure created by his predecessor. When Kennedy took office in 1961, he dramatically altered President Dwight Eisenhower's National Security Council (NSC) structure. The result was that the Joint Chiefs of Staff (JCS) had a much diminished voice regarding national security matters in both the Kennedy and Johnson governments.

This would prove to be a fatal flaw in decision-making going forward. "Kennedy's structural changes," McMaster wrote, "his practice of consulting frankly with only his closest advisors, and his use of larger forums to validate decisions already made would transcend his own administration, and continue as a prominent feature of Vietnam decision-making under Lyndon Johnson."[29] Both JFK and LBJ were wary of accepting input from the Joint Chiefs due to the failed Bay of Pigs invasion and the narrowly averted nuclear conflict with the Soviet Union during the Cuban Missile Crisis.[30]

The preeminent issue on the Johnson agenda from 1963 on was the outcome of the 1964 presidential election. What mattered most to Johnson was winning. "He wanted to be viewed as a 'moderate' candidate, so he resolved to take only those actions in Vietnam that bolstered his image."[31] Vietnam was an issue to keep under control, off the table and out of the American public's mind as much as possible.

LBJ's Republican presidential challenger, Arizona senator Barry Goldwater, repeatedly accused LBJ in the press of not being tough on Communism and being soft on national security issues.[32] Johnson's close advisers, like "Whiz Kids" Robert McNamara, Dean Rusk, and McGeorge Bundy (all holdovers from the Kennedy coterie of intellectuals),[33] agreed that their president could not seem weak or indecisive on the Vietnam War issue—not for the sake of American soldiers, but because he needed to keep his poll numbers up.

Johnson's secretary of defense, McNamara was the former president of the Ford Motor Company and one who, in his own words, came to the Pentagon with "a limited grasp of military affairs and even less grasp of covert operations."[34] A superb number cruncher, McNamara tended to ignore gut feelings, military intelligence, and military experience in favor of pure data. Historian David Halberstam characterized McNamara's approach to the Vietnam War as "the quantifier trying to quantify the unquantifiable."[35] Human emotions were taken out of McNamara's equations in favor of a "just the facts" approach. This would prove a fatal mistake.

This lack of interface between civilian and military in Washington extended to and encompassed those on the domestic military front. The wives, mothers, and other family members of lost military men were seen not as bereaved individuals who needed comforting but as the stuff of public relations nightmares, and potential liabilities for the POWs. Janie Tschudy remembered how State Department officials would act when they saw the POW or MIA wives in Washington. "Oh, no, here they come! They did not want us to rock the boat." At the beginning of the conflict, most American government officials were patronizing, placating, or just plain disinterested in the women's plight.[36]

As the POW and MIA wives would soon find out, the government departments they appealed to for help during the Johnson era were suspicious of one another and divided into military and civilian adviser camps. Instead of working together to help the bereaved families, American bureaucrats seemed to be focused on proprietary political wars against one another, making it difficult to obtain information about the missing or imprisoned men. Former deputy assistant secretary of defense Richard Capen remembered, "There was always friction between the State Department and the Defense Department. This got worse under Johnson as the Vietnam War went on."[37]

This problem again had its roots in the Kennedy administration. During JFK's presidential tenure, "a relationship of mutual distrust between senior military officials and civilian officials" had developed.[38] Under President Johnson, the divide continued to grow. The two groups and their respective departments began to build their policies in separate silos.[39] Many Vietnam POW wives, like Janie Tschudy, would later witness this split firsthand: "The war was run not by the military but by Washington," noted Janie. "The State Department and elected officials who had to please their constituents."[40]

Janie, Jane, and, later, other POW and MIA wives were dropped without warning into the alien landscape of Washington, much as their husbands were in Vietnam. The women had to negotiate a complex and secretive political climate that spoke in what would at first sound like a foreign language to them. Military and government doublespeak filled the women's ears with reassurances that the government knew exactly what was going on with the men, but at this stage information on the situation was scarce and incomplete. What would later be called "mansplaining" was almost always how men in power communicated with women. It would not even have been remarked upon or noticed. At the start of their predicament, POW and MIA wives accepted the men's word—and that of their government—without too many questions.

And most didn't care enough to do much about the ladies' plight. As POW wife Debby Burns Henry explained, unless you had a family member who was a POW or MIA and the issue directly affected you, Vietnam was just a faraway war that no one cared to know much about.[41] The country preferred to remain in denial and easily could, with the issue being so unpopular and so removed from American daily life.

In addition, the number of POWs captured in Vietnam would ultimately be relatively small compared with those captured in World War II and in the Korean War—and most were officers, not enlisted men. Although there were Army and Marine POWs, most Vietnam War POWs were Navy or Air Force pilots captured after F-4 Phantoms, A-4 Skyhawks, and, later in the war, B-52s were shot down. Handling these sophisticated planes and their equipment required years of training. Most pilots had a college education. Thus, American POWs in Vietnam tended to be highly educated men and career soldiers, not draftees or enlisted men.[42]

When men were taken prisoner, the women would begin their journey by running in circles around the Pentagon, trying to figure out whom to talk to and what to do next. Despite this frustration, they believed in their government. They trusted it. Averell Harriman, one of Kennedy's venerated "Wise Men" of U.S. foreign policy who was acting as the president's ambassador at large in the State Department, and scores of other government officials, both military and civilian, would soon dispatch soothing letters to the women as the crisis wore on, to tranquilize them. They worried most that the women would became hysterical. What if a male government official had to deal with a *crying*—or, worse, *screaming*—POW or MIA wife or mother in their office? God forbid that might happen. The truth was, when confronted with the Vietnam POW/MIA scenario and the women the men had left behind, neither Whiz Kids nor Wise Men knew what the hell to do.

On August 2, 1964, the destroyer USS *Maddox* reported that the North Vietnamese had fired upon the vessel in the Gulf of Tonkin. On August 4, the *Maddox* and another destroyer, the USS *Turner Joy*, claimed that a second attack had occurred. Though U.S. naval commanders could not confirm the second attack, and the situation was murky, President Johnson and his administration used this incident to justify air strikes against the North Vietnamese and officially enter the war.[43]

LBJ and his cronies tried to use the war as a political tool: by flexing their muscles against the Communists, they aimed to strengthen their American electoral support. The second Gulf of Tonkin incident was most likely a false alarm, but it presented the justification that allowed the president to escalate the war in Vietnam. For LBJ, it yielded a too-good-to-be-true political opportunity. "A one-time strike on North Vietnam would allow Johnson to continue as the candidate for peace while demonstrating he was neither indecisive nor timid."[44] He quickly ordered the strike, attempting (and failing) to time it with the evening news.

This "retaliation" resulted in short-term good publicity for Johnson, but it came at a human cost. Lieutenant Everett Alvarez Jr. achieved the dubious honor of being the first naval aviator to be shot down and captured by the North Vietnamese. A few weeks later, Lieutenant Richard C. Sather became the first U.S. naval aviator killed in action over Southeast Asia.[45]

As the last American pilot to leave the scene of the incident on August 4, Jim Stockdale was deeply conflicted about what he had witnessed. The air group commander would say many years later, "It was a bastard war from the beginning." What he saw there, or rather did not see, haunted him for years afterward. The lack of clear-cut evidence of Vietnamese aggression during the second Gulf of Tonkin incident left Stockdale feeling as though the war had been declared under false pretenses.[46]

After the Gulf of Tonkin, Jim's intellectual side began to spar internally with his warrior side. He was a professional soldier but also a trained philosopher with an unshakable ethical code. He realized that policy made in Washington did not always translate into good decisions on the ground. In response to this feeling of disillusionment, the pilot regrouped and formed a new mission. "Before the Gulf of Tonkin incident, I'd seen myself as a shield of protection between my pilots and the North Vietnamese; now I saw myself as a shield of protection between my pilots and McNamara's Pentagon whiz kids." After the Tonkin incident, Jim's biggest worry was that he would be captured and the North Vietnamese would beat a confession out of him that would result in international headlines reading AMERICAN CONGRESS COMMITS TO WAR IN VIETNAM ON THE BASIS OF AN INCIDENT THAT DID NOT HAPPEN.[47]

Just over a month after the Gulf of Tonkin incidents, Jim flew his final mission over Vietnamese airspace. On September 9, 1965, he was shot down in his A-4 Skyhawk, ejected, and was promptly captured by Vietnamese villagers. Although Jim's left leg was broken and his left arm and shoulder were terribly injured, he was still beaten to a pulp. Eventually he was operated on and then surreptitiously driven overnight to the seventy-year-old Hoa Loa Prison, in the North Vietnamese capital city of Hanoi. Here he would join his Naval Academy classmate Jerry Denton and Bill Tschudy; by now, the two had been imprisoned at Hoa Loa for almost two months.[48]

This was the same prison that the French had used in the First Indochina War to hold Vietnamese prisoners, and it had a fearsome reputation. Though Hoa Loa was most famous for its pottery, the name Hoa Loa had an alternate meaning in Vietnamese: "hell hole." The POWs soon decided to Americanize this horrific place, with all their gallows humor, and dubbed it the "Hanoi Hilton."[49]

Being locked up there was like being a guest at the Eagles' "Hotel California": You could check out anytime you liked, but you could never leave.[50]

Three

A GREAT SOCIETY FOR SOME, NOT FOR ALL . . .

WHEN PRESIDENT LYNDON B. JOHNSON was inaugurated for the second time, on January 20, 1965, his address to the nation mirrored his character: "It was pragmatic rather than poetic, utilitarian rather than inspirational," remarked the Associated Press. LBJ's delivery lacked the smooth theatrics and aristocratic cadences of JFK: "It was so slow and deliberate that one critic said it sounded as if the president was dictating to a stonemason."[1] In contrast to Kennedy's gossamer Camelot, the Johnson administration was clearly earthbound.

LBJ promised that all Americans would be part of his "Great Society," where everyone would be a valued part of the national community. Minorities would be respected, immigrants encouraged to rise, the environment protected. It would be a democracy where, he promised, "every man must someday be free."[2]

What about prisoners of war and those missing in action? They were barely on LBJ's radar at this point.

And American women? They did not even rate a mention in his speech.

Title VII of the Civil Rights Act of 1964 banned sex discrimination in employment along with race discrimination. But as the law went into effect, Johnson and his administration just rolled their collective eyeballs. "The sex discrimination part had been tacked on as a joke and a delaying maneuver," wrote Betty Friedan. "After the law went into effect, the administrator in charge of enforcing it joked about the ban on sex discrimination. 'It will give men equal opportunity to be Playboy bunnies,' he said."[3]

This attitude was typical of the time. In this pre-feminist era, women were expected to tolerate discriminatory jokes and innuendos without complaint. Highly educated women like Sybil Stockdale and Jane Denton accepted and embraced the concept that their primary duty was to be a wife and mother. How had these women arrived at that point of view?

When America was founded, women and men alike were just trying to survive. The defining of roles was of little concern to women initially as they endeavored to keep their families alive in the New World. By the eighteenth century, some women were beginning to think more critically about what their place in society should or could be. After allowing women a period of relative freedom in the pre–Revolutionary War era, American men once again tried to confine them, to categorize them and contain them as much as possible. More leisure time among the upper classes also allowed men more time to write about and define gender roles to their own advantage.

The American eighteenth-century concept of "republican motherhood" created "an ideology that gave women a political function, that of raising children to be moral, virtuous citizens of the new republic." Also called moral motherhood, this role did afford women a place in the new republic, although they were not allowed distinct political roles outside the home.[4]

American women's status in the nineteenth century devolved still further, reducing women (at least those of the upper classes who could afford it) to Victorian goddesses of the hearth whom society decided had no business being anywhere else. According to nineteenth-century lecturer and physician Dr. Charles Meigs, women had "a head almost too small for intellect and just big enough for love."[5]

Beginning in the 1820s, the "cult of true womanhood" gained precedence, reaching its peak after the Civil War. This cult identified four key womanly virtues: piety, purity, domesticity, and submissiveness. A woman's "job" was to act as the spiritual and moral guardian of the family.[6] Ideal Woman's next incarnation evolved slightly: the New Woman, with her pert Gibson girl nose and sporty mien, was more independent. Under the Nineteenth Amendment, women were finally granted the right to vote. Free-thinking "flappers" like Zelda Fitzgerald, Josephine Baker, and Clara Bow dominated literature, pop culture, and movie screens in the mid- to late twenties. Still, society's collective vision that a woman's ultimate objective should be marriage and children remained largely unchanged.

World War II presented a turning point for American women's history: Rosie the Riveter, the idealization of the can-do American female worker, arrived on the scene. Women were called to work in the factory, just as American women had been called to work on the farm during the Revolutionary War, to fill in for the men who'd gone off to fight. The war economy demanded that women use their brains and muscles for the good of America. But this independent, highly competent working woman would (at least temporarily) disappear as the need for female labor evaporated after the conflict.

The postwar economic boom of the fifties brought the relative luxury of automatic dishwashers, shiny new cars, and, most important, television. This magic square box updated and then further cemented the vision of women as domestic goddesses. Harriet Nelson, June Cleaver, Donna Reed—they were all Hollywood concepts pitched to and accepted by American consumers. Rosie the Riveter was plucked from her perch in the factory and set firmly into place in the household environment. Instead of her factory denim, she now sported a crisp shirtdress. Her bandanna headband was replaced by bouffant hair set with Dippity-do. This formerly powerful paid worker now stayed home with children and wielded a vacuum instead of a blowtorch. After one step forward, most American women took more than two steps back.

In the fall of 1965, Sybil was completely content. She did not see herself as oppressed, deprived, or downtrodden. She found her role as a mother and wife fulfilling. Her three oldest boys, Jimmy, Sid, and

Stanford, were all in school full time—only her youngest, Taylor, was home with her all day, so she was able to do a little tutoring in the afternoons to keep her mind occupied. The only thing she regretted was her husband's absence. Jim's deployment would be over in December, she reminded herself. Sybil had always been good at keeping busy: years as a Navy wife had taught her the value of distraction and constant activity, and finding those things was not a tall order with four energetic boys to manage.

On the afternoon of September 9, 1965, with the boys finally enrolled in school, Sybil accepted an invitation to see Carol Channing in *Hello, Dolly!* in San Diego—a play she and Jim had seen together in Japan that summer. The songs made her a bit sad as she thought about the romantic time she and Jim had spent together in July during his leave. No children, hot Japanese baths, cocktails! Now the boys were back to school and she was back to her daily routine in Coronado.

Sybil went home after the play, fixed a quick supper for the boys, and was shortening up the boys' pants for school at about 9 p.m. when her best friend, Doyen Salzig, suddenly appeared on the stairs. Startled, Sybil asked what in the world Doyen was doing there so late.

Doyen pulled Sybil close to her and whispered, "Sybil, Jim is missing," her voice cracking on the word "missing."

It was as if Doyen were speaking underwater or in another language that Sybil did not understand. What was she talking about? This made no sense at all. What the hell did it mean, "missing"? Sybil thought. You are either dead or alive. She felt sluggish, as if she were struggling through a nightmare.

"What do you mean, 'missing'? Is he dead?"

"We don't know, Sybil. His plane was shot down and they think he may have gotten out, but we don't know. The chaplain is downstairs talking to Jimmy."[7]

Sybil's reaction was more stoic than she herself would have expected: "No tears gushed forth. No screams of anguish. Just a puzzling sensation of shock that this was happening to me." Then, later, the panic set in. "I began to shake all over." Doyen ended up spending the night with Sybil and her boys on the sleeping porch.[8]

Then there was the terrible task of explaining the situation to her children. Jim Jr., a high school sophomore at the time of his father's shoot-down, tried hard to be a grown-up and help his mother. Sid, at eleven, cried his eyes out. Her youngest, Taylor, was too little to understand what was going on.

Six-year-old Stanford, or "Stan," was the one whose expression of condolence Sybil would never forget. Stan was a striking little boy with black hair and his father's big, round blue eyes. He snuck up on his mother quietly one day while she was doing the laundry. Looking Sybil straight in the eye, he said, "Mom, I'm so sorry about Dad." Sybil thought she might cry but managed to whisper back, "Thank you, sweetheart" as she wrapped him up in her arms along with the laundry.[9]

The POW/MIA children suffered from shock and despair just as much as their mothers did. When Jim Stockdale was shot down, his second son, Sid, was about to begin sixth grade. The day in early September of 1965 when he rode his bike to school to pick up the information packet for the first day of classes, "all the other moms were looking at me sympathetically and saying things like 'Isn't it sad that he's here all alone.'"[10]

How could Sybil explain to Sid and her other children that their dad might never be coming home? Perhaps all the Stockdales realized this possibility on some level, but it was best to shut the thought out, to lock it up and throw away the key to get through the day.

POW and MIA wives on the East Coast were struggling with the same issues as their West Coast counterparts like Sybil, and experiencing a bewildering silent treatment from the American government. After her Air Force pilot husband, Wilmer Newlin "Newk" Grubb, was shot down in January of 1966, Virginia POW wife Evelyn "Evie" Grubb knew immediately "that our children and I were an unwanted problem for the senior Air Force commanders in the United States. They didn't appear to have too much training in handling this kind of situation. I was expected to sit down, shut up, keep a low profile, and not bother them with questions."[11]

Some military husbands had the foresight to give their wives power of attorney when they departed for their tours in Vietnam. These wives were luckier than most. Without that (and even sometimes with that), POW and MIA wives could not complete day-to-day financial household management in the absence of their spouses. Some could not draw their husbands' pay, which accumulated in special accounts while they were held prisoner. Many could not buy or register a car, create and manage a mortgage, refinance, rent an apartment, or buy a house.

The women needed their husbands' signatures to do anything on their own. When your husband was locked up in the Hanoi Hilton, this signature was impossible to obtain. If your husband was shot down in the jungle and listed as an MIA, he generally did not leave a forwarding address. Without her husband's written endorsement, a POW/MIA wife and her family could be denied funds for their basic financial needs. Any legal bills that arose for these families from trying to combat such issues also had to be borne by the women.

When the Pentagon was asked to comment on the unique problems facing this population, a spokesman nonchalantly replied that these issues were "normal things that must be put up with when a man is missing or captured. Anyone with someone missing or captured will hit snags." This same spokesman advised POW/MIA families, "Don't write anything that would bring a flood of letters or calls . . . It would create unnecessary problems."[12]

These two important groups, women and POW/MIAs, were shut out from LBJ's Great Society. While the men lived in prison cells in Vietnam, their wives were trapped by their own service protocols, endemic societal prejudice, and, worst of all, their own government representatives. Most 1960s D.C. politicos didn't even bother to hide their disdain: What could women possibly know about war and diplomacy? The ins and outs of negotiation? Their husbands' fates?

As it turned out, plenty. By late 1966, the realization was sinking in among the POW and MIA wives that they were low priority on the Johnson administration agenda. LBJ happily appeared in photos with these wives (*Smile for the cameras, ladies!*), but he avoided meeting with them one-on-one or even in groups to discuss their concerns in depth.[13] Sybil realized early on that LBJ couldn't have cared less about the women and their concerns. "What truly infuriated her . . . was the Johnson State Department's benign neglect."[14] This neglect would turn out to be anything but benign, endangering the prisoners as time went on.

Though the State Department all but ignored the plight of the women, the military assigned a casualty assistance calls officer (CACO) to each POW and MIA family. These officers often acted like surrogate heads of the families. Some were helpful and dedicated, their presence greatly appreciated by certain POW and MIA wives. Dorothy McDaniel, whose husband, naval captain Eugene Baker "Red" McDaniel, was shot down in May of 1966, felt strongly that "Navy casualty assistance was . . . outstanding, and I was grateful to those who worked so diligently to make my life easier as the wife of a missing serviceman."[15]

Other wives were not as enthusiastic as Dorothy about their assigned CACO liaisons. Sybil soon informed the Navy about the inadequacies of the system. She felt the CACO officers meant well, but most were too young and clueless to know how to deal with the POW and MIA families sensitively. In September of 1966, she wrote to Captain James Andrews, assistant chief for morale services, warning him, "Don't forget that when you are talking about CACO's, you are talking about a group of very nice young men who usually know very little about the Navy. I don't for one minute think that regular solicitations by a CACO could begin to take the place of a periodic letter from Admiral Semmes and Company."[16]

Sybil was urging the Navy to make the wives a priority, not an afterthought. They deserved attention from the top brass, but this was not the treatment they were receiving. The women were often perceived as an annoyance by many in the military—hysterical females who just needed a shoulder to cry on now and then.

Even worse than the CACOs' general lack of experience was the seeming indifference some of them displayed toward the wives' legal, financial, and business problems. Some of these officers actively fought the women's right to make any decisions. Evie Grubb was appalled by her Air Force CACO officer's behavior after her husband, Newk, was shot down in January of 1965. "From the outset, [the CACO officer] adopted an attitude of suspicion and obstruction. It was as though his mission was to protect Newk from me and our children, as if we were the enemy, and he was on a mission to save Newk from us."

Although Evie had power of attorney, her CACO officer continued to question her right to access Newk's pay, and he was stunned to know that she had had any say about the couples' savings plan. How could he not realize, Evie wondered, that many military spouses had to manage family finances while the men were gone on long deployments? "I could not believe I had to get his permission to handle our money!" Evie fumed.[17]

Some of this attitude may have stemmed from experiences in the Korean War. There were instances among the Korean POWs of men who returned home to find that their wives had spent all their pay and wanted divorces. Protocols were then put in place to try to prevent this from happening again.[18] As Vietnam War POW and MIA wives like Evie found, these good intentions based on that earlier war were often misplaced and could hobble a POW or MIA family's finances.

Even as the wife of the highest-ranking Navy POW, Sybil Stockdale still had to fight hard just to get her husband's paycheck. After Jim was shot down, she trusted that she would get the money soon, but she quickly became concerned. Her mortgage was due (thank God she had bought the house during Jim's previous deployment) and she still had no paycheck from the Navy. Her friend Doyen's husband, Bud, also a Navy man, encouraged her to address the Navy sooner rather than later about the issue: "You can put up with that, but you don't have to."

After her conversation with Bud, Sybil threw down the dishes she was washing (she did not have a dishwasher yet) and, still covered with suds, called her legal officer, Commander Luddy, to inquire about Jim's paycheck. When she asked if he had heard anything about this matter, the commander nonchalantly said they had not been able to get Cleveland (Navy pay was processed out of there) on the phone.

By now Sybil's heart was pounding and her hands were shaking with fury. "I'll tell you how you can get Cleveland on the line," she told him, as she recalled in her diary. "You can get up at 5 o'clock in the morning and call them before the lines are busy . . . It won't hurt you to get up early for once. I doubt my husband is getting much sleep these days."

The officer began to protest, saying there must have been some misunderstanding, but he was no match for Sybil's rage and indignation:

> You're right, there's been a misunderstanding, and in my opinion, it's between you and your duties as a U.S. Naval officer . . . I've had enough of being backed into a corner and patted on the head waiting for you to get Cleveland on the line. I'll be fair though. This is Friday. I'll give you until Monday noon to get my financial status completely straight. If you can't handle it by then, I'll call Admiral Semmes, and see if he can get through to Cleveland on the wire.

Commander Luddy called Sybil on Monday at 9 a.m. Her financial status had been resolved.[19]

On Friday, April 15, 1966, something happened that improved Sybil's morale "1000%." As she was leaving the house to do errands with her youngest son, Taylor, the mail arrived. As she flipped through, it seemed at first as though there was nothing but circulars and junk that day. Then her heart stopped as she recognized something. *Hold on a minute,* she thought. *That handwriting looks familiar.* She looked closer and realized it was her husband's. The envelope bore stamps from Vietnam and a postmark that read "Hanoi." Then she discovered that there were not just one but two letters from Jim in the stack. Sybil hurried to a friend's house with Taylor to read the letters, just in case they contained bad news. On the contrary, she found out Jim was alive and well in a detention camp for captured American pilots somewhere in Vietnam.

One letter was dated December 26 and the other February 3. These relatively long missives indicated that Jim had been injured when his plane was shot down. The solitude was trying, he said, and he often dreamed of his family and their eventual reunion.[20] Even so, Sybil was ecstatic. She wanted to scream and jump up and down. "How incredible to get those letters from him out of the blue. How wonderful to know he was truly alive. How I thanked God for having watched over him."[21]

Sybil reported the letters to Commander Hill at the local Navy intelligence office and gave the staff her assessment of the contents. The San Diego–based intel specialists, impressed with her commentary, referred her along to Commander Bob Boroughs at the Office of Naval Intelligence (ONI), in Washington.

What was her and Jim's favorite song?

A bit taken aback, Sybil hesitated, then reeled off a list:

"Near You."

"Que Sera, Sera."

"Putting On the Style."

And finally, though she was embarrassed to admit it, "Fry Me a Cookie in a Can of Lard." Sybil thought that title would at least lighten things up a bit, but Boroughs did not react.

At the end of the conversation, Boroughs asked Sybil to come see him in D.C. to talk more—all expenses paid by the government. Thrilled, she planned to go see him in early May.

The evening of May 1, Sybil got another call, but this time it wasn't Boroughs. It was a commander from Naval Air Forces' Pacific headquarters, warning Sybil that Jim's capture had finally been announced. An article would run in the morning's paper, possibly with a photo of Jim.[22]

In the middle of that cold and foggy night, Sybil went to await the arrival of the *San Diego Union* on the Coronado dock. The dock lay just across from the Mexican Village restaurant, a popular Navy hangout where she and Jim always enjoyed going for their enchiladas and potent margaritas. She had continued to have girls' nights out with her POW/MIA wife friends here, at a familiar place where they could drown their sorrows. She even took her boys there sometimes for a quick bite. It was a total dive, but it reminded her of better times.

The fun and camaraderie of those evenings, contrasted with the horrible scenario she was trapped in now, seemed surreal. She felt like she was in a spy movie, but with no training and no idea of the intelligence she would receive. Sybil sat in the car shivering, waiting for the 2 a.m. boat while her oldest son, Jim, remained at home with the younger children. The newspaper didn't arrive on that shipment, so she had to go home and come back for the 4 a.m. delivery.

When Sybil finally had her hands on the paper, she saw a photo of Jim, unshaven, looking determined but wary.

The headline blazed in front of her: "Hanoi Claims S.D. Man Captive." Sybil later recalled that she was "relieved it was less horrible than it might have been. Very cautious about the press."[23]

Just in case Sybil had decided otherwise, it seemed the Navy was going to make sure that she was cautious in her public response. The article in the *San Diego Union* noted that "Mrs. Stockdale, at her home yesterday, would not comment, a family friend said."[24] When she read the article, Sybil was puzzled—who had the family friend been?

The "family friend" was almost certainly the Office of Naval Intelligence acting in accordance with the dictates of the LBJ government. Right now, Sybil and all her friends were terrified to speak to the press. As they had been told over and over, they might endanger their husbands and put their lives in jeopardy by speaking to the media. All the prisoners' wives could do for now was lie low, do what the American government commanded, and keep quiet.

Four

WIVES OR WIDOWS?

JANE DENTON WAS ABOUT to see her husband speak again after more than a year of separation. She had received a call from a Naval Intelligence officer based out of the Pentagon, Commander Bob Boroughs. A special broadcast would appear on the national evening news that night, he warned her. It was imperative that she tune in. Jane and her seven children dutifully gathered around the television that night, Mother's Day, May 8, 1966, anxiously awaiting whatever was to come. Watching the news with them were Jerry's father and stepmother; two men who had been on the flight detail with Jerry when he was shot down, Bill Salada and Bill Bowers; their wives, Betsy and Kay; and Janie Tschudy.[1]

Suddenly, Jeremiah "Jerry" Denton appeared in front of his family on the screen. He looked forty pounds lighter than when they'd last seen him. He seemed dazed by the bright camera lights. His oldest son, Jerry III, who was twenty years old at the time, recalled his mother's horrified reaction.

"When she saw his haggard look, my mother swore, 'Those bastards!' That shocked me. I had never heard my mother use a word like that in my life. We all yelled something, or cried, or sat in shocked silence."[2]

What was Dad doing with his eyes? the Denton children all wondered. He kept blinking violently. He looked as though he might be drugged. Jerry told his younger siblings that the Vietnamese had probably dragged their dad up from a dark dungeon and that the light might now be blinding him. The children were scared and mystified by their father's odd behavior.

Jerry's Japanese interviewer continued with his leading questions, attempting to get the American prisoner to betray his country on television, but Jerry slowly seemed to gather his strength. He clearly and firmly stated, "I don't know what is happening but whatever the position of my government is, I support it—fully. *Whatever the position of my government is, I believe in it, yes sir. I'm a member of that government and it's my job to support it and I will as long as I live.*"[3]

Jane and the older children knew instantly that these words might be his last. "I was horrified and haunted for years after, at the thought of what consequences he would pay for having done so," Jerry III said.[4] It would mean serious trouble for his father, for sure. Perhaps even execution. Despite their terror and fear for his safety, the family was so proud of Jerry, and so astonished at his courage, that they could barely speak.

The only glimpse of Jerry that Jane was permitted to see that night was her husband's zombie-like figure on television, a ghost of the larger-than-life naval aviator she had long known. This image would be seared into her brain and into the nation's consciousness for years afterward. But the question remained: What did Denton's strange appearance and behavior that night really mean? What happened next took Jane and her children years to fully understand, but it would eventually make Jerry Denton a national hero.

On May 1, the night before Jerry was forced to film what his captors had hoped would be his confession, he had managed to communicate about the situation with his friend and fellow POW James Robinson "Robbie" Risner, who was in a nearby cell. Both men had already faced horrific torture and repeated attempts at Communist indoctrination at the hands of the North Vietnamese. Risner advised

Denton to try to render the interview harmless. But Denton decided to do more than that with his interview opportunity.

"I'll go," Denton told his fellow POW. "I'll blow it wide open."[5]

By 1966, President Lyndon B. Johnson was utilizing attack aircraft such as A-6 Intruders, F-4 Phantoms, and A-4 Skyhawks to bomb the enemy. American POWs and MIAs in Vietnam were, consequently, those who had been sent on dangerous bombing missions like Jerry and Jim.[6] In these early days of the Vietnam conflict, Jane, Sybil, and their fellow POW and MIA wives—on both the East and West Coasts— trusted that the U.S. government would bring the men back quickly and safely. They had all been warned by the military to shun the media. Sybil was terrified to think that the press might swoop in and try to coerce her to speak publicly about her family's plight.[7]

Originally, Sybil felt "somewhat reassured by remembering that in a briefing about guidelines if your husband was taken prisoner, the commander said our government believed that the men being held were well-treated. If I kept quiet, the Navy felt that the Communists would continue to treat the men in a humane and civilized way. I felt sure our government had reason to insist on this 'Keep Quiet' policy."[8]

Official military guidelines for Vietnam-era POW and MIA wives were stark and not very comforting. The women were not allowed to speak with anyone outside of their immediate families about their husbands' personal history and military service. They couldn't write to Communist leaders or heads of state to plead for their husbands' release. Neither the Department of Defense nor the Department of State would share much additional information.

Above all, the American government admonished the women never to speak to the press. The government warned POW and MIA wives that any information they gave the newspapers, TV, or radio might be used against the men. These dictates might be given in person or they might arrive by a Department of Defense letter or telegram. Adding to the devastating nature and sometimes impersonal delivery of these admonitions was the ominous suggestion that accompanied them: "Any violation might result in harm to a wife's husband."9

After receiving these terrifying warnings, these wives were instructed to go about their daily lives as if nothing had happened. They were told to go to the grocery store, to church, and to school to pick up their children with smiles plastered on their carefully made-up faces. With their bouffant hairdos perfectly set, the women had to present a good front to the world while living in limbo. The women and their children were condemned to a purgatory for months, or even years, in which they did not know where their husbands and fathers were, or if they were dead or alive. And by some superhuman fortitude, these military wives and families were supposed to keep this situation TOP SECRET!

Of course, the "keep quiet" policy was a farce. Within the naval aviation community, word spread fast about what was going on. The men had gone to school together, at Annapolis or elsewhere. They had trained together and gotten drunk together (probably more than once). When a high-ranking officer—a group commander like Jerry Denton or Jim Stockdale—went down, everyone in his home community, as well as those in other naval aviation communities, heard about the loss sooner or later.

This familiarity between Navy pilots extended to their wives and families as well. The women tended to stay at their home base while their husbands were deployed, which facilitated widespread support when needed in their local Navy community. The main "home port" naval aviation bases were Coronado, Lemoore, and Alameda Naval Air Stations on the West Coast, and Naval Station Norfolk and Pensacola Naval Air Station on the East Coast. This handful of towns played host to most Navy pilots and their families.10

In the early spring of 1966, POW wives all across the country were praying that their husbands' North Vietnamese captors were following the tenets of the Geneva Conventions. These women lived in a constant state of high anxiety: Were their husbands being starved? Tortured? Interrogated for government secrets? In dire need of medical care?

Those whose husbands were listed as MIA were just praying that their spouses were alive. Many women in this quandary, particularly the MIA wives, were asking themselves: *Are we wives, or are we widows?*[11]

What the women feared—and, on a gut level, strongly suspected—was that the Third Geneva Convention, "Relative to the Treatment of Prisoners of War," first ratified by the North Vietnamese[12] in 1949 then again in 1957,[13] was being ignored in the Vietnamese prisons. This part of the Geneva Conventions had established guidelines for humane treatment of war prisoners that included decent food, clothing, shelter, and medical care. Communication with those outside the prison camp was to be allowed at regular intervals. Prompt next-of-kin notification of capture and imprisonment was also a firm requirement.

The visceral feeling among the POW wives that all was not well had just been graphically confirmed on television by Jerry Denton's eerie interview. Military families were startled by Denton's scarecrow-like appearance. He looked malnourished and possibly drugged. Dorothy McDaniel, whose husband, Red, was also a Navy pilot stationed in Virginia Beach, remembered seeing the broadcast: "I thought he looked horrible and the film made me even more worried about sending Red off to war." Red had another perspective: "I thought he looked pretty good considering what he had probably been through."[14] Both realized almost immediately that Jerry was being badly treated.

What Naval Intelligence would soon confirm, thanks to this broadcast and other bits and pieces of intelligence, was that the downed American aviators were being treated as war criminals, not as prisoners of war. They would later learn that the men were put in leg irons for up to sixteen hours a day, stretched into cruel contortions by rope torture, and beaten to a pulp on a regular basis to force "confessions" from them. They were frequently isolated from their fellow American POWs for months, and sometimes for years.[15]

Though Jane, her children, and the American public did not realize it at the time of the broadcast, in May of 1966, Naval Intelligence operators almost immediately grasped what Jerry Denton's strange blinking meant.

Dah, dah-dah-dah, di-dah-di, dah, dit-di-dah, di-dah-di, dit. It was Morse code for "torture."[16]

Pat Twinem, Bob Boroughs's assistant at Naval Intelligence at the Pentagon, viewed the Denton film along with Boroughs and many others there before the ABC broadcast. Decades later, Twinem recalled with raw emotion the immediate reaction he and his fellow officers had upon watching it:

"We just cried."[17]

Their worst fears regarding the POWs were real.

Just days after the Denton interview aired, Sybil was on her way to Washington to meet with Commander Bob Boroughs—the same man who had warned Jane about Jerry's Mother's Day television interview. Sybil had talked to Boroughs on the phone days before, but she was still puzzled by his interest in her. What could she possibly offer the government that they didn't already have?

What Sybil did not realize at this point was that she could be a crucial government asset. Being Jim Stockdale's wife made her the wife of the highest-ranking Navy POW. Intelligence officials desperately needed a link to the prisoners, someone smart, a quick learner, a potential collaborator in the fight to save the men. The intelligence officials had identified her for just this purpose. She could be a covert tool of the American government, they figured, if she would cooperate.

More important than her cooperation, though, was that she possess the "right stuff," the same bravery and confidence a Navy pilot like her husband had to have to survive in hostile territory. That part was still to be determined. Right now, Sybil thought, she didn't know if she had the strength to do anything but make it through each day.

The day after Sybil landed in D.C., she arrived at the mall entrance to the Pentagon for her arranged rendezvous with Boroughs. She wondered idly: Would he look like a spy? What would a spy even look like? Then she saw him.

He was not a spy in the James Bond mode. This secret agent was not wearing a tuxedo or bringing her a dry martini, as Sybil might have hoped. Instead he was inconspicuous, wearing a striped suit rather than a uniform, to blend in with the crowd. He looked to be about five foot nine, with blondish hair and a receding hairline. Boroughs possessed a reassuring, calm manner that immediately put Sybil at ease.[18] Despite his serious tone on the phone, his gray eyes seemed to contain a mischievous glint.

Robert Sams Boroughs Jr. was a southerner, born in Greenville, South Carolina, in 1925. A skinny seventeen-year-old with a crooked grin, he enrolled in the Navy Reserve as an apprentice seaman in 1943. Through the Navy, he attended the Georgia School of Technology beginning in 1943 where he earned his B.S. By 1945, he was appointed an ensign in the Navy Reserve. He was a veteran of both World War II and the Korean War. He showed an early aptitude for intelligence work, with many of his superiors noting his talent in this area.

Boroughs was trained in air intelligence, security of classified matter, national security, and many other facets of intelligence tradecraft. He became a lieutenant in 1951, a lieutenant commander in 1956, and a commander in 1961 in the Navy Reserve. He consistently scored top marks in his classes and received numerous military commendations and awards. His background in air intelligence and weapons analysis was highly sought after by the Navy.

By October of 1962, Boroughs was deep into intelligence work at the Pentagon. He was acting as an intelligence duty officer, heading up the Targeting of Intelligence Requirements and the Coordinating Section of ONI as well as the Targeting Unit for Air Warfare Intelligence. His job plate was already overflowing when he met Jane, Sybil, and the other POW wives and families. Scenarios with American POWs and MIAs in Vietnam were just beginning to unfold. This Navy Reserve commander was about to become a key player in the drama.[19]

Boroughs's job at the Pentagon brought him into frequent contact with POW and MIA families. He could see and feel the purgatory they were all in on an almost daily basis. Boroughs had observed the runaround the women were experiencing, and, unlike most of his peers, he also noticed how smart and capable these wives were. He had a particularly good head for thinking out of the box, finding creative solutions to difficult problems. He loved puzzles of all sorts.[20] The POW puzzle and how to solve it would prove to be Boroughs's biggest challenge. He connected the dots early on that the wives might be the missing link.

After he picked up Sybil at the mall, Commander Boroughs did not waste a minute of her time. He had urged Sybil to meet first with representatives in the State Department. Boroughs's assistant, Pat Twinem, escorted Sybil over to her first meeting with Philip Heymann, an assistant to Averell Harriman, ambassador at large in charge of POW matters. Sybil almost went ballistic when they arrived at the appointment to find two staffers reading over Jim's letters to her from Vietnam. Sybil was taken aback by what she considered a total invasion of privacy. She recalled, "I had my conversation with Mr. Heymann and heard lots of bla bla bla about what the U.S. State Department was doing about the POWs. When I got back to Boroughs office, I lit into him but good about letting my letters get over there and put him on notice that one more mistake like that and he'd never hear from me again."[21]

After that mishap, Sybil would send copies of the letters directly to Boroughs's home address in Arlington.[22]

Perhaps the State Department visit was meant to show Sybil what Boroughs already knew: that the department was operating as a separate silo. It did not want interference from ONI at the Pentagon or anyone else on POW issues. A collaborative approach was frowned upon. Twinem and Boroughs were no fans of Harriman, about whom Twinem noted, "He didn't interact with us or Naval Intelligence." Twinem also lamented that there was "too much competition between departments. We had less to do with the State Department than anyone else."[23]

Sybil and the other wives would find Boroughs to be the straight shooter they had been searching for in a sea of government bullshit and bureaucrats. He would never tell them more than he was permitted to, but he *would* tell them what others would not: the truth. Boroughs would soon become known as "Uncle Bob" among the POW wives for his kindly demeanor and willingness to be honest with their families.

The commander was also a bit of a rogue agent who would go over, above, and around if needed, using his government contacts and friends in other departments to get the best results. Twinem noted their team approach to problem-solving regarding the POWs: "We would meet often with contacts in other agencies like the CIA and DSA to share info on the POWs and MIAs. *Not* with the State Department, though!"[24]

After Sybil had calmed down from her disastrous meeting at State, Boroughs got down to real business. He asked Sybil if she would consider working with him to pass secret messages along to her husband in prison. All those questions Boroughs had asked Sybil on the phone about songs she and Jim both liked now made sense: Naval Intelligence would translate the couple's personal history into symbols for covert communication. "That sounds dangerous," Sybil gasped. "What if he gets caught?"

"He'd be on his own," Bob replied calmly. He advised Sybil to think long and hard about covert communication and her involvement in it. It was a critical decision, and not one she should jump into without serious reflection. If Jim were caught, he would surely be executed on the spot. Working covertly with Naval Intelligence on such a dangerous mission could mean the difference between life and death for Jim and the other POWs. Sybil's decision had to be made carefully, but soon.[25]

By July of 1966, even more evidence of American POW mistreatment presented itself; this time it was the North Vietnamese themselves who inadvertently alerted the world to this fact. Sybil and her four boys were at Sunset Beach, Connecticut, that July, per their usual routine. She, Jim, and the children had always gone there every summer to visit her parents at their beach cottage. One hot evening, as Sybil sat on the seawall watching a particularly gorgeous sunset, she was startled to see her parents rushing toward her with concerned looks on their faces.

They had just watched the evening news, which showed grim-faced, malnourished POWs being forced to march through the streets of Hanoi. The news commentator had talked about the possibility of the men being tried for "war crimes." Though her father had not seen Jim in the footage, he described what they had just witnessed on TV.[26] As Sybil would find out years later, Jim did not participate in the march: he was locked up in solitary confinement. The North Vietnamese did not want Jim, a senior officer, to spend any time with his men. Instead they continued to torture him for information while he was isolated from his fellow POWs.[27]

The North Vietnamese had filmed the march on July 6, and it was broadcast on American television a few days later, when Sybil's parents saw it. Fifty-two American prisoners were put on public display and marched through the streets of Hanoi. The men were handcuffed, beaten, and led through hostile and violent crowds, who attacked some of the men during the march. By some estimates, the North Vietnamese who lined the streets of the city that night numbered 100,000.[28]

Though the men were "guarded" by Vietnamese soldiers with bayonets, the angry mob attacked the prisoners repeatedly, hitting Jerry Denton in the groin and pushing fellow naval aviator Robert H. "Bob" Shumaker into a brick wall, rendering him unconscious. Despite this brutal treatment, Denton reminded Shumaker and the other prisoners, "You are an American! Hold your heads up and show your pride!"[29] Shumaker later remembered thinking that the prisoners "were not going to make it." He counted himself lucky that he was knocked out—when he awoke late that night in his cell, it was to the sound of the screams of the other POWs, who were being tortured.[30] All the men sustained head and facial injuries, "nursing loosened teeth, broken noses, blackened eyes, and various bumps, bruises, and lacerations."[31]

The North Vietnamese Communist captors were constantly attempting to "break" the American prisoners, to turn them against their own government and military. Then, they felt, they could use the American POWs as political pawns and instruments of propaganda.[32] Jerry Denton, his copilot Bill Tschudy, Bob Shumaker, Everett Alvarez, Porter Halyburton, Robbie Risner, and many other POWs forced to participate in the Hanoi March made sure this approach back-fired.[33] Denton's "screw you" Mother's Day broadcast, coupled with the POWs' military bearing during the Hanoi March, conveyed their unwillingness to be turned.

While not planned by the POWs, the march also helped the men's chances of release. It showed the world both the brutality and the il-legality of prisoner-of-war treatment in North Vietnam. In the wake of Denton's television appearance and the march, television and news-papers became the greatest allies of the POWs and their wives. Once the film and photos from the Hanoi March surfaced, the North Viet-namese treatment of the POWs was widely condemned all across the globe. Secretary-General U Thant of the United Nations, Pope Paul VI, British prime minister Harold Wilson, Indira Gandhi, and many other world leaders called for this maltreatment to stop immediately.[34]

World leaders also spoke out against the notion of a "war crimes" trial for the POWs, as the North Vietnamese had earlier threatened. Soon after, LBJ warned of consequences that would follow if any such trial were held. Secretary of State Dean Rusk and Averell Harriman worked behind the scenes to reach a diplomatic solution. On July 24, North Vietnamese president Ho Chi Minh announced, "There was no trial in view," backing away from his original plan.[35]

Jerry Denton correctly predicted to the North Vietnamese that the march would backfire. The Hanoi government's attempt at producing a film to be used in their "psywar"—psychological warfare—against the American enemy created an enormous international backlash. "The organizers' intent was to show cowed Americans slinking cravenly through the streets of Hanoi before the jeers of a victimized but or-derly populace. What they got instead was footage of manacled pris-oners comporting themselves with admirable dignity and courage against an unruly mob."[36]

Jerry, Jim, and most of their fellow POWs had yet another card up their sleeve in their resistance plan against the North Vietnamese. They possessed special skills and training that could mean the difference be-tween life and death for them in the prison camps. As noted earlier, naval aviators flying into combat zones were required to attend SERE school, based on the experiences of Korean War veterans who had been held as POWs. President Dwight D. Eisenhower prescribed this training for all first-line carrier pilots.

As such, Jim attended SERE school twice, first in the San Diego mountains in the late 1950s and then again right before he deployed to Vietnam. He spent a week in the wilderness learning to survive and a week in a mock prison learning how to resist his captors. The SERE training was created within the Code of Conduct, which reminded POWs that if they were captured, the American chain of command remained intact within the prison walls.[37]

Once Jim was shot down in Vietnam, he, Jerry, and the other senior POW officers realized that what they had been taught in survival school had to be adapted to a new sort of enemy, much different from the one the country faced in the Korean War. In Korea, American captives had learned that if they could hold out and not crack in the first month or two, their jailers would put them aside as a waste of time and leave them alone.[38]

By the time of his May 1966 filmed interview, Denton also knew the game was not a traditional one. Though he was not taught specifically to use his eyelids for Morse code, he was taught in SERE school to use any methods necessary to survive, evade, resist, and escape. Any hope hinged on the men's ability to outsmart this new enemy, who was not going to play by any established rules of warfare.

A different approach was clearly required on the home front as well. Sybil saw this almost immediately. With Bob Boroughs's help, she would become the first trainer, administrator, and public relations director in the POW and MIA wives' version of survival school. But the first obstacle she had to overcome to communicate with the outside world was that of her own government.

Five

A RELUCTANT SORORITY

SYBIL, JANE, AND THEIR fellow POW/MIA wives continued to get the runaround when they visited Washington, desperately trying to find out more information about their husbands.

Fortunately, the women soon gained a powerful ally in Robert F. Kennedy, brother of slain president JFK, former attorney general of the United States and now a New York senator, who urged further investigation of the POW/MIA issue. The result was the creation of the Interdepartmental Prisoner of War Committee in April of 1966. This group comprised one representative each from the State Department, the CIA, the Joint Chiefs, and the Office of the Secretary of Defense (OSD). By May 18, a government dictate designated Averell Harriman, a longtime friend and ally of RFK's, as "the single spokesman for the government on all PW matters."[1]

Despite vivid confirmations of POW mistreatment in the Hanoi March footage in July, President Johnson and Ambassador Harriman did not act. They had known about incidents of abuse for months by the time Sybil made her way to D.C., but they decided to keep this intel under wraps. What Johnson and Harriman feared most was that POW wives and families might go public with the story. If the media knew about the POW situation, they rationalized, their chance for a diplomatic solution would be lost.

Harriman repeatedly shut down Department of Defense proposals to share evidence of the POWs. In one 1966 Interdepartmental POW Committee meeting, he declared that "no useful purpose would be served by publicizing torture." Further, he felt that any acknowledgement of this abuse would further taint the diplomatic atmosphere, making negotiations more difficult. "We did not advertise the cruelty we knew existed there because we didn't want to make propaganda. It was a conscious decision not to go public. We didn't use it to stir up the American people."[2]

President Johnson, such a powerful force in politics at home, was indecisive when it came to this foreign war. He would not fully commit to a clear position regarding Vietnam. Desperate to implement his Great Society domestic policies, and already conscious that this seemingly insignificant war could be his political undoing, Johnson did not want to highlight the predicament of the captured servicemen. What good would it do for his presidential image? "Without hope of bringing them home, Johnson had little to gain and much to lose by drawing attention to their plight."[3]

Johnson's "keep quiet" policy was also based on the American experience in World War II and the Korean War, where prisoners of war were kept for relatively short periods of time. As the American prisoners in Vietnam already realized, and as their wives would soon find out, this was not your parents' war or even the war of ten years past. It was uncharted territory, further complicated by the fact that the Vietnamese considered the men "air pirates" and political criminals. Since the United States and the Democratic Republic of Vietnam (DRV) were not yet technically at war when the first pilots were captured, the North Vietnamese refused to recognize captured Americans as true prisoners of the conflict.[4]

The Vietnamese were a different kind of foe than the Germans or the Koreans. They seemed to be in the torture business for the long haul. This game didn't just have different rules from those of previous wars—it seemed to have no rules at all. Although the North Vietnamese had signed the Geneva Conventions in 1949 and again in 1957, they decided to toss this agreement out the window even after the

United States officially entered the war after the 1964 Gulf of Tonkin incident. Many American pilots knew instinctively that if they were shot down, the chances that the North Vietnamese would honor the Geneva Convention tenets were slim to none. Charles W. "Chuck" Stratton, an American Air Force pilot who would later be listed as MIA, told his wife, Sallie, that the Geneva Conventions card he carried would not be worth the paper it was printed on should he be captured.[5]

The POW and MIA wives would find similar scenarios on the home front. None of the old rules of wartime were valid during Vietnam. After months of "keeping quiet" and obeying their government's dictates, they could see that nothing was moving forward for their captured or missing husbands. Sybil Stockdale later revealed: "I set out to get our own government to acknowledge that we had prisoners who were being mistreated in North Vietnam. Johnson knew this would emotionally involve the American people in the war and they did not want that. They wanted to keep the people as separated from the war as possible."[6]

Harriman and his State Department lackeys held to their party line, urging the president not to stir things up by going public with the POW scenario. They could surely solve the problem by diplomatic means. Harriman was old school, following the template of his negotiations in previous wars. He had been encouraged in this line of reasoning by the positive results he and Secretary of State Rusk had seemed to generate regarding the notion of a "war crimes" trial. Their clandestine efforts both before and after the Hanoi March did help to dissuade the North Vietnamese from this approach in the summer of 1966.[7] But what the two diplomats seemed not to realize (or perhaps did not want to admit) was that their work was only a secondary factor in halting the trial.

Silver-tongued diplomacy got you only so far: media coverage of the prisoners' plight during the Hanoi March was what immediately caught the world's attention. The embarrassment the footage caused was the primary factor in the Communists' decision to back off the threat of a war crimes trial. While Rusk, Harriman, and Johnson congratulated themselves on their diplomatic success, they had missed the bigger picture. The media, especially television, would more effectively spotlight diplomatic issues as the war went on. Groups on both sides of the conflict were only just beginning to realize how the international press could be used for message amplification and for outright warfare against the enemy during Vietnam, the "first television war."

While diplomacy had seemed to work in the initial stages of the conflict, it would soon prove to be a futile, frustrating, and dangerous approach where the POWs and MIAs were concerned. Though the war crimes threat had passed for the moment, the notion of a trial would continue to hang over the heads of the American government like a sword. "From time to time . . . the North Vietnamese reasserted their right to try pilots as war criminals."[8] Diplomacy had only provided a flimsy Band-Aid for a wound that would be opened and reopened throughout the war.

Back at Sunset Beach, Sybil finally broke down after the Hanoi March news. She sobbed in her mother's arms: "I can't stand it. I can't stand it . . . What am I going to do?" Her mother advised her to cry it out for her boys' sake. The emotional release did her good. Sybil could see that, as individuals, the POW and MIA wives' voices were ineffective and ignored. No one seemed to listen. It was as if the ladies were shouting into a hurricane, their cries for help drowned out by the diplomatic and military machines of their own government.

Determined to try to change things, Sybil devised a plan, inspired by one of Jim's favorite sayings: "When in doubt, see a manager." Sybil added her own axiom to this, one that would serve her well in the coming days: "Nothing can take the place of a personal visit."[9]

A few weeks later, Sybil returned to Washington. She had appointments lined up with Ambassador Harriman; Admiral David McDonald, chief of naval operations; and Admiral Semmes, head of the Bureau of Naval Personnel (BuPers). Boroughs again served as her escort, meeting her at the airplane. On the way to the Pentagon, Sybil told Boroughs that she intended to work with Naval Intelligence to send covert letters to her captured husband. Boroughs grinned broadly—now, he thought, they were really in business.[10]

The West Coast POW wife was particularly nervous to see Harriman.[11] Long known as one of JFK's foreign policy Wise Men, Harriman was also hailed as the "Lion of Diplomacy." Patrician and handsome, Harriman came from Union Pacific Railroad money.[12] With his charm and polished manners, he had been a magnet for women in his youth, including (the married) Pamela Churchill, Winston Churchill's daughter-in-law. The two carried on a torrid affair during Harriman's stint as head of FDR's lend-lease program in Britain during World War II. (Some thirty years later, Pamela would become Harriman's second wife.)[13]

This venerated diplomat, former governor of New York, and world-class snob possessed a hard edge that those who worked with him came to know all too well. "His episodes of impatient snapping in the genteel atmosphere of the White House caused [fellow Wise Man and LBJ national security adviser] McGeorge Bundy to liken Harriman to an old crocodile arousing from a feigned doze with snapping jaws." Far from taking offense at this moniker, Harriman embraced the characterization and collected all manner of crocodile figurines, which he kept on his desk in the State Department. He often used "Crocodile" as his code name.[14]

One thing Harriman did not possess was on-the-ground combat experience. While most of his college classmates immediately enlisted in the Great War, he chose to stay home and profit from his merchant shipping business, purchased with his mother's backing. "The fact that Harriman had chosen to profit from World War I, rather than fight in it, was also held against him. Some of his friends from Yale considered his behavior shameful; several would not speak to him for years."[15] Perhaps Harriman's constant striving to become top diplomat in World War II, and trying to stay relevant in an ambassadorial role in Vietnam, may have been attempts to assuage his guilty conscience over not enlisting. Like McNamara, he found that his skills lay in the business arena: the dirty work of war and military combat was an abstract concept to him.

The other, even more fatal flaw in Harriman's makeup? He "was renowned for his lack of a sense of humor, especially about himself."[16]

When Sybil met with the Crocodile that July, she was intimidated but determined. His quarters in the State Department, with their sense of opulence, reinforced his reputation. The office was fit for a king, with its plush carpets and ornate furniture. Harriman's lair was guarded by a secretary "who postured like a *Vogue* model," Sybil remembered.[17] Exactly the habitat one would expect a Wise Man—or a Crocodile—to inhabit.

Although Sybil later described Harriman as an elderly gentleman who wore a hearing aid, she understood that he wielded great power in Washington and in the world of international diplomacy. Sybil realized that she had to play her cards carefully with him—that he could turn out to be a valuable ally if she engaged him correctly. She spoke clearly and deliberately and maintained steady eye contact with the aging diplomat, deferring to most of his opinions.[18]

The POW wife immediately noted Harriman's keen interest in how the Pentagon was treating her. "You would have thought they were all from different countries the way they kept checking up on each other," she noted of the State Department and the Pentagon. This did not reassure her, and, despite the debacle over her letters from Jim on her last visit to ONI, Sybil resolved not to "air any dirty Navy laundry in public . . . I told him the Navy treated me like a queen." Her instinct was to protect her service branch just as all military wives had been trained to do, but Sybil soon realized that the ambassador at large had never even *seen* a letter from a POW, even though he was head of the entire POW/MIA welfare operation, eroding her confidence even further.[19]

Harriman assured Sybil that everything possible was being done for the men but that he could not tell her exactly what those efforts involved. Still, Sybil recalled, "That two-hour visit with Ambassador Harriman meant a lot to me, and afterward I wrote to Jane Denton to the effect that his big points were (1) the things we are trying to do on behalf of the prisoners can't be discussed publicly but the activities cover a wide range and (2) he was encouraged Hanoi has muted its threats about war crimes trials."[20]

The next day, Sybil visited with Admiral David L. McDonald, chief of naval operations, and Admiral Paul D. Miller, deputy chief of naval operations. Both seemed receptive to her wives' newsletter idea (Harriman had been also) and to her idea of an anti–North Vietnamese propaganda campaign by the Navy.

She also talked to Admiral Semmes, the head of BuPers, and urged him to have the Navy write the POW/MIA wives often to keep them updated about their husbands' status. Sybil's argument may seem dated today, but it was cunning in its emotional appeal: "You know you're dealing with the female psyche in this situation and I remind you that it's somewhat different from your own. For example, if on your wedding day you told your wife you loved her and then considered that job done, you'd be in for trouble. You have to tell her you love her over and over again. It's the same with the wives of the men who are prisoners and missing—you need to tell them they're being remembered and their husbands also."[21]

Sybil left Washington satisfied that she seemed to have made an impact. She wrote the other wives: "I came away from my recent visit feeling that our husbands' lives are in the hands of master statesmen who will do and are doing everything in their power to assure the safe return of the prisoners and bring the conflict to an early close."[22] Was Sybil trying to reassure not just the other wives but herself about the American government's efforts in this department? She had seen more than one indication that all was not well. She was aware there were issues, but she had not yet completely absorbed the depths of the Washington political swamp, nor the gaping divide between the State Department and the Pentagon. Only months later would she begin to see things as they truly were: Admiral Semmes's office would finally send her "newsletter" out to the wives, reworked into unrecognizable gobbledygook, "a say-nothing bureaucratic letter, which satisfied no one."[23] Semmes would soon become the focus of her ire and mistrust.

Not happy about this feeble attempt to placate the wives, Sybil finally wrote an open letter to the POW wives herself. She eventually got the Navy to distribute the letter for her without releasing the POW families' names or addresses. The letter was sent not just to Navy POW wives but also to the wives of senior-ranking POWs in other military branches. MIA wives were not included in this initial letter, but Sybil did offer to provide more information to any MIA wives who might be interested.

Jane Denton was one of the recipients of this first communication from Sybil, as were her friends in Virginia Beach Janie Tschudy and Louise Mulligan, whose husband, Jim, was shot down on March 20, 1966. The letter first apologized for invading the families' privacy. "If I am invading yours at this point by all means file this in the trash can and let me know you want to hear no more." For those women who cared to read further, she suggested, "Many of us might benefit from sharing some of the knowledge and experiences which others in our position have had."[24]

The relief of the wives who received this letter in the mail in the late summer of 1966 was palpable. Finally, there were others they could talk to who shared their daily grief, frustration, and lack of information. At last there was a wives' "grapevine" where the women could help one another and communicate. Initially, the wives' get-togethers were casual events, sitting around kitchen tables. They might have a potluck supper, share a casserole and wine together, play cards, and vent about feeling like a "fifth wheel" at social gatherings. But at least now they were not so alone.

While the POW/MIA wives received great comfort from connecting with one another, they were all still suffering from their government's lack of concern regarding their financial support. Many of the women, just like Sybil and Jane, had already experienced major problems getting their husbands' paychecks and cashing checks. Then came what many wives considered the final blow: the introduction of a savings plan created for the benefit of American servicemen who were fighting in combat zones, whereby their pay would accrue 10 percent interest per year tax-free. On August 14, 1966, Public Law 89–538 established this plan, but it did *not* include the POWs and MIAs lost in North Vietnam.[25]

When POW and MIA wives found out about this glaring exclusion, they were dumbfounded. Their husbands were not only deployed to a combat zone—they were *jailed* or *missing* in a combat zone. Why would the men and their dependents not be included automatically in the savings plan? The ladies assumed this was simply an oversight. The matter was quickly brought to the attention of the government by the Navy, only to garner a negative ruling from the comptroller general:

"This action would not serve the purpose of the Act since amounts credited to the member's pay account while he is in a missing or captured status would not ordinarily enter the economy of the country in which he last served and therefore would not affect the balance of payments position of the United States in any way." Furthermore, the serviceman's dependents would also not be allowed to make any deposits in his name into a 10 percent savings account.[26]

Sybil and her fellow San Diego POW and MIA wives, like Debby Burns, as well as the East Coast wives, like Jane Denton and Janie Tschudy, all received this same letter, a further confirmation, in their eyes, that the military could not have cared less about their husbands, and cared still less about the welfare of the men's families. Public Law 89–538 and the legislators who created it had not even considered the missing men in the first place; upon appeal, these men were still denied access to the 10 percent savings plan.

POW/MIA wives all across the country were stunned at the sheer cruelty of this pronouncement. Many women already felt socially ostracized from their local military communities when their husbands became POW or MIA. But now their federal government was disowning them, setting them adrift on a choppy financial sea without the 10 percent savings lifejacket that other servicemen in combat zones had received.

All these variables were adding up for the women. They could see that the numbers were not compounding in their favor. If they continued to cling to their government officials and to toe the party line as they had been doing, what would be their reward? Their husbands' reward?

The answer was: nothing.

The women knew this, just as they knew the men were not being treated humanely. Jane Denton wrote Harriman to this effect, upset by reports she had read from unidentified State and Defense Department officials that the POWs held in Vietnam were being well taken care of. Anyone who had seen her husband's film on May 8, 1966, could surmise that was not the case. "I am convinced that, on the contrary, they [the POWs] are being badly treated . . . I feel that we should show indignation and inform people both here and abroad of the violations which are being committed by the government of North Vietnam."[27]

Jane further strengthened her case by referring to a Chilean newspaper report that stated that Jerry was being kept in solitary confinement. Even more chilling was the case of American POW Dieter Dengler, who had escaped from brutal treatment by the Pathet Lao—Laotian resistance fighters backed by the North Vietnamese Communists. Dengler was severely tortured and within twenty-four hours of dying when he was finally rescued in June of 1966.[28] (The movie *Rescue Dawn* is based on Dengler's story.) After reading the gruesome reports of Dengler's treatment, Jane wrote to Harriman of her astonishment at the "apathy of the American public on this subject. Where was the compassion for him and his fellow prisoners?"

Jane boldly urged Harriman to take this information and run with it: "I ask you to consider the wisdom of publishing the injustices which the captured American servicemen are enduring thereby arousing world opinion, and hopefully getting better treatment for them."[29]

Like the appeals regarding the 10 percent savings plan, Jane's entreaties fell on deaf ears.

On Friday October 7, 1966, a group of thirteen Coronado Navy wives entered the charming 1950 Tudor bungalow, covered in twisting vines of roses, at 547 A Avenue, Sybil's cozy home base. The women settled in around the massive oak dining room table that had come with the house. Medieval-looking, it was so heavy and long that it could never be moved. Sybil served the ladies lunch—perhaps her famous Tacos à la Casa Stockdale, one of her specialties.[30]

East Coast Navy wives were more formal, but here things were as laid-back as they could be in a military community. The women were casually dressed, as they often were in California even in this era. Some women wore pedal pushers with pearls. Athletic Sherry Martin came straight over from her tennis game still wearing a tennis skirt. She hadn't had time to change before lunch.[31]

The women were all 1960s Navy wives at ease with the military dictates that governed their day-to-day lives. They met regularly for squadron wives' lunches, baby showers, and cocktail parties at the officers' club. They accepted the prescribed rules and regulations regarding what to do, say, and wear for every occasion without question or protest. Until recently, the military rule book *The Navy Wife* had been their bible. But today, none of these protocols applied.

All the ladies who attended the luncheon that day had recently experienced the stomach-churning sight of an official-looking black car in their driveways. As Sybil noted, "The chaplain always came to tell you about death in a black sedan."[32] The sight of that car was what led all these women to Sybil's rose-covered cottage for lunch. The women who had young children had all gotten babysitters; the discussion was not going to be child friendly. Some wives were so traumatized that they could barely drag themselves out of bed to get their children off to school. A few of the women had received some vague information about their husbands' whereabouts, but many had no idea where their spouses were.

In the naval community, a wife's status mirrored the rank of her husband, and according to this long-standing protocol, Sybil was by default the wives' leader on the home front. To the younger Navy wives whose husbands went missing, she was also a maternal figure. Sandy Dennison was a twenty-year-old San Diego Navy officer's wife with two small children when her husband, Terry, was shot down on July 19,

1966. She felt like Sybil became her second mother.[33] POW wife Karen Butler described her friend Sybil similarly: "Sybil was many things . . . She was a natural leader with an indomitable spirit, a loving presence always, especially when you needed it, and a mentor who helped others to cope and stand strong."[34]

The women were still talking at Sybil's home at 5 p.m. that evening. Sybil remembered later the "outpouring of exchange of information—who was being told what, and so forth. We agreed to meet on a regular basis as regularly as squadron wives would meet every month."[35] Structure might just save their sanity.

When Sybil and the other POW and MIA wives first received news of their husbands' shoot-downs, some had panicked, gone numb, or taken tranquilizers to get through the awful, unending first night — or week or month or year—of this new life in limbo.

Swiss psychiatrist Elisabeth Kübler-Ross's 1969 work *On Death and Dying* was the first to study the human condition of grief from a clinical perspective. This seminal work was published five years after the Vietnam War began and soon became well-known in popular culture. As Sybil became aware of Kübler-Ross and her theories, she later realized that what she, like the other POW/MIA wives and their children, experienced was also a kind of death—the death of their normal life and existence.

In retrospect, she would define the POW/MIA wife experience using the same terms Kübler-Ross employed. Sybil observed six stages that she and the other POW/MIA wives seemed to pass through after they received word of their husbands' shoot-downs: shock, confusion, assessment, learning, planning, and action.[36] In these early days of the war, only the first two stages would apply.

The first state was shock as she herself had experienced it. Utter disbelief, denial, and, in some cases, a dissociation from reality for a time seemed to affect most of the women. This could last a few days, a few weeks, or even longer. There was often a period of self-medication among the women, with sleeping pills being the drug of choice. Sybil's advice to wives in this scenario? "Be pessimistic: watch out for 'all will be fine.' Don't count on your intuition about [your husband being] dead or alive."[37]

The second stage was confusion. What was really going on? What do we know? Who can we trust? The wives were not the only ones who were confused. Very often, the Naval Intelligence "experts" who came to tell the women about their husbands' shoot-downs had little information about the missing pilots' whereabouts. This was an era before GPS systems, before cell phones, before Twitter and Facebook. The lack of information was compounded by the secrecy surrounding the American pilots flying bombing missions in Vietnam.

The bombings had two goals: to disrupt the North Vietnamese supply routes on the Ho Chi Minh Trail and to aid U.S. allies in North Vietnam against the Pathet Lao. The Ho Chi Minh Trail also ran through parts of Cambodia and Laos, and these countries suffered huge amounts of collateral damage among civilians. LBJ did not want Americans to know the ugly truth about the extreme loss of human life or his strategy to take out the North Vietnamese.[38]

Sybil's counsel to her wives during this stage was still pessimistic, but it offered some practical advice: "Find other wives in your same situation. You will probably get no government help. Invest in a phone message machine so you can listen and answer to messages as you feel like it." And, perhaps most important, "Don't exhaust yourself being nice to people. Save all your strength for you, your family, and the fight ahead."[39]

Sandy, Sherry, and Patsy Crayton, a young POW wife whose husband, Render, had been shot down February 7, 1966, had contacted Sybil early on, as well as the twenty-seven other San Diego POW/MIA wives, to form a "reluctant sorority." As Sherry put it, they were an exclusive club that "no one wanted to belong to."[40] These "waiting wives" had begun to develop a sisterhood—something that went beyond their relationships with their blood families, something that often meant more to them and their children than any prayers the Navy chaplain could offer them.

At their first few meetings, they proceeded through stages one and two of their new normal. Their goal at this point was simply to get through the day without losing their sanity. No formal agreements were signed, no bylaws created, no roles assigned. But this incubation period was crucial. The women learned to trust one another, rely on one another, and communicate with one another discreetly, since they were not allowed to speak publicly about their plight.

Soon, other women joined the sorority, with several of them moving to Coronado and the surrounding area from Lemoore naval base. Their backstories were all eerily similar, taking place before these Navy wives had even met Sybil. Jenny Connell was one of these women. Her husband, James "J. J." Connell, was lost July 15, 1966, just two weeks before his scheduled return home. A Navy A-4E Skyhawk pilot with attack squadron VA-55 aboard the USS *Ranger*, J.J. was flying a mission along the Red River south of Hanoi when he was shot down and taken prisoner. Petite and brunette with a wide smile, Jenny was a twenty-five-year-old stay-at-home mom with a two-year-old, James, and a three-year-old, Ruth, at the time of her husband's shoot-down. She and J.J. had been married for only five years. Her naturally optimistic nature would help keep her and many of her fellow POW and MIA wives afloat.

Three months later, Jenny heard about Debby Burns, also a Lemoore Navy wife, whose husband, Doug, had been shot down on June 30. Blond, beautiful Debby was also a stay-at-home mom, with three children: Scott, age seven, Steve, six, and Linda, three. Jenny went to "call" on her. "I recall Debby saying she was shocked that I could laugh and joke. She was still in a raw and vulnerable state."[41]

It would not be long before Debby was in Jenny's position, comforting yet another Navy wife in Lemoore. She remembered: "I was still in Lemoore & in our little cul-de-sac of 6 boxy Navy 'houses,' 3 of the men were shot down! Paul Galanti, Mike McGrath, & Doug. When Mike was shot down I heard Marlene [his wife] scream so I ran over & gave her some of the 'Librium' they had given me the night I was told about Doug."[42]

Jenny also met Karen Butler at Lemoore. Karen was a vivacious registered nurse whose husband, Phillip Neal Butler, had been shot down on April 14, 1965. She got a knock on her door at six thirty one morning and opened it to see two men in Navy uniforms. She was told he was missing, presumably killed. But she was soon called by a hysterical friend who informed Karen that her husband's photo had just appeared on the *Today* show—he was now listed as captured.[43] Karen had one daughter, two-year-old Diane, who had been born just one month prior to her husband's shoot-down.[44]

Jenny, Karen, and Debby would soon meet Sybil and be brought into the POW/MIA wife fold, which was becoming more regional than local as more and more Navy pilots fell from the Vietnamese skies. Sybil recalled that they did not differentiate between POW wives and MIA wives: both were welcome. "Our meetings weren't sad, sober-faced affairs, but frank and open-hearted exchanges about feelings and information. We always drank wine and laughed. We knew some of our behavior might seem ghoulish to others, but among ourselves we felt free to do and say whatever we felt. Being together gave us all strength."[45]

An undercurrent of female subversion was also floating in the crisp California air. Sybil and her San Diego–area POW wife friends Karen and Jenny were aware of the rising feminist movement and books like Betty Friedan's *The Feminine Mystique,* published in 1963. Friedan's book outlined "the problem that has no name." She vividly described for her readers a malady prevalent at the time among suburban housewives: "As she made the beds, shopped for groceries, matched slipcover material, ate peanut butter sandwiches with her children, chauffeured Cub Scouts and Brownies, lay beside her husband at night—she was afraid to ask even herself the silent question—is this all?"[46]

Though most POW/MIA wives would never be feminists à la Friedan, some would take a page from *Mystique*—ditching the "problem that has no name" for activism, in response not to a husband's indifference but to their own government's maddening neglect. Prejudice against women in general was an intrinsic part of the fabric of American culture. Women had so often been treated as second-class citizens that most military wives barely noticed and did not often complain.

But when their gender started to affect the outcome of their husbands' fates as prisoners or missing in Vietnam, a revolution slowly began to simmer, bubbling just under the surface among POW/MIA wives. It would be a long, slow burn, but eventually it would hit a boiling point.

A few days after the Navy wives' first meeting at her home, Sybil coded her first letter per Boroughs's instructions. She was terrified and almost physically ill at the thought that she literally had her husband's life in her hands. Twice, she rode her bike to the post office and returned home again without mailing the letter. She knew the North Vietnamese would kill Jim if they somehow figured out the letter was coded. Even so, she knew he would want her to take the risk. She and Boroughs had worked references into the letter that Jim would know to be flat-out lies. In this first letter, Sybil wrote about Jim's mother flying out to see her and the boys, taking a taxi, and swimming in the ocean—none of which were things she would ever do. "All your Mom needs is a good soak," she wrote. A Polaroid photo was also included in the letter, showing a woman who resembled Jim's mother; the idea was that these false statements would clue Jim in to soaking the photo, inside of which a CIA specialist had inserted a secret message.

If Jim soaked the photo, he would find a note explaining that the letter had been written on a kind of "invisible carbon" paper that could be used to write his own veiled responses back to America. By writing firmly but not enough to indent the page underneath, Jim could leave invisible messages literally between the lines of his letters home. The CIA could then reveal the hidden messages. This carbon paper could be used multiple times.[47] It all sounded like something James Bond's gadget master Q would come up with. Now all that the Qs at Langley needed was for their James Bond—Stockdale—to figure out their ruse.

Finally, Sybil gathered up her resolve and thrust the letter into the outgoing mail box. "When I finally heard the letter drop to the bottom of the box I thought, 'for better or for worse, it's done now. Please God, let it be for better.'"[48]

As it turned out, Sybil was not the only one coding letters for "Uncle Bob." Sybil strongly suspected that others in her San Diego group with POW husbands, like Lorraine Shumaker, were doing the same. She would be correct about Lorraine and others, like Debby and Jenny, who would also work with Boroughs as time went on.[49]

The West Coast ladies were not alone in engaging in spycraft for Naval Intelligence. Uncle Bob had more "Jane Bonds" on the East Coast. Jane Denton and Janie Tschudy were two of the earliest ones in Virginia Beach to participate in the coding. Though Jane and Janie were both coding for Bob, they almost never talked to each other about it. Janie remembered, "It was ingrained in us to be so careful . . . I trusted Jane implicitly, as she did me, but you felt you were being too risky" if you talked about the coding to anyone else.[50]

As they began their engagement in covert intelligence work, the women grew even more skeptical of the State Department and the Navy's generic communications. These women were already realizing that a cover-up was being employed to give the higher-ups room to negotiate with the Communists.

When Jane and the other POW/MIA wives received a form letter from Admiral B. J. Semmes, the head of naval personnel, in March of 1967, they had to be completely disgusted. The letter belatedly suggested guidelines for the POW/MIA families about how to write to the prisoners, urging them, above all, to "try to be cheerful." Wives should write about sports, entertainment, and family activities and avoid any discussion of the prisoner's situation, accounts of other losses, the U.S. government's position on Vietnam, or foreign affairs in general.

The letter then stated that recently published statements from American POWs Nels Tanner and Dick Stratton that the North Vietnamese were using coercion and drugs were likely false. The State Department still clung to its party line: "The prisoners are treated humanely, are well-fed by Vietnamese standards, and receive medical treatment commensurate with the Vietnamese capability."[51] This statement rang false to the women: they knew that American prisoners of war during the Korean War had suffered from terrible torture and starvation: 43 percent of them had died in captivity. Many of these POWs had even instructed the women's husbands in SERE school before they deployed to Vietnam. Based on this data, the American government's assumptions seemed worse than placating to the wives. Statistics didn't lie. The U.S. government and military, however, might.

As one MIA wife noted, "There weren't any 'how to' books to give us direction, no other role models we knew how to emulate."[52] Perhaps some of the women then turned to their protocol guides out of desperation. *The Navy Wife, The Air Force Wife, The Army Wife, The Marine Wife*—these books had been their go-to manuals, dispensing advice on every issue they might encounter as a military wife. But when the POW and MIA wives desperately searched in the index for entries on "prisoners of war" and "missing," their dog-eared guides were blank. They might as well have made a bonfire with those books, adding their government's letters on top. Instinct and common sense were rapidly taking the place of protocol among the wives. Over their communal cups of coffee in the morning and their potluck dinners at night, the women finally began to air their discontent.

The State Department had had its turn with quiet diplomacy and failed. It was time now for the women to take the controls and organize in earnest.

Six

NEW GIRL VILLAGE

BY 1967, POW AND MIA wives had become more comfortable running the show at home and in public. Changing fashions reflected their newfound independence. The bouffant lacquered hair, heavy makeup, hose, and tweed skirt suits of the early 1960s now seemed dated. Hippie culture blossomed, with "butterfly bohemians" and a more natural (and frequently bra-less) look. During 1967's "Summer of Love," flower children flocked to the Haight-Ashbury neighborhood in San Francisco to smoke pot, experience "free love," and protest the Vietnam War.

Musical happenings like the Monterey Pop Festival sprang up everywhere like magic mushrooms, the psychedelic drugs favored by the hippie crowd.[1] In November of 1967, Jann Wenner published his first issue of *Rolling Stone* magazine, which covered both the music and the politics of the day.[2] Wenner later explained the central role of late-sixties music festivals like Monterey: "I think we felt we were all at the center of something special. As casual, informal and irresponsible as it was, it had a higher purpose . . . it was evangelical."[3]

Blond, long-haired Michelle Phillips of the Mamas and the Papas, exotic-looking, brunette actress Ali MacGraw, and sexy, raven-haired Grace Slick of the band Jefferson Airplane were among the female pop icons of the era.[4] Their photos appeared often in *Rolling Stone, Vogue,* and *Harper's Bazaar,* illuminating an updated "New Look" for the late 1960s. "Standards for fashion and physical appearance underwent a drastic makeover. Clothes became more comfortable, colorful and dramatic."[5] Miss America, once the icon of apple-pie American femininity, was now considered hopelessly bourgeois. In her stead, folk singer Judy Collins, with her long, straight hair, was the ideal. Exotic socialite Talitha Getty (married to playboy oil heir John Paul Getty Jr.), who sported elaborately patterned caftans and dangling earrings sourced from the bazaars of Marrakesh, was the epitome of laid-back cool. Talitha became a muse of French couturier Yves Saint Laurent, who translated her allure into bohemian luxe gowns on the runway.

In 1966, Saint Laurent again "broke ground when he proposed that women wear trousers with suits, such as his 'Le Smoking' tuxedo-style outfit." This was still seen as shocking and inappropriate by many. Even as late as 1969, Representative Charlotte T. Reid would incite a frenzy (mostly among her male colleagues) when "she showed up in Congress wearing a pantsuit, the first time a woman had worn pants there."[6]

This late-sixties iteration of the New Woman was sophisticated, internationally aware, and outspoken even in the halls of Congress. Her clothes signaled that she was not going to accept the status quo, the party line, or men telling her what to do. Instead, she might venture into political activism, public service, or a music festival with impunity. And, best of all, a woman could finally be comfortable while she took on the world, whether in a caftan or in pants.

Conservative military wives in their forties, like Sybil and Jane, were not as quick to adopt such radical sartorial changes as the younger wives in their twenties and thirties. West Coast wives like Jenny, Debby, Karen, and Patsy arguably took more chances with their fashion choices than more conservative East Coast wives, like Jane, Janie, and Dot McDaniel. But whether you were on the East or West Coast, whether you skewed younger or older, it was impossible to ignore the sweeping cultural changes taking place. The clothes, music, and movies of the time reflected the struggles taking place both domestically and abroad. The Vietnam War was always at the epicenter of these debates.

POW/MIA wives had begun to ditch their prim suits and pearls for Pucci shifts and plastic beads. They would soon begin to storm Washington in attempts not only to reform the ineffective policies of stuffy pinstriped government officials, but also to reject the veil of silence forced on them by the current and previous administrations.

In early 1967, information regarding the POWs coming from the American government remained scarce. The International Red Cross was not allowed to inspect prisoner-of-war camps: its usual role as an intermediary in wartime conflict had been neutralized. Soon into the conflict, they were completely shut out by the Communists in North Vietnam. In the past, the IRC had overseen mail delivery to and from the early prisoners of war in the camps.[7]

But as the conflict continued, this avenue also seemed to be narrowing, with less and less correspondence getting through to the prisoners' families in the United States. POW wives were getting more and more desperate for information and reassurance of their husbands' health and safety. The American government was having little to no success in its efforts to obtain clear lines of communication in and out of the prison camps.

Jane hadn't received a letter from Jerry in months. She had hoped for a Christmas letter from her POW husband, but this was not to be. She and the other POW wives knew now not to expect much in terms of delivery through traditional Red Cross channels.[8] With no Jerry at home to help her with discipline, she felt that her rambunctious younger children were getting out of control. On Sunday, January 8, she spanked all of her little ones after church. She recalled later that the children "weren't really bad, but they weren't really good—too wiggly and I decided they should learn. Right now I feel I have allowed myself to be too lax and all the children are showing it. I'm trying to be more strict—maybe I'm just being mean."[9]

However, other POW wives would soon receive communications from their husbands from an unexpected source. On January 10, four American women, affiliated with Women Strike for Peace (WSP), a

D.C.-based peace group, brought twenty-one letters home from American POWs. This organization was founded in November of 1961 with a one-day national peace protest, led by a small group of mostly middle-class white women from Washington. "They came from liberal to left political backgrounds, having been pacifists, Quakers, New Deal Democrats, socialists, anarchists, Communist sympathizers, and Communist Party members."[10] The fear of nuclear war and its consequences initially drove the organization.

Like many of the POW and MIA wives, WSP women were well-educated and well-heeled and had many more options than their mothers had had when it came to working outside the home. Like their military wife counterparts, though, "the women who joined the peace strike . . . made the choice to devote themselves to live-in motherhood."[11] These women had much in common with the POW and MIA wives from an educational and socioeconomic standpoint and shared the same domestic focus. But the two groups were diametrically opposed politically. This divide seemed to be unbridgeable in the early days of the war. Conservative military wives, along with the press and the general public, saw WSP women and other female peace protesters as "kooks," "commies," and even "housewife terrorists."[12]

WSP had been the first group to stage a mass protest at the Pentagon, in the winter of 1967, when "twenty-five hundred women carrying enlarged photos of napalmed North Vietnamese children under the slogan, 'Children are Not for Burning,' demanded to see the Pentagon generals who were responsible for the killings." The women literally banged on the doors of the Pentagon complex with their shoes to make their point. The WSP women specifically wanted an audience with Secretary of Defense Robert McNamara, who promptly barred the door. This story received huge amounts of media attention and publicity.[13] Jane, Sybil, and the other POW and MIA wives on both coasts knew exactly who these women were. How could they miss them? They were so *out there,* so loud and pushy! But the POW wives were now finding that more frequent lines of communication were coming not from their own government but from the government protesters they so reviled.

The WSP would become the first American women's peace group "to establish person-to-person relations with the Vietnamese. Vietnamese leaders concerned with external relations began to think of the WSP women as very dear old friends."[14] When WSP brought back precious communications from the POWs that January of 1967, Jane's close friend and fellow Virginia Beach POW wife Janie Tschudy was one of the lucky few to receive a letter from her husband, Bill. In Coronado, Sybil's spirits rose at the receipt of a letter as well. At the same time, she was infuriated by the mail's bearers and their motives. She sniped that the Women Strike for Peace crowd were "welcomed in Hanoi by the North Vietnamese and then came home and babbled the North Vietnamese propaganda line about treatment of prisoners like so many wind-up robots."[15]

The Vietnam War and its growing issues would breed a new version of the WSP woman, one militant in her beliefs and much more sympathetic to the Communist regime in the North. Cora Weiss, one of the leaders of Women Strike for Peace, was to become the archnemesis of the POW and MIA wives as the war raged on.

Cora's father, Fabergé perfume empire magnate Samuel Rubin, was widely reputed to be a member of the Communist Party. (His son Reed, Cora's brother, was named after John Reed, the first American Communist representative to the Soviet Comintern, 1919–1920). Cora and her husband, lawyer Peter Weiss, were steeped in Rubin's political views. After Rubin sold the Fabergé business in 1963 for $25 million, he established the Samuel Rubin Foundation to further causes aligned with his political views. Daughter Cora and son-in-law Peter doled out Rubin Foundation funds to support left-leaning causes in the United States.[16]

Peace demonstrators and antiwar activists were the opposition in the minds of most military wives like Sybil and Jane. They often tried to force their views—and propaganda pamphlets—on grieving military families. As time went on, these "peace" groups essentially held the POW wives—and their husbands—hostage as they became the sole pipeline for letters and information about the POWs. "We were over a barrel," noted West Coast POW wife Jenny Connell Robertson.

The POW wives were "wanting the letters yet not from groups we thought could do more harm than good to the men."[17] But for the moment, most of the twenty-one POW wives who received letters rejoiced just knowing that their husbands were still alive.

Jane Denton would have to wait until February 4, when she finally received a letter—through the American government, not the peace activists. "A red letter day!" she exclaimed. "We got a letter from Jerry. Thank God. He says he's all right and seems all right. His message is short and written on a greeting card—he didn't have room to say much but all the important things are there." Later that night, Jane wrote, "Today I was at last alone—children outside—and I poured a glass of sherry and toasted Jerry. I felt he was with me—just the two of us. It was a quiet, happy, confident feeling. I felt like we had licked all kinds of odds and the end was in sight. We couldn't lose. I can't really explain it. The main thing was I felt we were together and sharing, really sharing, the moment."[18]

Jane admitted that getting a letter from Jerry made her eldest son's imminent departure for Army training camp a bit less painful. But her elation would be short-lived. Two days later, Jane tearfully sent Jerry III on his way. The younger Jerry's best friend, Bill McFarland, had been killed in combat earlier in the Vietnam conflict. Soon after Bill's death, Jerry had decided to train as an Army helicopter test pilot at Fort Eustis, near Newport News. He decided to enlist "to honor my Dad and Bill McFarland and so someone else wouldn't have to fill my billet."[19]

(On July 20, 1969, young Jerry would land in Vietnam the same night that Neil Armstrong landed on the moon.[20] The next day, he headed for Bien Hoa Air Base and his new assignment with the 334th Armed Helicopter Company, the only armed helicopter unit in Vietnam.) Jane understood why her oldest son felt he had to go; she didn't try to stop him from serving. How could she say no as a military wife and mom? But now, not one but two of her dear ones were in harm's way. She must have wondered if she would ever see her son or her husband—or either of them—return. Would they arrive safely in an aircraft carrier's passenger seat or in a coffin draped with the American flag and stored in the aircraft cargo hold? Many rosaries would be said and many tears shed before these homecoming scenarios would be resolved.[21]

Sybil had started a teaching job at the end of January in the Chula Vista School District. She reveled in her work, which kept her busy and intellectually engaged. Her boys were happy in school—Taylor had just started kindergarten. As the children grew older, she was beginning to have more time for both her job and her activism. Her frame of mind was cheerful and more confident that Jim would be home soon and that she was doing everything possible to help the government with this effort. In her diary, she wrote, "Classes began and I <u>love</u> the students. I also <u>love</u> having lunch in the cafeteria, All the teachers <u>very</u> nice. The day flies. Such a blessing."[22]

When she learned that Bob Boroughs would be visiting her in Coronado at the end of February, Sybil was elated. She had been coding letters to Jim for months now. Finally, the fruits of this covert activity might be ripe for a reveal. She took a day off school to pick up Boroughs at the airport and spend the day with him at ONI in San Diego. She chatted away about her teaching and her four boys while Boroughs stayed mostly silent on their car ride to ONI. Sybil's optimism suddenly felt misplaced.

When the POW wife and the Naval Intelligence officer finally arrived at ONI, a low-slung building surrounded by a high chain-link fence, Boroughs led Sybil to a small, spare room, leaving her alone to read a chemically developed secret message from Jim. "I sat there, on one of those cold folding metal chairs and remember so well looking at the words 'EXPERTS IN TORTURE HAND AND LEG IRONS 16 HOURS A DAY,' along with a long list of names who had been captured or were there in person."[23]

Sybil felt the bile rise in her throat. Thank God she had spotted a trash can in that barren room in case she had to throw up. She surely would have thought about not only Jim but also the other POWs, like Jerry Denton, her husband's friend and Naval Academy classmate, who were surely suffering the same fate at the hands of the North Vietnamese. It was clearly even worse than she, Jane, and the other POW and MIA wives had imagined.

After what seemed like hours, Boroughs finally opened the door. Sybil angrily demanded, "Why did you show this to me?" He replied evenly, "Wouldn't have gotten those names and the truth without your help and I thought you'd want to know the truth." He was right: she did want to know the truth. But the burden of the truth—and of that kind of classified knowledge—came at a high price.[24] How would she keep this knowledge to herself? Away from her boys and her POW and MIA wife friends like Patsy in Coronado? And Jane in Virginia Beach? They couldn't know. No one could know. At least, she comforted herself, the government now knew exactly what was going on over there. *Now the administration will surely do something to help them,* she thought. *Please, God, let them help my poor Jim.*[25]

As the months wore on, the POW and MIA wives on both coasts continued to hew to their routines as much as possible. The women in each community already knew one another well. "They attended many of the same functions, served on the same boards, shopped in the same post exchanges, sent their children to the same schools."[26] However, many were feeling less and less welcome at their home bases. Without their husbands, their place was uncertain in the military community. Some senior commanders asked POW and MIA wives to leave base housing, because of "the emotional impact they might have on the community of wives waiting for their husbands' return."[27]

Perhaps it was a feeling of impending doom that caused some military wives to exclude POW and MIA wives from their gatherings. Any aviator could be shot down anytime. In the minds of some non-POW military wives, if they didn't include those women whose husbands were prisoners in their social events, they could deny the danger their own husbands faced and magically keep the same fate from happening to them. Sybil was very conscious of this attitude between the POW/MIA wives and other military wives: "We made the other wives very uncomfortable . . . Because they would look at us and say, 'Oh my gosh that could be me.'"[28]

The POW wives themselves at times avoided social gatherings with other military wives—it depressed them and they felt out of place. Jane Denton wrote about such a meeting in her diary in March of 1967. "This morning, I went to a VA 75 coffee—the first time since Sept. '65. They've been nice about inviting me almost every month—but I don't like to go. Janie [Tschudy] went also—it was a farewell for Judy Kenny and Ellen Mott—the last of the girls I knew and liked and both have been very kind to me. All new group otherwise—of course, Rita was there—she took me. I enjoyed it in a way but it was definitely the last Navy wives' activity I want to or will go to—All that business seems like a . . . *cruel?)* make-believe game."[29]

Thankfully, the POW and MIA wives had begun to find one another and to forge their own unique communities. They no longer fit in the traditional military structure, so they had to fashion a new community to support their radically changed circumstances. In December of 1967, Jenny and Karen would move to La Jolla, in north San Diego. Debby would also move, to a few hours north to Fairmont. Karen was working as a registered nurse in Hanford, California, several days a week and finishing up her college degree. All three women had little children. Karen and Debby worked as nurses to make ends meet.[30]

For this reason, the POW and MIA wives tended to cluster together socially. Fellow POW wife Patsy Crayton had become one of Sybil's dearest friends as they bonded over their lost husbands. Patsy was younger than Sybil, worked for a lawyer in town, and had no children, but she often hung out with Sybil and her sons. The women lived close to each other in Coronado, and the Hotel del Coronado pool became their oasis. Patsy recalled one day when the stress overtook Sybil. "In the beginning, we would go to the Hotel del Coronado to the pool and we'd sit there and talk, and the boys, whoever was around, would go swimming. And one day, we hadn't been there very long, and Stanford [Sybil's third son] yelled out, 'Mom, Taylor [the youngest] has the ball, and he won't give it back to me!' And she said,

'Life's not fair and the sooner you figure it out, the better off you'll be!' The entire pool crowd stood up and clapped."[31]

Like the Amazons of Greek mythology, these women formed an almost exclusively female world where their lives centered around coping with war. Like the women of that mythical tribe, the POW/MIA wives were single parents, filling both maternal and paternal roles. Many of these women, like Patsy, Karen, and Debby, were earning income from jobs outside the home. The situation compelled these wives to "assert themselves, to gain control of the family, and to establish themselves as the rightful and legal representatives of the absent husband and the family." As they did this, they gained experience, confidence, and more power.[32]

Over in Vietnam, the POWs had quickly set up their own network, despite their frequent separation from one another by thick concrete prison walls. Even there, they bonded and established a "tap code" to communicate. Through the code, Jim Stockdale, Jim Mulligan, Jerry Denton, and many others were also able to retain their command structure, even in solitary confinement.[33]

Another way the men coped was to give their prison camps tongue-in-cheek American names. In addition to the Hanoi Hilton, camp wags identified sections within the larger camp with other American-themed names. Newly shot-down pilots were typically processed and housed within the confines of "New Guy Village." Here, the newbie prisoners learned the ropes—literally, from rope torture, and figuratively, by entering the Vietnamese prison system. Then there was "Little Vegas," composed of buildings named after Las Vegas Strip hotels: Riviera, Stardust, Desert Inn, Mint, and Thunderbird.[34]

In Coronado and in Virginia Beach, the POW/MIA wives were establishing their own version of a bonded community. New Girl Villages began to take root. Here the women figured out their strategy. They realized that, alone, they were tilting at windmills in a quixotic quest to be heard. But together, as a unified group, their voices might gain resonance and their distress codes might eventually transmit a significant message their government could no longer ignore.

Seven

THE LEAGUE OF WIVES

Shy, intelligent Phyllis Galanti, who had always been afraid to speak publicly, got a crash course in Government Runaround 101 in the months and years that followed her husband, Paul's, shoot-down and imprisonment in North Vietnam in June of 1966. Phyllis, an Army brat from Roanoke, Virginia, had graduated with a degree in French from the prestigious College of William and Mary, but she would not teach in a classroom. The very idea of standing up in front of a roomful of students and talking to them made her nauseous.[1]

Now she did not have the luxury of avoiding public discourse. Speaking out or choosing not to had become a matter of vital importance for the POW and MIA wives. She had kept quiet, had followed the rules set down by her government, and nothing was moving forward. Did anyone *really* know what was going on with the men? She didn't see how government officials knew anything at all, since the Red Cross was not being allowed into the POW camps for inspections.

By March of 1967, Phyllis was making regular trips to Virginia Beach to meet with the other POW/MIA wives living there. On March 2, Jane Denton noted in her diary that she had talked to Phyllis on the phone. She had invited Phyllis to Virginia Beach on Saturday, March 4, to have dinner with other area POW/MIA wives. Jane and Janie Tschudy were the hostesses. Though it was a "school night," stiff drinks like G&Ts would have been available, along with white wine.

The guest list included Jenny Keller, Janie Marick, Pat Fellowes, Phyllis Galanti, Carol Brett (Air Force), Louise Mulligan, Louise Brady, and Betty Yarborough. As the wife of the highest-ranking Navy POW in the Virginia Beach area, Jane knew it was her duty to host the women. But she had hesitated to do so. Jane was very private and not one who loved to entertain. She often had to force herself to go out socially after Jerry's shoot-down.

In her diary, she recalled of the dinner, "It was time I did this— I'm glad I did, but I'm glad it's over, I think it went off alright. Every-one seemed to like getting together. I'm trying to analize [sic] my feelings. I felt a stimulation and a sort of 'I will be gay' feeling—I tried hard to be encouraging, determined and optimistic as the oldest one of the group and also as the one who [with Janie Tschudy] has been in this situation for the longest time."[2]

The women talked about everything and seemed to agree on many aspects of the situation. Jane noted that all the ladies enjoyed imag-ining what it would be like when (not *if*) their husbands finally returned. Would there be ticker-tape parades for the returning men? they wondered.

Still, Jane's sharp eye had already discerned certain divisions and differences of opinion in the group. The strain was slowly beginning to peel off the veneer of politesse. Personality traits that had been sub-merged in military wife protocols began to emerge more clearly and more forcefully in some of the women. Jane and Louise, in particular, often had differing viewpoints on the war and the men's role in Vietnam.

"Louise and I differed on the one matter as we usually do . . . whether or not professionals [meaning those who had chosen the mil-itary as a career] only should be fighting this war. I don't feel strongly on this point, but Louise and I frequently disagree on one or another aspect of the war." Jane continued, observing of Louise, "She's a very positive person and I think it bothers me because she touches a tender spot of doubt in my mind which I want submerged. I don't know whether I believe and have faith in our commitment and conduct of the war because I really believe [in the war] myself, because Jerry has instilled faith in me or because I want to believe."[3] Perhaps Louise was forcing the more traditional Jane to take a harder look at a conflict she had not questioned previously. Jane seemed to be questioning the whole military code, her government, and the war itself as months without news of Jerry dragged on.

After the dinner was over, the dishes were cleared, and the women had said their final goodbyes, Jane and Janie collapsed. Jane was relieved all had gone well, but she was also completely worn out. Her instinct after social gatherings with the POW/MIA wives was often to retreat to her bedroom. "Now I have the feeling I would [have] to get in a shell and not see or speak to anyone for days. This reaction is the usual thing for me after making myself project."[4]

While Jane was more soft-spoken and initially hesitant to comment publicly about the war, Louise was more forceful. A fiercely intelligent, no-nonsense New Englander, Louise was skeptical of Washington rhetoric regarding the POWs from the start. As the war wore on and she received letters from the government that she thought were giving her the runaround, she used a special stamp on them: it spelled out BULLSHIT. She wished she could send them back to the government without getting sued, surveilled, or both.

It wouldn't be long, though, before she would be putting her own verbal stamp on things by speaking out on behalf of her husband and the other POWs and MIAs.

By April, the nerves of the POW and MIA wives in Virginia Beach were seriously frayed. Agitation was in the air—many of the wives had now gone two years without their husbands and with scarce updates from their government. Harriman belatedly picked up on the smoke signals. On April 4, the Crocodile finally sent two State Department officials to brief Navy and Air Force wives in the area. The reaction of two POW wives who were becoming prominent activists was courteous but skeptical.

Louise Mulligan took issue with the government's positions. She noted that after two years of the "soft-sell," political negotiations "have not produced anything but more lives lost and more commitment" in Vietnam. Louise, like Jane, held up the war crimes trial incident as an example of the power that world opinion held over the North Vietnamese. "Cannot pressure be leveled in this direction to better prisoner relations?"[5]

Phyllis had traveled to Oceana for the meeting that day. Like Louise, she was not falling for the government runaround. She wrote to Harriman, "I am still not convinced that the prisoner situation is receiving the priority due it by our government and by the International Red Cross." IRC was assigned the duty of regulating the mail traffic between the prisoner camps and the families and was failing spectacularly at its job, as Jane had correctly surmised after meeting with Washington IRC reps when her husband was first shot down.

Like Sybil and Louise, Phyllis also highlighted the inadequacy of State Department communications with the POW/MIA wives and families. They were both infrequent and impersonal. Washington continued to overlook the emotional impact this dearth of news had on the community. "It would be so reassuring to the wives of the prisoners if we could just be contacted periodically by the State Department . . . As I said before, we are vitally involved and we are starved for any news that may concern our husbands."[6]

In her diary on the night of the April 4 meeting, Jane Denton recorded her impressions of the edgy meeting:

I learned nothing new but feel the meeting was very worthwhile in that it gave us an opportunity to discuss all aspects of prisoner situation with them —and altho' much of the comment and info is based on speculation and indefinite info it does add to our understanding and knowledge to discuss with them. They also learned from us. There were a number of details which we have learned

*and told them—most important we had the opportunity to show
how informed and alert we are to what they're doing.* We are no
longer a faceless group.[7]

As Sybil had also noted earlier, there was no substitute for a face-
to-face meeting. Government officials had avoided these meetings as
much as possible. Now the ladies had both faces and voices, and they
were refusing to be ignored.

The party line was still that the prisoners were being treated well, despite much evidence to the contrary. When the government officials still
insisted this was true, even Jane Denton, traditional, deferential, and
respectful of the military, felt her hackles rise: "I vehemently disagreed
today when Mr. Flotte said they [*sic*] POWs are being treated well."

Jane continued her own personal debriefing in her diary, again trying to figure out the players and how the pieces of government ma-
chinery all fit together: "I cannot understand the lack of cooperation
between Navy and State and I don't know where to place blame. Navy
has same traditional attitude that State is made up of ineffectual
elete / efete (sp)—I don't really feel this is deserved—Navy accuses them
of not being cooperative—I don't know what State's side is."[8] These
tensions and cracks in the government's facade were already evident to
the women who were working with them. Collaboration among the
departments, even when it was a matter of life and death for the prisoners of war, seemed near impossible to most government officials.

It took those intimately concerned with the POW/MIA situation—
wives and family members—to zero in on the issues that mattered.
The problems were obvious, the solution muddy. But it did not take a
genius to see that few in Washington were paying adequate attention
to the missing and imprisoned soldiers. The State Department saw the
POW/MIA wives as a nuisance, an afterthought and a political
liability for the Johnson administration.

Sweeping POW torture under the rug bought the State Department
and Harriman time to do the "soft sell," but, as Louise Mulligan noted
early on, this method had serious flaws. There was no open-door policy
for the POW/MIA wives when it came to their president or to most of

his staff. Like their Women Strike for Peace counterparts before them who had banged their shoes on the doors of the Pentagon, conservative POW and MIA wives who had sacrificed their husbands for their country found the door to their government officials similarly barred.

As LBJ continued to build up the U.S. ground troops and ratchet up the air war with Operation Rolling Thunder, the bad news spread across the country to wives from all branches of the armed services. Whereas the East and West Coasts were hubs for naval aviators, the interior West was the nerve center for Air Force men and their families. Colorado Springs, Colorado, once best known for its role in the Pike's Peak Gold Rush, was now home to the Air Force Academy and its large community of Air Force personnel and their families. These aviators were heavily involved in the same dangerous bombing missions as the Navy pilots. They were just as vulnerable to being shot down as their Navy counterparts.

On April 24, 1967, Helene Knapp, wife of Air Force pilot Major Herman "Herm" Knapp, was in her kitchen cleaning and happened to look out the window. She saw her neighbor Marion Kunce gazing at a blue car that had just pulled up in Helene's driveway. Out stepped an Air Force colonel and an enlisted woman. Helene knew immediately that the news could not be good, and her stomach knotted up. She invited her guests into her living room, where they proceeded to give her some terrible news.

"Ma'am, your husband, Herman Knapp, has been shot down over Vietnam. He has not yet been found."

"You must mean he is dead," Helene said, her voice trembling. Suddenly Helene's son Robbie burst into the room, having been awakened from his nap by the strange voices and the commotion. "Mommy, did these people come to shoot us?" Robbie asked, his lips quivering. "No, honey, of course not," Helene responded soothingly as her son nestled close to her on the sofa.

The newly minted MIA wife listened skeptically as her military visitors told her that Herman could be alive and a POW, but that she should not tell anyone about his circumstances. Helene's immediate gut reaction was, "This was ludicrous. How does one live a daily life keeping such a life-changing situation a secret?" Without her consent, she had just entered the same reluctant sorority that many of the East and West Coast wives had been initiated into some months before.[9]

Dot McDaniel, in Virginia Beach, was another POW wife who was quickly becoming more forceful in her efforts on behalf of her POW husband, Red McDaniel. Like Jim Stockdale, Red was a friend of Jerry Denton's and a fellow Navy pilot shot down in North Vietnam, during a routine bombing run on May 19, 1967. He had written Dot numerous letters and sent audiotapes about his growing disillusionment with the leadership in Washington. He felt the bombing targets had been chosen by Washington, for political reasons, not by military commanders in the field. Though the bombing runs were extremely dangerous, the targets were insignificant. The feeling among many of the experienced pilots like Red was that "we're fighting this air war with our hands tied behind our backs. It's a tough way to fight a war. And it's probably going to last a long, long time."[10] Like Jane and Louise had noted before, there was a huge divide between military men and non-military government officials about how the war should be fought, which was making the airmen's job nearly impossible.

As the months wore on after Red's shoot-down, Dot grew more resentful of government POW policy. "Our whole world had collapsed, but we weren't supposed to talk about it. That made it really hard to explain to people what had happened." Her children, Mike, David, and Leslie, were her primary concern. Her two boys did not understand why they could not tell anyone what had happened to their dad. "Is there something wrong with being shot down?" Mike asked. Dot simply did not know how to answer her son without compounding his worry.[11]

When Dot made her first pilgrimage to Washington to talk to State Department and Pentagon officials, as Sybil, Phyllis, Jane, Janie, and many other POW and MIA wives had before her, she, too, returned home shocked and disillusioned. "The man in the State Department told me he had 'reason to believe' our POWs were being treated well, but he couldn't tell me what made him think so." Even worse were congressmen and senators on Capitol Hill who hadn't a clue. Most knew little about the war and nothing about the POWs. One congressman suggested that Dot contact the Red Cross about getting mail through to her husband. Dot politely told him, "The Red Cross isn't allowed into Vietnam." She mentally noted that all the government folks seemed to parrot the same script—"we will do everything we can"[12] to help, they all said, like mechanical dolls or puppets. But Dot, like all the other wives, knew that there was no substance or knowledge of the situation behind this generic claim.

Dot quickly became a friend and an ally to both Jane and Janie. They were all trapped in the same horrible scenario, desperately trying to figure things out. They knew of Sybil Stockdale and her work within the San Diego community, of course. Sybil was frequently in Washington, pressing the flesh with senators, congressmen, State and Defense Department staff—anyone who would talk to her about the POW/MIA plight.

Sybil and Jane had talked many times on the phone since Jim's shoot-down, but on July 18, Sybil arrived in Virginia Beach to see Jane in person and to meet with some of the other POW/MIA wives in the area. July 18 just happened to be the second anniversary of Jerry's shoot-down. Jane's diary recorded the visit with the momentous date at the top of her mind:

2 years today. I wouldn't have believed this could go on like this. It's all a nightmare that never ends. Sybil Stockdale flew down here today and I spent several hours talking to her. We had so much to talk about and have like thoughts, concerns and, of course, hopes. I like her and we think generally alike. She isn't as positive as she seems to be in letters but is as confused as I am about like things.

We agree that prisoners are not being well treated at all and want
everyone to be aware of this and gov't to use all possible force to get
better treatment. She heard about and has corresponded with ex-
prisoners and gave me copies of letters. We're going to try to work
on best possible arrangements being made now for repatriation and
rehabilitation, so that past mistakes will be avoided. Navy is work-
ing on this—we want to be sure they're giving it top priority.[13]

Though there was still a divide between Jane and Louise Mulligan, Sybil encouraged both of them to work with her—and the other West Coast women—for the POW/MIA cause, though no formal group had been created just yet. Dot had recently joined the group and remembered the tension between the two senior officers' wives. "Louise Mulligan and Jane Denton were always arguing with each other: they had very different points of view."[14] Though the meetings were always civil and respectful, they were also tense.

At thirty-four, Dot was a seasoned military wife but still a good bit younger than Louise and Jane. She felt more like a spectator at these early, informal get-togethers. She watched the two older women debate the pros and the cons of "keeping quiet" versus "going public" with their husbands' scenarios. It was a bit like a tennis match, watching the ball being hit back and forth between two wives who were polar opposites personality-wise. At this point, Jane and Louise possessed totally different opinions about how to proceed in the murky waters that surrounded them all. Jane was a "stabilizing force," wrote Dot, who considered Jane her role model. She described her as a real lady, dignified, "but she was always scared we would lose our dignity and the men's if we did something wrong."[15] Louise was more willing to put herself out there publicly. As Dot put it, "she would tear the roof off the White House" to get results. "She was brash, in your face. She did not care about manners, the niceties, she wanted to get things done." Dot also remembered that Louise would always quote Sybil to the group as the authority on the POW/MIA issues.[16] Sybil and Louise were two of a kind. Both New Englanders, they did not have the deference that many southern women of the time were raised from birth to project. Sybil may have sensed a certain reluctance in Jane to come forward early in the crisis. Jane and the other wives had good reason to mull things over and to think before jumping into the fray. More traditional women like Jane were important in the group dynamic. They kept the peace, held the group together, and smoothed the path for Louise and others who were more willing to speak out.

What the Virginia-area POW/MIA wives would find was that they needed the yin and yang of Louise and Jane to make their efforts a success. These two senior wives provided checks and balances for each other. Each would strengthen the women's cause in different and valuable ways.

Sybil and Jane had a key friend in common, though they would not have discussed this connection at their July 18 meeting. On July 31, Jane went to D.C. to visit with Bob Boroughs at Naval Intelligence. She was desperate for new information about Jerry, but Bob had none to offer that day. Jane also visited representatives in the State Department—they also came up empty-handed, as did the Bureau of Naval Personnel. Jane felt even more hopeless after this latest visit.

"I feel no progress has been made toward peace or treatment of prisoners. It's [*sic*] seems so damn empty and bordering on hopeless—I can only pray—what else—can't someone untangle this damn mess. I made it clear that I consider the present state of affairs unexceptable [*sic*]—something new must be tried."[17]

Jane's growing feeling that the government was not doing their job well in terms of the men was compounded by an August 8 article by syndicated columnist (and later Pulitzer Prize winner) Jack Anderson, titled "Disturbing Reports on U.S. Prisoners." In the article, Anderson reported: "Disturbing whispers have leaked out that the Johnson administration has not done all it could to arrange better treatment of American prisoners in enemy hands."

The columnist, who cultivated lower-level State Department officials to get the straight scoop on D.C. politics, revealed: "One high official complained to this column that prisoner problems have been given low priority in the State Department." Ultimately, Anderson concluded, "The great Pentagon hush-up seems to be aimed less to protect the prisoners than to protect the authorities from criticism."[18] The article dovetailed with what Jane, Sybil, Louise, Dot, and other wives had noticed at State Department meetings. After reading a copy of the column in the *New Haven Register,* Sybil immediately sent telegrams to Secretary of State Dean Rusk and Chief of Naval Operations (CNO) Admiral Thomas Moorer. Moorer, who was relatively new to his job, had refused to see Sybil before. Now she had thrown a hand grenade that might allow her to blast down the CNO's office door.

It worked. Two days later, she had not only a response from Moorer, but an invitation for lunch on August 16 in Washington.[19] At the luncheon, Sybil was surprised to be having lunch with not only Admiral Moorer and his wife but also the outgoing CNO, Admiral Semmes, whom she had deemed worthless in the past. Though Sybil liked Moorer and found him a vast improvement over Semmes, she was shocked and infuriated when Semmes blatantly tried to buy her off by offering her a job working for him. "Keep quiet" had reached a new low—now hush money seemed to be on the table.

Sybil would have none of it. "I thought, 'Why you smooth article, you're trying to buy me off.'" She shocked herself when she exploded at Semmes: "If I told the other wives the truth about how I feel right now about your help they'd leave feeling worse rather than better." This, of course, made for a very awkward lunch meeting. Moorer's wife tried to smooth things over, which a grateful Sybil appreciated. But the meeting only deepened her distrust and strengthened her resolve to take POW/MIA matters into her own hands. She would soon transmit word of her latest D.C. debacle to the other wives—and effectively mobilize their support.[20]

Sybil had been corresponding with Phyllis since soon after Paul's shootdown, sharing information about the POWs from her sources and writing Phyllis personal notes of support.[21] When Phyllis received an update from Sybil in mid-August of 1967 about her meetings with

Averell Harriman and Admirals Semmes and Moorer over the summer, she immediately telegraphed Sybil's information to other POW and MIA wives on the East Coast.

"We have been told by the State Department that every attempt is being made to secure [humane] treatment. In spite of their assurances, we have achieved nothing in that area; and the treatment of our men are still great unknowns." Phyllis continued, gaining momentum as she wrote: "We wives who are vitally concerned must convince our government that we are not willing to sit idly. Time is precious to us, and we must have more decisive action than what we have seen to date." Phyllis urged her fellow wives to write to Harriman and "convey to him our dissatisfaction with the lack of progress regarding the prisoners."[22]

By late October of 1967, POW/MIA wives' groups on the East Coast began meeting more formally. Virginia Beach, where Naval Air Station Oceana was located, quickly became the hub of the East Coast wives' activity. They were a small group at first, perhaps thirty or forty women, but their numbers soon began to multiply.

Phyllis steadily ramped up her involvement in the movement. She and the tenacious Evie Grubb, from Petersburg, Virginia, first met at a regional POW/MIA wives' meeting hosted by Louise Mulligan at her home in Newport News on October 23, 1967. Paul Galanti had been captured just five months after Evie's Air Force pilot husband, Newk, was shot down. Evie recalled, "All this time I had been feeling so alone and lost, as had Phyllis, and we were living only 30 miles apart!"[23] The two women quickly became good friends and began driving to Virginia Beach together for the regional POW/MIA gatherings. The East Coast movement was spreading fast—flourishing, in fact, under the umbrella of Sybil Stockdale and her West Coast wives.

Month after month, in seemingly idyllic Coronado, the San Diego–area wives had written individual letters to the State Department, begging for someone—anyone—from the State Department to come talk to them and update them about what was going on in Vietnam.

These letters were met with a deafening silence.[24] No one cared much about an individual wife and what the government considered small problems. Harriman and his crew had sent reps to talk to the East Coast POW wives in April—wasn't that enough? The West Coast was perceived to be so far from Washington as to be almost irrelevant, despite the high concentration of POW and MIA wives there.

Fueling the West Coast women's concerns was intel from the Virginia Beach wives. Several of them had talked to State Department representatives who told them they believed their captured husbands were being held in private homes in Vietnam and were teaching English to the Vietnamese. Sybil was incensed: how could they possibly be so gullible?[25]

At the Pentagon, however, there were some who recognized the women's plight. Bob Boroughs at Naval Intelligence continued to demonstrate his concern about the West Coast POW/MIA wives. He saw the neglect going on and the anguish these women were suffering. He also knew the State Department was not doing a proper job. He and his assistant Pat Twinem had observed firsthand how the State Department often refused to share information on the captured men with the Pentagon.[26] Bob had worked in the Navy long enough to know how things worked, how to solve conundrums. Here was an issue Boroughs realized had a simple solution.

The Naval Intelligence agent was convinced that Sybil needed to have the West Coast wives organize formally. They needed to establish the group legally, elect officers, create bylaws, print stationery. The group needed to legitimize itself so the top brass at the Pentagon, as well as the functionaries at the State Department, would be forced to take their cause seriously.[27] Boroughs called Sybil on the phone that fall and, in a low, monotone voice, said, "Organize!" "Why now?" said Sybil. "I'm running a three-ring circus already." In the same voice, Boroughs, always a man of few words repeated, *"Organize."*[28]

By October of 1967, the West Coast POW and MIA wives did just that, under Sybil's command. The women chose the name League of Wives of American Vietnam Prisoners of War and instantly, almost magically, became a "real" group. Sybil was away for the first two meetings, tending to Jim's sick mother in Illinois. In her absence, three of Sybil's cohorts, Karen Butler, Jenny Connell, and Sandy Dennison, elected officers and finalized their organization's name. When she returned, not only were these items taken care of, but Sandy, now the League's first secretary, had rented a post office box for the group and ordered organizational stationery.[29] Shirley Stark, who also worked at the Bank of America branch at NAS North Island, became the organization's treasurer. (The group started with $19.)[30] Debby Burns was also in the mix now, doing as much as she could to help the League cause.

Soon after its inception, the group received some good news. By November, Congress had at long last amended Law 89–538 so that it would now include POWs and MIAs in the 10 percent savings plan.

The group's next move generated more surprising results. Sybil recalled, "Our secretary wrote to the State Department on our printed stationery, asking someone to come to San Diego and talk to us. The same request by the same few people, but now with our organization's title. Three weeks after she mailed the letter, Averell Harriman's assistant [Frank Sieverts] was in San Diego talking to us."[31]

Finally, things seemed to be moving in a positive direction. Washington was starting to prioritize the West Coast POW/MIA families. Bob Boroughs's advice to "organize" had galvanized the women. Their new status as a "legitimate" entity transformed them from a group of grieving housewives into humanitarian lobbyists.

Sybil laughed as she later recalled that the League "had become so by my magic wand, naming us as such."[32] Sybil was not only the League's founder; she was its fairy godmother, changing their pumpkin into a coach. Someday, they just might be invited to the ball.

Eight

INCREDIBLY SCREWED UP

On Tuesday, October 31, 1967, A Avenue in Coronado was crawling with costumed kids. Casper the Friendly Ghost, NASA astronauts, and Frankenstein monsters patrolled the streets, grasping pillowcases bulging with Swedish Fish, Pixy Stix, Astro Pops, and Fruit Stripe Gum.[1]

High schooler Jim Stockdale Jr. was enrolled at Mercersburg Academy, a boarding school in Pennsylvania, so he missed the Halloween fun at home that year. In his stead, Sid was tasked with staying home at 547 A, running the Stockdale Haunted House in the basement and handing out the candy while his younger brothers, Taylor and Stanford, hit the streets. The two younger boys knew exactly what to do, thanks to their older siblings' expert training.

Like all kids their age, Taylor and Stan's primary goal was to get as much candy as possible. Their secondary goal was to eat as much candy as possible before Mom attempted to regulate their sugar intake, or Sid demanded tribute. Perhaps they could hide out in the Stockdale Haunted House when they got home to gorge on it all. The makeshift haunted house was so small you had to crawl through it, providing a safe haven for the little boys from Mom and their older brother.[2]

On Halloween, the two youngest Stockdale boys were just like any kids on their street. When they had their costumes on, the neighborhood's other parents and kids might not even know who they were. On this one night, no one thought to pity them as the children of a Vietnam prisoner of war. It was a joyful, mad rush for candy, in costume, under cover of darkness. The anonymity of the evening and being part of the crowd, not a kid people felt sorry for, must have been a welcome feeling for both Taylor and Stan.

After Halloween, the school year zoomed into high gear. Sid was obsessed with flag football and played the drums for the school band. An amused Sybil wrote to her husband that Sid "is interested enough in girls to thoroughly enjoy his Cotillion dancing but otherwise has no time for them now."[3] Kindergartener Taylor had learned to ride a two-wheel bike. Second grader Stan was a busy bookworm and read to the family each night.

Though the boys were flourishing, Jim's mother had been ailing for months, and she died of leukemia that same fall. Sybil wrote Jim to tell him the news, but she was not sure he would ever receive her letter—she had not heard from her POW husband since the previous January. In addition to being a single parent to four boys, a teacher, and the head of a newly formed POW/MIA group, Sybil now also became the manager of a 222-acre farm in Illinois, as executrix of her mother-in-law's estate.[4]

A harried Sybil was exhausted by the time the holidays arrived. The so-called most wonderful time of the year was typically rock bottom for POW and MIA families. Inevitably, everyone was melancholy and the world seemed gray. That feeling was the new normal for the families of prisoners and missing men. "It was like a big black pall had descended over our family," said Don Denton, one of Jane and Jerry's older boys. The pall began when Jerry was shot down and hovered there. "Every year we said, 'He'll be home next year,'" noted Jim Denton, Don's younger brother.[5]

What caught Sybil by surprise when she opened the mail one sunny December morning, however, was not the posed postcards of families full of holiday cheer: she had already steeled herself for those. Instead,

she had received a letter from the Bureau of Naval Personnel inform-
ing her imprisoned husband, Jim, that he had been selected for "deep
draft command" and that the Navy would attempt to place him in
his new role as soon as possible. After the disbelief wore off, she raged,
"Jim's been a prisoner for over two years and I've certainly tried to
impress them with this fact in Washington. Still, they're so discoordi-
nated [*sic*] they send him this letter to Coronado now?"[6]

She wondered both to herself and to her League friends about the
Navy and the supposedly omniscient American government. "How
could they be so incredibly screwed up?"[7]

Like the POW wives, the American media were beginning to home in
on the Johnson administration's mixed messages regarding the war.
Walter Cronkite was perhaps America's most trusted and beloved journalist. As the anchor of the *CBS Evening News,* his was the voice and
the opinion most trusted by Americans. He was "an apple-pie American, a Missouri boy who expressed the mood of the heartland as much
as he presumably influenced its pulse beat."[8]

"Uncle Walter" was rapidly becoming a much more trusted figure
to American families than anyone in the Johnson administration. The
POW and MIA wives turned to Cronkite—not their government, nor
their military—for the real story of the conflict. Vietnam became
known as the first television war, where viewers saw the fighting and
heard the casualty reports each evening on the news. The war's bloody
battles played out nightly in people's living rooms.

After an eye-opening visit to Vietnam during the Viet Cong's Tet
Offensive, launched at the Vietnamese New Year, in late January of
1968, Cronkite decided to do something extraordinary. In what would
become known as a watershed event in American journalism, the
anchor prefaced his February 27, 1968, evening news broadcast by
acknowledging that his analysis that night would be "speculative,
personal, and subjective." Cronkite's take on the Vietnam War that fate-
ful February evening? "It seems now more certain than ever that the
bloody experience of Vietnam is to end in a stalemate."[9] What

Cronkite had witnessed firsthand was that, despite the U.S. military's claim that the United States was winning the war, American troops were losing ground against a formidable—and far more committed—Communist enemy. With this pronouncement, Cronkite dealt a mortal blow to U.S. policy in Vietnam. The "most trusted man in America" had publicly announced that the U.S. military could not win the war in Vietnam, and many Americans agreed with him. LBJ despaired when he heard the broadcast, saying something to the effect of: "If I've lost Cronkite, I've lost Middle America."[10]

Public opinion about the war became increasingly bitter after the Cronkite telecast. The heightened conflict provided fewer and fewer opportunities to get American troops—along with those imprisoned in Vietnam—back home safely. There seemed to be no clear exit strategy that would preserve the country's honor, or any exit strategy at all.

Many, including *The Washington Post*'s diplomatic correspondent in Vietnam, Don Oberdorfer, attributed the erosion of public support to the credibility of the Johnson administration. The president's office regularly issued rosy pronouncements at odds with the tactical ebb and flow on the battlefield.[11] The public was becoming more and more wary of such cheery proclamations in the face of the bloody realities they saw on television and in the daily body counts from Vietnam.

Antiwar forces were gaining momentum in the face of such hopelessness. Even staunchly conservative military wives were beginning to consider other options. Perhaps, some of the women thought, the POW families should explore alternative avenues of communication with Hanoi. Regular channels of diplomacy were all but worthless, and time was running out for some of the prisoners who were in dire need of proper medical care, food, and clean water.

One of these prisoners, Navy Lieutenant Commander John S. McCain III, had been shot down October 26, 1967, from his A-4 Skyhawk bomber. He suffered severe fractures in his right knee and in both arms upon ejection from his aircraft. After being stripped and repeatedly beaten by his captors, McCain was finally given some minimal medical treatment at a hospital in central Hanoi, only because his captors realized that his father, Admiral John Sidney

"Jack" McCain Jr., was the commander in chief of the U.S. Pacific Command.[12] Even so, the younger McCain's mosquito- and rat-infested living quarters and the amateur doctoring he received initially did little to ameliorate his desperate condition.

The young pilot spent weeks in a makeshift hospital, undergoing nightmare medical procedures. Despite the primitive medical aid, McCain was one of the lucky ones who received any medical treatment at all.[13] The downed pilot was soon moved into a filthy prison cell at the "Plantation" prison camp, in northeast Hanoi. Sleeping eighteen to twenty hours a day, his wounds festering, McCain's chances for survival looked slim.[14] How long could prisoners like him, in such dire circumstances, hold out? McCain later recalled of his fellow Vietnam POWs, "A lot of men died who shouldn't have, the victims of genuine war crimes."[15] How many more would have to suffer and die before a POW rescue finally occurred?

January 31, 1968, dawned cold and gray in Virginia Beach. Jane Denton read in the morning newspaper that a group of prominent antiwar activists were planning to go to Vietnam to meet with Communist leaders. She immediately called her Naval Intelligence contact, Bob Boroughs, and asked if she could go find out whether the group would take letters to the POWs and search for information about their whereabouts. Boroughs gave Jane the thumbs-up, and she and her good friend and fellow POW wife Janie Tschudy scrambled to collect as many letters and photos as they could from area POW and MIA families.

The next day, the two nervous but excited women flew to New York and were met by Naval Intelligence agents who drove them to the headquarters of *Liberation* magazine.[16] David Dellinger founded the far-left magazine and still served as its editor. A lifelong pacifist, he was "the most visible antiwar activist, and appeared to be its intellectual inspiration and strategist."[17]

Antiwar activists were viewed as homegrown Communists in the

eyes of most American military wives. One of the largest such organizations, the National Mobilization Committee to End the War in
Vietnam (aka "the Mobe"), was composed of left-wing activists like
Dellinger, Tom Hayden, Boston University professor Howard Zinn,
and the Catholic left priests (and real-life brothers) Daniel and Philip
Berrigan. Founded in the summer of 1966, the Mobe focused on
organizing large-scale antiwar rallies. The New Mobilization Committee to End the War in Vietnam ("the New Mobe") would continue
this work after its founding on April 15, 1967, organizing huge dem-
onstrations in New York City and at the Pentagon that same year.

Mobe members soon began traveling to Hanoi, interacting with
Communist officials, and occasionally facilitating prisoner exchanges.[18]
The intersections between the POW/MIA wives and the antiwar ac-
tivists, at one time unthinkable, were about to become more common.

As Jane and Janie pulled up to a dirty, ancient building with no el-
evators, they both wondered, *Is this really the correct address?* As they
walked up the three flights of creaky stairs, Jane made the sign of the
cross on every step. When they reached the *Liberation* office, they
found it was a messy hole in the wall, with only a typewriter, a copy
machine, one male staffer, and one female staffer. Jane and Janie were
shocked. Jane recalled, "So this was the cell that the oft-quoted, in the
media, and influencing antiwar propaganda was emanating from?"

The women explained the reason for their visit. The staffers were
helpful and made a phone call to arrange a meeting that same day with
Dellinger, Hayden, Father Daniel Berrigan, and Howard Zinn, the
group who would soon be traveling to Hanoi. The women thanked
the workers and scrambled down the stairs, pleased with their progress.

The intelligence officers next drove the two ladies to an apartment
only a block from the *Liberation* office. The two POW wives were
warned to stay no longer than thirty minutes—or their escorts would
come in and get them. To their surprise, Hayden answered the doorbell and invited them in. They sat down in the living room and were
soon joined by Berrigan, Dellinger, and Zinn.

The ladies explained their mission and gave the men the POW/

MIA families' letters and photographs. Jane recalled that "Hayden was casual and relaxed. Dellinger, the older one, let me know he had been an activist all his life. Father Berrigan sat on a chair somewhat removed from the group and stared at us in a suspicious, hostile way."

The entire meeting was over in a matter of minutes. The antiwar activists agreed to take the letters and try to find out what information they could about the POWs and the missing men. Hayden escorted the women to the elevator. Jane then asked what Naval Intelligence had instructed her to find out: "What route do you plan to take?" Hayden answered, "Via Russia." While this was not much of a secret, it further confirmed the Mobe's close ties with the North Vietnamese.

Jane later remembered, "The elevator door opened, we stepped inside, and it closed behind us. Janie and I almost collapsed, and we laughed too. We had made our effort to get information on our husbands and their comrades. It might or it might not work. But we had succeeded in one thing for sure: we had found out the route they were taking for Naval Intelligence."[19]

Jane and Janie didn't realize it at the time, but their clandestine work on behalf of their husbands would facilitate POW communication with their families and help provide some accounting for the missing. The two POW wives had done something extraordinary— something all the famous diplomats in D.C., with all their expertise, found impossible to achieve. They had broken through to the other side. To hell with diplomacy and government protocol: the women's goal was to get the men out, alive, using any means necessary.

Three airmen who had been prisoners of war were released from Hanoi that winter through the efforts of Berrigan, Zinn, Dellinger, and Hayden. Zinn later recalled the meeting with Jane and Janie from his perspective, noting that the POW wives "showed only a slight tension at meeting objectors to a war their husbands were waging; it helped perhaps that one of the emissaries [Berrigan] was a Jesuit priest and the other [Zinn himself] a professor who had been an Air Force bombardier."[20]

Berrigan and his band were just beginning to grasp the idea that they were becoming power brokers in Hanoi. They were used to being in the background, working behind the scenes. But now *they* were the diplomats. They finally had currency. "In the peace movement, you got used to being without power; that was your name. Then the invitation from Hanoi—and suddenly, what power! . . . Why we were doing what all the king's armies and all the king's men couldn't do. We were going where Mr. Rusk couldn't go, or Bundy, or the President himself."[21]

In addition to Jane Denton and Janie Tschudy, Berrigan and Zinn had one other unexpected pre-flight visit that February night they flew to Hanoi. Averell Harriman had sent one of his State Department staffers to meet with the group. Zinn remembered that the staffer "offered to validate our passport for travel to North Vietnam, an officially forbidden destination." All the same, Berrigan and Zinn declined—they had mutually agreed not to recognize any government's right to approve or deny their travel.[22]

Sybil was always curious why Bob Boroughs had told her that the State Department was too cozy with the antiwar activists. "He thought that some State Department officials were too friendly with those Americans who happily spread North Vietnamese propaganda in the United States."[23] In desperation, Harriman and his men were counting on Berrigan, Zinn, Hayden, Dellinger, Cora Weiss, and others in their network to aid them in the early releases of American prisoners. Harriman even hosted Hayden and Dellinger at the State Department to discuss their ideas.[24]

Though he didn't tell Sybil, Boroughs knew of the February 1968 meeting between State and antiwar leaders—as well as others who happened under the radar. Despite his dislike of the antiwar lobby, Boroughs realized that he, too, had to use any means necessary to get word of the POWs. Writing to Sybil from D.C. on February 12, 1968, the Naval Intel officer awaited the release of the three POWs and their escorts, saying, "Let's hope Berrigan and Zinn come out with a suit-case full of letters. It's been a long dry spell. Keep your fingers crossed."[25]

Other POW wives were not only meeting with the perceived enemy and passing messages—they were becoming full-fledged "Jane Bonds." Boroughs recruited numerous POW wives to assist Naval Intelligence in its efforts to gain more information on the captured men. Dot McDaniel recognized Boroughs as an ally almost as soon as she met him. "I had a strong suspicion that I had found a maverick bureau-crat, one who didn't buy the 'keep silent' rule."[26]

Many of Dot's friends on the East Coast—Jane, Janie, and Phyllis among them—worked with Boroughs at Naval Intelligence to produce letters into which code could be inserted.[27] Most of the women were terrified to talk to one another about what they were doing. They were, after all, risking their husbands' lives by participating. It was perhaps a Faustian deal, but the women had all seen firsthand that doing noth-ing was even more dangerous.

Sybil was one of the few women who wrote about her experiences coding secret letters, recording them for posterity. She began working with Boroughs on the West Coast in 1966, coding messages into her letters to Jim. She later recalled how exhausted she was after produc-ing these missives for encryption. It took tremendous time, effort, and careful thought.

In her diary, she recorded that her letter to Jim of May 25, 1967, looked "simple as you read it, but it took me all that time to write because almost all of it is in a cryptographic code." She continued, ad-dressing her four sons as she recorded her work for posterity, "Save your time boys, and don't try and break it [the code]. I never could, even having the formula I worked from. As I wrote, I knew that one mistake would throw the whole thing off, and oh how I labored over those words."[28]

Some of the POWs who knew these same techniques taught them to other prisoners so they could also send information back to their wives via coded letters. The men shared names of other prisoners in the POW camps, information on MIAs, reports of the torture they were undergoing, intelligence about possible North Vietnamese military plans, the location of camps, and potential nearby targets.

Jim Stockdale's son Jim Jr. would later reveal that his dad and many of the other POWs "used invisible carbon techniques, cryptography, and (at the very end) microdots to reach beyond their prison cells to the offices of Naval Intelligence and beyond."[29] The women received these seemingly innocuous letters from their husbands and promptly passed them on to Naval Intelligence for decoding.

If caught, Jim Stockdale, Jerry Denton, Paul Galanti, and numerous others who wrote and sent coded letters faced torture and probable execution. Their wives would become widows. The stakes for POWs and their wives/encryption partners were much higher than anything Sean Connery faced in the Cold War–era James Bond films playing in theaters at the time.[30]

The Pentagon, the State Department, and the Department of Defense were increasingly at odds. No one trusted anyone else, and each department kept a tight grip on its own secrets and military intelligence. Different branches were often disinclined to work together. Boroughs was uniquely positioned to see this problem. During 1967, he served on both Harriman's Interdepartmental Committee on Prisoner Matters and Defense Department general counsel Paul Warnke's DoD Prisoner of War Policy Committee.[31] Boroughs was not supposed to talk to his friends in the CIA or share intel with other government departments. But he often did. "When Bob Boroughs of Naval Intelligence reached out to other clandestine services in 1967 for their expertise, the challenge was significant. But persistence, risk-taking, and cooperation led to a durable communications network."[32] The POW wives were the bedrock of this enterprise, the conduits through which intel could pass unnoticed by the North Vietnamese.

Boroughs would also use the antiwar activists as couriers to find out as much information about the POWs and MIAs as possible. He was forced to think outside the box and to use all available outlets to get messages through to American prisoners of war. The women's former existence as military wives had strict but clear codes of conduct. Their frightening new existence involved scenarios of espionage, political intrigue, and strange wartime bedfellows the wives could not have imagined before the Vietnam conflict. Once a crisp black-and-white, the POW/MIA wives' world was now painted with many shades of gray.

Sybil, Louise, Jane, Janie, Phyllis, Dot, and many other POW wives decided to use whatever methods they had at their disposal to help their husbands. Other military wives (not just POW wives) hesitated. Sybil noticed this early on, writing later that "the officer's wives' clubs connected with different bases were hesitant to get involved because the policy had been to not say or do anything for so long." She also surmised, "I think a lot of them were afraid that if they got involved with us that perhaps it would hurt their husbands' careers."[33]

As the years dragged on, the highest priority for most of the wives became bringing the men home honorably. While this did not indicate that the POW and MIA wives supported early release for the prisoners (this was against the military Code of Conduct, though the U.S. government would consistently ignore this and allow early releases through the peace groups), it did mean communication via any possible route. As Louise Mulligan, Dot McDaniel, and many other POW wives later emphasized, "We were willing to make a deal with the devil if we had to to get our husbands back."[34]

Nine

YOU SAY YOU WANT A REVOLUTION?

IN JANUARY 1968, JUST before Jane and Janie entered their unlikely alliance with Tom Hayden, David Dellinger, and his band of radical activists, an incident took place at the White House that the POW/ MIA wives surely took notice of. Glamorous singer and *Batman* TV series star Eartha Kitt single-handedly took on the Johnson administration when she was invited to a White House luncheon on crime issues. The young star criticized LBJ's Vietnam policies in front of the fifty or so other women at the event. Kitt was so forceful in her comments, she made the First Lady, Lady Bird Johnson, cry. "You send the best of this country off to be shot and maimed," she told her fellow guests. "They rebel in the street. They will take pot . . . and they will get high. They don't want to go to school because they're going to be snatched off from their mothers to be shot in Vietnam." Kitt was just getting warmed up. She then told the First Lady that young Americans felt alienated because "they can't get to you and they can't get to the President, and so they rebel in the streets."[1] After her comments, the CIA would put Kitt under surveillance and ruin her career for a decade.

The young people weren't the only ones who couldn't get near Johnson. The POW/MIA wives and their cause were not on his agenda, either. The alienation Kitt described was reflective of what the wives were feeling also. Though Sybil, Jane, Louise, Helene, and the other POW/MIA wives would not have approved of Kitt's approach or her politics, they must have admired her courage. Revolution was brewing. The White House was beginning to burn down from the inside out. Kitt was not going to keep quiet anymore—and soon, neither would the much more rule-conscious POW and MIA wives.

On January 23, the USS *Pueblo,* an American naval intelligence collection ship sailing in international waters in the Sea of Japan, was attacked and then boarded by North Korean patrol boats. The armed North Koreans wounded several of the crew members and killed one during the assault. The *Pueblo*'s commander, Lloyd M. Bucher, and eighty-one other crew members were taken hostage before American forces could intervene.[2] The men were just beginning an eleven-month ordeal of imprisonment in North Korea. Johnson would do nothing in response.

The North Koreans, however, would do quite a bit with their prize hostages. "Communications technology had given the ancient practice of hostage-taking a whole new purpose as a tool of propaganda," wrote historian Amanda Foreman.[3] They proceeded to use them as a beacon from which to broadcast their political position. The ensuing press coverage of the incident dissected every detail of the plight of these American prisoners. Though the U.S. presence in the Sea of Japan was not illegal, "the North Koreans, by the exercise of extreme brutality and what seemed to Bucher and his men to be a credible threat of death, extracted 'confessions' that the spy ship had violated the coastal zone." Johnson still did nothing. The only way the United States was finally able to rescue the American naval crew was by submitting a formal apology to the North Koreans, while simultaneously repudiating the apology in the international media. (This could be done only on account of North Korea's ironclad control of its domestic media—the North Korean public heard only the U.S. apology, not its denial.)[4]

During their captivity, the men had found a way to communicate their ill treatment to the world: in a famous photo of eight crew members that appeared in the international press in August of 1968, all the prisoners were giving the camera the finger. They had told their captors this was the "Hawaiian good luck sign." While the Koreans didn't get it, the American press certainly did.[5] POW Paul Galanti had done the same thing in *Life* magazine in October of 1967. These images were a powerful symbol. Even in captivity, American soldiers retained their SERE skills—and their sense of humor. Still, some of the American prisoners eventually broke due to ongoing months of abuse and torture, making forced false "confessions" to satisfy their captors.

When the *Pueblo* crew finally returned home to San Diego on December 23, 1968, there was talk of court-martial for Commander Bucher and some of the crew. Though this did not happen, the military Code of Conduct came under intense scrutiny. The general conclusion was that in certain hostile and brutal situations, prisoners could be forgiven for signing false confessions. No disciplinary action would follow, given the prolonged and harsh treatment by the enemy. This would later have a great impact on the Code of Conduct regarding servicemen held in captivity in North and South Vietnam. The military had long cautioned the men to "keep quiet" themselves, to accept torture, punishment, or even death before they gave the enemy any information. Things would change as the length of prisoner captivity increased in Vietnam.

Even more significant to the POW/MIA cause at the time, however, was the intense media coverage of the *Pueblo* encounter. Sybil noted, "It was a fantastically frustrating experience . . . to have all the 'hullabalu' about these prisoners going on in the press while nothing was being said by our Government about our own men in Vietnam."[6] The inconsistent way LBJ and his staff handled this incident chipped away even more at the fragile layer of trust that the women still had in the current administration. They could also see how disengaged their president was from the prisoner issue, letting the men suffer indefinitely at the hands of the North Koreans. The president's lack of action and engagement with the *Pueblo* prisoners did not build their confidence in Lyndon Johnson or his government. The wives were watching, and they did not like what they saw.[7]

On February 29, 1969, only a few months after the *Pueblo* incident wrapped up, Robert McNamara left his position as secretary of defense. Rumor had it that McNamara was close to a nervous breakdown. But perhaps closer to the truth was the public perception that McNamara had gone from Whiz Kid to washout. "McNamara had been a model cabinet officer for Johnson—able, conscientious, discreet, and above all, loyal. But Johnson was ruthless, and McNamara had become a liability."[8] Conservative Arizona senator Barry Goldwater and many others supported LBJ's decision to fire the Kennedy appointee, proclaiming, "McNamara was to me the most dangerous man we've ever had in the secretary's job."[9]

Sybil didn't agree with LBJ on much, but she did agree with his decision to give McNamara the ax. She saw the former secretary's flaws clearly through a prisoner-of-war lens. After his departure, Sybil remembered hearing McNamara "say something on the radio to the effect that no one would have dreamed this war could last so long. I thought to myself, anybody who fights a war the half-baked way you do, should know it can go on almost forever."[10]

That same winter, another young woman was about to join the reluctant sorority of POW/MIA wives. Raised in New York City, Andrea Rander was petite, stylish, and smart. Born in Harlem, she later moved to the South Bronx, where she attended a diverse high school, mixing with students of different nationalities, ethnicities, and religious backgrounds. Andrea was African American and had Jewish and Italian friends from school. She loved New York and the mix of cultures there that were part of her daily life. She recalled her neighborhood and its streets fondly and had a happy childhood and adolescence there. Her parents regularly took her to the Met and to Broadway shows and to events like the Macy's Thanksgiving parade. These experiences provided her with a wide exposure to art and culture that helped form her outlook on life.[11]

Andrea had moved to Baltimore while her husband, Army sergeant Donald "Don" Rander, was deployed in Vietnam. Now he was close to finishing up his deployment, and stationed in the city of Hue. Unbeknownst to his wife, Rander had received special intelligence training. Andrea had been a little surprised, in late January of 1968, when she got a call from her husband at home. He had called from one of the fancy military phones that high-ranking officers typically would use. He told her not to worry about him: "Things are busy here, but we're ok."

This would be the last thing she heard from him for years.

Though she thought the call was a bit strange, Andrea did not have time to ponder it too much at the time. She had a full-time job in Baltimore as a para-professional in a mental health clinic, where she monitored the crisis hotline. Later, she would also work for a pharmacist running a poison control line—managing scary scenarios was part of her daily routine. She had two young daughters at home, Donna Page and Lysa. She was doing double duty as a career woman and a single mom.

A few days after her husband's cryptic call, a secretary in Andrea's department at work called with instructions for Andrea to go immediately to the head of her department. The young wife and mother followed orders, and found her doctor and several men in Army uniforms waiting for her in another office. One of the Army officers told her to have a seat as she wondered to herself, *Why are they here?*

The servicemen told her there had been an insurgency in Hue and that the city had been taken over by Communist forces during what would later become known as the Tet Offensive. Rander's whereabouts were unknown; he was now classified as MIA. This was a huge shock: Don had been in Vietnam for only three months. This terrible announcement would soon be followed by another revelation, but one that included some welcome news.

A month later, escaped Army POW Bob Hayhurst told his debriefers that Donald Rander had been captured in Hue. Andrea rejoiced—he was alive! His status was reclassified from MIA to POW. After her shock wore off, the mental health advocate and now POW wife wondered, "So how do I plan my life now?"[12]

In March, another political bombshell fell. LBJ announced that he would not be running for a second full term as president. Sybil and many other POW and MIA wives were thrilled. "When Johnson announced at the end of March that he wouldn't run again, I rejoiced. I felt strongly we had to have a change of party in order to have any change in policy."[13]

Coincidentally, Bob Boroughs noticed Sybil's increasing clout in his communications with the Office of Naval Intelligence Analysis Department on her behalf. On April 16, he wrote, "Such service we never had before: I put a copy of your 'official' note to me along with the original of your 19 December 1967 letter and it was enough to move this to the head of the line."[14] Boroughs had always known how valuable Sybil was. Only now was the Navy catching up with his original assessment. She was a valuable intelligence asset and one the Navy could not afford to ignore.

Meanwhile, the Vietnam War and LBJ's indecisive response to it had nailed his political coffin shut.

Washington and Hanoi spent March and April of 1968 bickering over the location of formal peace negotiations that aimed to end the war. Geneva, Vienna, New Delhi, Jakarta, Rangoon—would any of these locations suit the North Vietnamese diplomats? Hanoi turned them all down in favor of Paris. Foreign Minister Xuan Thuy headed the North Vietnamese delegation, while American ambassador Averell Harriman, from Team LBJ, controlled U.S. negotiations.[15] In the United States, the mere fact that negotiations had begun sparked hopes that the war might be brought to a peaceful and rapid conclusion.

Upon their arrival in Paris, the American diplomats discovered that they were not the only ones dealing with protests in their streets. A cultural, social, and political revolution was sweeping the Left Bank.

Chic female students wearing low-slung belts and Sonia Rykiel knits, accompanied by bearded male students in bell-bottom jeans, had taken over the Sorbonne.

A general revolt was under way against what young people and the intellectual left perceived as bourgeois postwar society, ruled over by Charles de Gaulle. Though General de Gaulle, savior of the French during World War II, had failed spectacularly in France's own war with Vietnam, as the French president he had proved a popular, if paternalistic, leader. He subscribed to the old order in France, whereby "women couldn't wear pants to work and married ones needed a husband's permission to open a bank account. Homosexuality was a crime. Factory workers could be fired at will."[16]

By May 13, the first day of the Paris peace talks, "students joined forces with the trade unions to proclaim a general strike. Paris appeared to be on the brink of an authentic French revolution."[17] Harriman, Xuan Thuy, and their deputies would have heard popular anthems of this revolution like "Il est Cinq Heures, Paris S'Réveille" ("It's 5 a.m., Paris Wakes Up"), "Paris Mai" ("Paris May"), and "Déshabillez-Moi" ("Undress Me") streaming through the streets. "L'Internationale," the Communist anthem, also played frequently, to the probable horror of Harriman and the equally probable delight of Xuan Thuy. Cars were strewn everywhere, barricades were up. Even at the world headquarters of diplomacy, where protocol was paramount, disorder was the order of the day.

In the middle of this French mêlée, American and Vietnamese diplomats met each Thursday at the Hotel Majestic (today the Peninsula Paris), on the Avenue Kléber in the Sixteenth Arrondissement of Paris. The routine resembled an existential farce, with each side spouting demands and the opposing negotiators refusing to compromise. Everyone went through the prescribed verbal gymnastics, followed the rules, and got absolutely nothing accomplished.

American hopes of a quick diplomatic fix were dashed.

"Predictably, the talks went nowhere. It was the old story. The North Vietnamese wanted an unconditional halt to the bombing. Harriman had been told to get something in return."[18] Time and time again, the

venerable American ambassador was stonewalled by the North Vietnamese, who seemed not to care how long they had to hold out to win
the war.

Harriman's own biographer noted that his much labored-over
speeches to the North Vietnamese were "so laden with boilerplate quo-
tations of LBJ that he sounded more like the mouthpiece of a totali-
tarian regime than the ambassador of a democracy."[19] There was no
movement at all during the public peace negotiations, except at a point
halfway through the day when the diplomats broke for tea and cakes.
Even secret negotiations between the two nations proved pointless.[20]

Britain's prime minister, Harold Wilson, and his diplomats worked
hard behind the scenes to help the Americans and North Vietnamese
reach a peace agreement, despite his frosty relationship with Lyndon
Johnson. Wilson, like the Americans, was repeatedly frustrated by
North Vietnamese diplomats' elaborate stalling techniques. "The British schemes to broker a peace [did not] achieve much, either in terms
of easing tensions between the Americans and the North Vietnamese
or in terms of enhancing British standing in American eyes."[21]

Diplomats from all sides felt that each day was a repeat of the previous
one. They must have felt like actors in the Samuel Beckett play *Waiting for Godot*. (Spoiler alert: in the play, Godot never shows up.) There
seemed to be no end to the mind-numbing Paris peace talks or the
plight of the American POWs in sight, nor an accounting of the MIAs.

Months after the February releases, the U.S. government decided to
bring one of the returned POWs to San Diego to reassure the area
POW wives that he had been treated well in the camps. Sybil knew
from her coded correspondence from Jim that this was rarely the case
unless the prisoner had been purposely set apart by the enemy. "No
one pointed out that this man's release, good condition, and reason-
able treatment were part of the enemy's propaganda campaign."[22] Sybil
and the other POW wives knew just as well as their prisoner husbands
that "our Code of Conduct forbids military men to accept parole and
come home early."[23]

"Stockdale's frustration with the Johnson administration stemmed above all from its inability to counter POW propaganda. Knowing that her husband had been abused for his refusal to denounce the war, it angered her that his captors rewarded prisoners and peace activists who willingly did so through early releases."[24]

The U.S. government also continued to inflate the hopes of the POW wives that negotiations with the North Vietnamese were progressing.[25] The Paris peace talks were stalled, but the American government felt it had to give the POW and MIA families some hope to keep their complaints at bay. The last thing the now waning LBJ government could take was a full-scale revolt, like the one that has just occurred in Paris, among the POW/MIA wives and families.

Well aware that Sybil Stockdale was a political liability for them, the government kept her under a wary watch. After all, she knew the truth of the matter because of her coded correspondence with her husband. She fully realized that the current administration was covering up the POW abuse and then lying to the American public about it. When might she blow the whistle? And she was not the only one they had to worry about. Many of the other West Coast POW wives also felt they were being constantly surveilled. The women noticed a faint but constant clicking on their phones—all suspected they were being wiretapped by their own government.[26]

No one was supposed to say a word about their missing or imprisoned husbands, even now. On the East Coast, Andrea recalled that the Army told her "not to open my mouth to anyone about anything. Just name, rank, and serial number." She was forbidden to speak to anyone but immediate family about her situation. When friends asked her about Donald, all she could say was "I don't know."[27]

Sybil decided to dedicate that summer of 1968 to learning everything she possibly could about the Communist treatment of prisoners throughout history. This would help her decide if she should break with military tradition and the "keep quiet" policy and go to the media with her story. During what Sybil called her "Branford Library summer," she pored over tracts on this topic at the library near her family's summer cottage in Connecticut during the dog days of July and August.[28]

The Korean War (1950–1953) was the most recent American war in which prisoners of war were taken and thus a major focus of her studies. The conflict began when the North Korean Communists invaded democratic South Korea. The North Korean army, armed with Soviet tanks, took over South Korea, and the United States quickly came to South Korea's aid. The way the North Koreans treated American prisoners of war and the subsequent changes to the U.S. military's Code of Conduct were of great interest to Sybil.[29]

The common perception among Americans both during and after the Korean War was that the Communists were masters of "brainwashing." The idea that the Communists possessed some secretive and irresistible method of indoctrination that turned American prisoners of war into their obedient zombies became a lasting myth in the States.

However, a 1956 Senate investigative Committee on Government Operations found that this popular perception was false. (JFK and RFK served on this committee and the Permanent Subcommittee on Investigations, respectively.) The report noted that the Communists did not possess any magical formula for breaking down their prisoners of war. But they did employ a time-tested practice, "based on the simple and easily understood idea of progressively weakening an individual's physical and moral strength." The Communists, however, exploited this idea that they had special training in "brainwashing." A psychologist testifying at the Senate hearing noted that "the aura of mystery and fear which has long been associated with Communist methods of interrogation and indoctrination is, in itself, a major factor in their effectiveness."[30]

In the Korean War, a total of 7,090 American troops were captured by the Communists—6,556 were Army, 263 were Air Force, 231 were Marine Corps, and 40 were Navy. Of this number, only 4,428 of the prisoners were repatriated to the United States. Several thousand prisoners either died or were murdered in the North Korean military prison camps.[31] The total number of prisoners taken in the Korean conflict was much larger than in the Vietnam War. However, the total duration of imprisonment in North Korea was relatively short in comparison with the lengthy captivity American POWs would face in Vietnam.

A major lesson learned by Americans fighting in the Korean War was the vital (and long-overlooked) need for a uniform military protocol for American prisoners to follow. On August 17, 1955, President Dwight D. Eisenhower issued an executive order that established this new U.S. military Code of Conduct. American servicemen now had a beacon and a road map to guide them if imprisoned by future Communist regimes.

An intensive training program was developed to support this code throughout the military, placing "great emphasis on military discipline, esprit de corps, and morale." All personnel were trained to resist Communist indoctrination in any form, to develop moral character with support for religious beliefs, and to appreciate their American heritage and program goals.

Part of the program was soon taught formally in the SERE (Survival, Evasion, Resistance, and Escape) schools to all individuals and units heading into combat zones. "It stresses means to evade capture, and then escape and survival. The serviceman is taught how to combat and survive the physical and mental conditions which he might face under Communist control. He is taught how to deal with informers and collaborators. He is trained to combat interrogation and indoctrination techniques." Most American POW and MIA wives took some comfort from knowing that their husbands had attended SERE school and received intensive training in this area.[32]

However, Sybil continued to wrestle daily with the thought of going to the press with her story about Jim's torture. Her entire career as a Navy wife told her *not* to say anything and to keep her opinions to herself. But Sybil was an avid student of history, and what she found in her deep dive into the brutal Communist treatment of prisoners of war was clear-cut. She decided that "a consistent, gruesome pattern was clear and I had to conclude that the worst way to influence the enemy to accord our men humane treatment was to keep quiet about the truth."[33]

That same summer of 1968, Sybil made another trip to Washington, with a side trip to see Jane Denton and Louise Mulligan in Virginia Beach. Over dinner one evening, Sybil asked Louise to be the "area coordinator" for POW/MIA efforts in the Virginia Beach area.[34] Louise was trying to organize women there and all over Virginia to speak out about the POW issue. Jane had ramped up her own involvement with the nascent organization and thrown off some of her initial inhibitions. The younger women around her, like Louise, had made an impact on her more traditional approach. The prisoner and missing scenario was too dire to sit at home and wait for a rescue. Jane was now more willing to shed some of her well-honed manners and to add different approaches—like working with the antiwar activists—to the wives' arsenal.

After debating the matter all summer, Sybil was still undecided. Should she go to the press with her story, risk her reputation and her husband's, or stay silent? After reading an article in the *San Diego Union* on September 1 that claimed the POWs were being treated horribly in North Vietnam, she sent Harriman a telegram asking him what steps were being taken to prevent Geneva Convention violations. Harriman quickly responded, but his reply astonished her.

SEPTEMBER 6, 1968
FOLLOWING MESSAGE TO YOU RELAYED FROM PARIS:
DEAR MRS. STOCKDALE. I APPRECIATE YOUR SHARING
WITH ME YOUR CONCERN REGARDING THE RECENT
COPLEY NEWS SERVICE ARTICLE ON OUR PRISONERS
OF WAR IN VIETNAM. I CAN TELL YOU THAT WE HAVE
NO INFORMATION TO SUBSTANTIATE THE ASSERTA-
TION IN THE ARTICLE THAT OUR PRISONERS WILL BE
EXPLOITED IN CONNECTION WITH FUTURE NEGOTI-

ATIONS ON A SETTLEMENT IN SOUTH VIETNAM. IN
FACT, NORTH VIETNAMESE REPRESENTATIVES HERE
HAVE INDICATED TO ME THAT THE RELEASE LAST
MONTH OF THE THREE PRISONERS WAS A GESTURE
OF GOOD WILL. I HAVE URGED THEM TO GIVE SERI-
OUS CONSIDERATION TO FURTHER RELEASES, IN-
CLUDING THOSE PILOTS THAT HAVE BEEN HELD THE
LONGEST TIME AND THOSE THAT HAVE BEEN IN-
JURED. I AM SURE YOU REALIZE THAT THE WELFARE
AND THE EARLY RELEASE OF YOUR MEN HELD IN
PRISON CONTINUES TO BE UPPERMOST IN MY MIND.
SINCERELY W. AVERELL HARRIMAN.

Sybil was furious. Her immediate reaction: "No Ambassador Harriman, I thought when I finished reading the message, I'm not sure I
do realize the welfare of the men is uppermost in your mind, nor do I
think you should be advocating early releases, which are a violation of
the Code of Conduct."[35] Of deep concern to Sybil was the complete
lack of understanding among diplomats like Harriman and State Department staff of the military's code—its very bedrock, especially in
times of conflict. Harriman's urging for the early release of American
captured servicemen took an ax to the military's foundation. "The U.S.
government was encouraging the military to disobey its own Code."[36]

In her diary later, Sybil further dissected the LBJ government's response to the prisoner issue and its misguided strategy of early prisoner releases. "Our Government was mushy and mealy-mouthed on
the subject of our prisoners, playing straight into the hands of the
Communists and allowing them to exploit and torture the majority
of them at will. A few prisoners were always kept separate and treated
well of course so that they could talk to those Americans who kept
traveling to Hanoi and mouthing the Communist propaganda line for
the people in this Country."[37]

Harriman had unwittingly made Sybil's difficult decision for her.
He was the match that lit her bomb fuse.

It was time to go public with her story.

Boroughs must have turned the POW/MIA problem over and over in his mind, like the puzzles he so loved to do in his spare time. He was nervous about the idea of Sybil—or any of the wives—going to the press. General publicity about the POWs and MIAs was a good thing, he thought. But Sybil knew so much, she was so deep into the covert coding—if she went to the press, would she endanger Jim and all the others? He wasn't sure. But Harriman and his State Department stooges were making a royal mess of things. Hell, they would rarely talk to him or his assistant Pat Twinem. Maybe this was the key, the answer to a complicated issue that the current administration had shown little aptitude for solving. He decided to give Sybil his blessing.

On October 28, Sybil finally went public, giving an interview to the *San Diego Union* and breaking the "keep quiet" rule. "The North Vietnamese," Sybil declared, "have shown me the only thing that they respond to is world opinion. The world does not know of their negligence and they should know!"[38] Sybil did this not only with the approval of Boroughs but also with the full approval of Naval Intelligence, making "no reference to our covert communication."[39] The primary reaction among most POW and MIA wives across the country? Massive relief.

The news spread like wildfire among the POW and MIA wives. Sybil had found the magic words that allowed the women to begin to throw off their invisible chains. Now the wives began to flee their prisons without walls. Each new story emboldened other POW/MIA wives to tell their stories as well. By January, five other West Coast Wives had had their stories published in the press. Sybil soon received an avalanche of mail from all over the country, including from other POW/MIA wives and mothers.[40]

The West Coast POW and MIA wives also began to speak at public meetings about the POW plight, to write articles for newspapers and magazines, and give television interviews about what it was like to live alone, without their husbands, their children and families living in limbo while their husbands and fathers rotted in dank jungle prisons eight thousand miles away. A June 4, 1969, *San Diego Union* group interview described the wives' special purgatory: "The great majority of women left behind do not know if they are wives or widows. And the years of uncertainty stretch on. There can be no planning for the future in this lonely limbo." In the article, Sandy Dennison said that "Going Public" was one of the hardest decisions she had ever made. "We live in fear of many kinds. We were frightened that if we told our stories it might somehow be used against our husbands. But the world must know the truth about our prisoners." In addition to this terror, many wives felt frozen in time, unable to plot their way forward. Debby Burns admitted that for two years after her husband Doug's shoot-down, she did not plan anything beyond the next morning. "I could not picture more than 24 hours ahead," she said quietly. "The most I've ever looked ahead is six months and that is because I had to sign papers on a house."[41]

A fire had been lit on the West Coast in 1968. From Coronado, the POW wives' revolution spread quickly to the East Coast. Louise Mulligan would be first to carry the torch there.

Louise and many other POW/MIA wives in the Virginia Beach area were angry. They were tired of empty promises made by their government. The women realized that little was being done to help their husbands, though they were constantly told that every effort was being made. They would have to move the ball forward themselves and force the government's hand.

Until Sybil spoke out, the Virginia Beach wives had been afraid to go public and had stuck to what they considered "safe" letter-writing campaigns. They had asked the media to talk about the POW/MIA issue, but they were afraid to speak out themselves. Louise changed all that one Friday evening, hosting a POW wives' get-together. Her friend and fellow POW wife Dot McDaniel recalled, "Several of us agreed that sooner or later, to make our writing campaigns more effective, we would have to make speeches and agree to media interviews.

We decided there would be safety in numbers; if several of us went public at the same time, no one's husband would be singled out for special harassment."[42]

Louise soon rounded up other area POW/MIA wives. Together they wrote a joint letter and made an appointment with Paul Warnke, the assistant secretary of defense. "A letter was drafted by the wives calling on the Defense Department to put international pressure on North Vietnam. Mrs. Mulligan delivered it in person to the Pentagon."[43] Louise recalled that she then read Warnke and his staff at the Pentagon the riot act, as drafted by the East Coast wives:

"We want to go public, and we will take responsibility for our husbands, and they [the DoD] didn't object. And, even if they had, well, we weren't military, we didn't have to follow orders."[44] Warnke and his staff were stunned.

Now who was in charge?

Ten

"NIXON'S THE ONE!"

THE YEAR 1968 HAD been a murderous period on the American home front. On April 4, civil rights leader Martin Luther King Jr. was killed by a sniper's bullet as he stood on the balcony of the Lorraine Motel, in Memphis. Riots broke out all across the country in response to the murder. You couldn't even see the U.S. Capitol building the next few days due to the thick smoke generated by the rioters' fires. General William Westmoreland, commander of U.S. troops in Vietnam, happened to be in Washington then. He recalled that the riots had left D.C. "looking worse than Saigon did at the height of the Tet offensive."[1]

Andrea Rander, who was living in nearby Baltimore, was told "not to come to work. Stay put, don't leave your house" in the wake of the riots. "We lived in a whirlwind" in that fatal spring of 1968, she recalled. "We felt like we were losing control over our lives."[2] But this was just the beginning of what would become an infamous killing season.

On June 5, shots rang out again, this time at the Ambassador Hotel, in L.A. JFK's younger brother, New York senator and former attorney general Robert Francis Kennedy, was assassinated while celebrating his win in the California Democratic presidential primary, a key victory toward achieving the nomination he sought. (Vice President Hubert Humphrey had chosen not to enter the primaries.) Still hanging heavy over the American psyche was JFK's assassination, on November 22, 1963, in Dallas, Texas.

Harvard psychiatrist Dr. Frank Ochberg, originator of the term that applied to so many Vietnam veterans later, post-traumatic stress disorder (PTSD), would write, "Surely it was the triple slaying of those particular men, JFK, MLK and RFK . . . that focused my emotions and attention on human cruelty and tragic loss." Ochberg and many others deemed 1968 "the darkest year" of the decade, featuring race riots, a mounting battlefield death toll in Vietnam, and widespread recreational drug use among young people turning to serious abuse among segments of the population.[3]

The nation mourned deeply for both the slain King and its second lost Kennedy. The country seemed to be enveloped in a gloomy, poisonous fog.

With RFK gone and other potential Democratic nominees lagging far behind, LBJ's vice president, Humbert Humphrey, won the Democratic nomination by collecting the most delegates in the non-primary states. (Only fourteen states had primaries at the time.) Though he was a strong choice, the former Minnesota senator lacked the Kennedy glamour. He was also an integral part of an administration that was increasingly tainted by the unpopular war. He continually tried to get his nerve up to tell his boss, LBJ, his feelings about the war, but every time they met, he "chickened out."[4] The POW and MIA wives knew by this time that Johnson's administration had given low priority to their husbands' fates. The women wanted fresh blood, a new leader who would put their husbands' welfare high on their presidential agenda.

Enter Richard Milhous Nixon.

Born in 1913 and raised a Quaker in a humble Southern California household, Richard "Dick" Nixon was an unusual young man. He was highly intelligent, a fine debater, and an actor. Despite these gifts, he could also be petty, sour, and aloof. He would never quite fit in socially.

The bright young man attended Whittier College, in his hometown, due to a lack of funds. (He was admitted to Harvard and Yale, but his family could not afford the tuition.[5]) After an outstanding college career, he was thrilled to receive a scholarship to Duke Law School. Even so, after graduation, he was not able to procure a job with a law firm on the East Coast and was forced to return home to Whittier to practice law.

But there was a silver lining: the young lawyer soon fell in love with Whittier Union High's business teacher, also a sometime Hollywood bit player and model, Thelma Catherine "Pat" Ryan. Though Nixon's mother, Hannah, felt that she was not up to snuff in terms of social class,[6] Pat was sought-after, smart, and beautiful. "Lithe and graceful, she wore fashionable skirts with bright blouses and sweaters that set off her luxuriant red-gold hair, her fresh-complexioned face, and her high cheekbones. And she wore lavender perfume. Student Robert Blake remembered, 'Miss Ryan was quite a dish.'"[7]

In 1941, the young couple married and moved to Washington, where Nixon worked as a bureaucrat at the Office of Price Administration.[8] Despite his Quaker background, Nixon enlisted in the Navy. In his memoirs, he later noted, "The problem with Quaker pacifism, it seems to me, was that it could only work in the face of a civilized, compassionate enemy. In the face of Hitler and Tojo, pacifism not only failed to stop violence, it actually played into the hands of a barbarous foe and weakened home-front morale."[9] Nixon's religion informed his worldview, but it certainly did not dominate it. After a boring stint serving in Ottumwa, Iowa, the young soldier asked to be transferred to a war zone and was sent to the South Pacific, where he became an air transport officer, experiencing bombing raids, poisonous insects, and dangerous living conditions.[10]

Nixon's Quaker conscience had not allowed him to stay out of war. However, this cast of mind seemed to make him reflect longer and harder than many other presidents on the human costs of battle. "Years later, remembering, Nixon saw war as 'the catalyst' that had transformed his interest in politics to a sense of mission."[11] Nixon achieved the rank of Navy lieutenant commander at the end of World War II and was awarded the Asiatic–Pacific Campaign Medal, the Navy Unit Commendation, the American Campaign Medal, and the World War II Victory Medal upon his return home.[12]

While he was not a notable war hero, Nixon's wartime experiences had a major impact on his worldview. Death during war was real to him: body counts were not simply a statistic to be quantified and explained away as the cost of doing business, per Secretary of Defense Robert McNamara's cold calculations. Nixon scholar Irwin Gellman noted that Nixon personally knew many men during the war who were killed or maimed. "He was sensitive to the amount of people who were survivors." And to their wives and loved ones.[13] In Nixon's own words, his war experiences showed him "the ultimate futility of war and the terrible reality of the loss that lies behind it."[14]

After the war, Nixon once again found himself in Washington, this time as an elected official. In November of 1946, he was elected to the U.S. House of Representatives from California's Twelfth Congressional District. He would serve in this capacity from 1947 to 1950, quickly climbing the ranks to become his state's U.S. senator from 1950 to 1953. Known as a vehement anti-Communist, Nixon next became vice president under President Dwight D. Eisenhower, serving the country in this capacity from 1953 to 1961.[15]

As the POW/MIA wives had already begun to realize, politics, like war, made for strange bedfellows. As freshman congressmen, working-class Nixon and über-privileged John F. Kennedy met and unexpectedly became friends. They shared a shy nature and were mutually intrigued with each other. Despite their personal connection, the men's friendship changed irrevocably when JFK and Nixon faced off in the 1960 presidential election. In a campaign full of "muckraking" and "dirty tricks" on both sides, Kennedy won, but only by the slimmest of margins. "So ended the tightest election in American history. Both candidates had gone to bed not knowing who won . . . Nixon had lost by less than 1 percent."[16]

Many, including Nixon, believed the race had been won thanks to illegal votes, cheating, and fraud. Nixon considered asking for a recount but then decided against it.[17] He and Pat left Washington after the inauguration, regretfully. But Nixon somehow knew this would not be the last he saw of D.C. "I suddenly stopped short—struck by the thought that this was not the end—that someday I would be back here."[18]

From 1961 to 1967, Nixon remained a private citizen, working as a lawyer. In November of 1963, his old colleague President Kennedy was assassinated. Always a bit of a fatalist, Nixon was saddened but not surprised. He wrote Jackie Kennedy immediately to express his condolences and offer his help to her. She wrote him back a few weeks later. Her words now seem eerily prescient:

> *I know how you must feel—so long on the path—so closely missing the greatest prize—and now for you, all the questions come up again—and you must commit all of your family's hopes and efforts again—Just one thing I would say to you—if it does not work out as you have hoped for so long—please be consoled by what you already have—your life and your family.*[19]

Despite his friend's assassination, Nixon plunged back into the national scene within a few years, campaigning for president on the promise of ending the war in Vietnam. He had no "secret plan to win the war," as was widely reported at the time. Instead he broadly declared that he would "*end* the war and win peace in the Pacific."[20]

Military force would always be valued by Nixon. When he visited Vietnam in March of 1964, just a few months after the assassinations of both JFK and Diem, what he saw there convinced him that LBJ's Vietnam policy was a failure. During that same trip, Nixon was the houseguest of Chinese Nationalist leader Chiang Kai-shek, now leading his government in exile after being kicked out by Communist dictator Mao Zedong. Chiang Kai-shek was acutely aware of the flawed American approach to North Vietnam and the Communists and gave Nixon some advice about their common enemy: "It is the familiar fallacy that economic development will defeat the Communists . . . only bullets will really defeat them!"[21]

Richard Nixon represented a classic American archetype: the underdog. He was not glamorous or telegenic like his frenemy JFK. But like Kennedy, he had a "low tolerance for the back-slapping and hand-wringing" that went along with American political life.[22] He did not have LBJ's macho manner or effortless deal-making abilities. But what he did have was grit. Staying power. And an iron will to survive in the jungle of D.C. dirty politics. He would get knocked down, dust himself off, and live to fight another political day many times over.

Nixon's personality, his experiences as a naval officer in World War II, and his resulting empathy for war veterans led to an intense and immediate connection to the POW/MIA wives and their fledgling cause. The wives, like Nixon, knew what it was like to be ignored, underestimated, and just plain overlooked.

Nixon displayed a strong attachment to the women in his adult life. His mother, Hannah, his wife, Pat, and his daughters, Julie and Tricia, were the ones he most wanted to please. "It was the women in Nixon's life who gave him the determination to go on and do what it took to win."[23] Practical, "can do" women with conservative values appealed to him. "From his mother to his wife to his daughters, he was drawn to examples of feminine strength."[24] His support of the Vietnam War's POW/MIA wives—led, as they were, by women like Sybil Stockdale, Jane Denton, and Louise Mulligan—was a natural fit for the new president.

Presidents Truman and Eisenhower introduced the American presence into Vietnam.[25] JFK and LBJ armed the country and propelled the United States into the Vietnam War. It was now up to Nixon to get America out. POW/MIA wives like Sybil, Jane, Louise, Helene, and Phyllis voted for him hoping that he would be their champion and the one who finally ended the drawn-out conflict in Southeast Asia.

After Nixon's victory at the polls in November of 1968, Sybil could wait no longer. She was itching to take action that would lead to real change in Washington. She was convinced that "Nixon's the One!," as his famous campaign slogan read.

Sybil had read that President-elect Nixon would be attending the

Republican Governors Conference in Palm Springs on December 6 with the governor of California, movie star turned politician Ronald Reagan. She immediately placed calls to both Nixon and Reagan and was told she could not talk to either. Fuming, she fired off a telegram to Reagan, "telling him I had been told I could not talk to him on the phone and asking him to tell President Elect Nixon about our plea for help." Busy with her boys and a million other obligations, Sybil promptly forgot about the telegram.[26]

A week later, she got what she thought was a prank call.

"Mrs. Stockdale, this is Ronald Reagan."

Sybil recalled, "I thought it was a friend trying to fool me and almost said 'Yes, and this is Sophia Loren, what would you like to do tonight?'"

But something in his deep, resonant, movie-star tone made her stop in her tracks and reconsider.

It was him! He was really on the phone, and he seemed to take her concerns seriously. Reagan promised Sybil that the president-elect was completely aware of the problem. Reassured and heartened by the thoughtful personal call, Sybil thought, *Maybe the Republicans really will turn things around.*[27] She could not help but mentally compare this change of tone with President Johnson's one brief stop through San Diego years earlier to shake hands with the POW wives. "There was no chance to say more than 'how do you do?' It seemed almost as if we should feel privileged he had taken the time to shake hands with us while changing airplanes on North Island."[28]

Earlier that fall, Andrea Rander had gone to a Nixon presidential rally in Baltimore. She felt she had to go to represent the POW wives and to make sure this candidate would truly do something to help. At the rally, she yelled, "Don't forget the POWs!" She felt good to have a voice after being told to keep quiet so often. Years later, Andrea would laugh, saying she had decided after the rally that her action would surely make an impact on Nixon. "I *know* he's going to do something now that I've talked to him!" She was beginning to be more outspoken about her beliefs and starting to speak her mind in public.[29] Feeling even more emboldened by Nixon's victory, the wives refused to keep their individual stories quiet anymore—not for the Army or the Navy, not for the U.S. government, not even for the sake of traditional diplomatic methods. Shining the media spotlight on the POWs and MIAs was critical, and perhaps the only way to force the North Vietnamese to account for their husbands. They had gained worldwide support for their cause in this way, and they did not intend to relinquish the upper hand they had so painstakingly cultivated.

By the end of 1968, most of the wives had relegated the "keep quiet" policy to the trash bin. Even highly patriotic and rule-conscious Jane reveled in her new government-approved freedom of speech.

On the West Coast, Sybil took a page from the civil rights and feminist movements spreading across the country. "Sit-ins" had become a well-known technique used by activist groups to gain attention for their causes. Sybil's version of this activism was to coordinate a grassroots "telegram-in," where she urged POW/MIA wives and family members to deluge newly elected President Nixon with telegrams, reminding him to put the POW/MIA situation at the very top of his agenda. The new president received more than two thousand telegrams from Sybil and her cohorts.[30]

Nixon quickly realized the power these women held in their hands. He and his staff took pains to reply personally to each telegram. Phyllis Galanti got not one but *three* replies to her telegram: from Richard Nixon, Secretary of State William P. Rogers, and ambassador to South Vietnam Henry Cabot Lodge Jr., the chief negotiator at the Paris peace talks.[31]

Nixon and his new staff deemed it crucial to win the war of domestic public opinion. Integral to this victory was the support of those who could unify the country through the POW/MIA cause. Sybil, Jane, Janie, Louise, Dot, Phyllis, Helene, and hundreds of other POW/MIA wives and families were forming a powerful and influential lobby that the new Nixon administration desperately needed on its side.

What lengths would the new government go to to support them? Would it be any better than the previous administration? Was Nixon really "the One"?

Eleven

GO PUBLIC

THE NEWLY INSTALLED NIXON administration had gotten the message loud and clear from the POW/MIA wives that they had better take notice of their husbands' plight. *Right now.* The women and their families were Nixon supporters and voters—at least for the moment—and the administration wanted to keep them in that camp.

Sybil was pleased to see the direct results of her January telegram-in. "I was encouraged to be notified that a group from the Nixon administration in Washington was coming to San Diego (to the Naval Air Station Miramar Officers' Club) on March 26 to talk to us about the prisoners and missing. What a change—they were actually coming to talk to us without our having to browbeat them!"[1]

Attendance at the meeting was restricted to wives and parents of the POWs and MIAs from the area. It was to be held on a "no publicity" basis, and Sybil noted in her diary that she warned all invited attendees, "I cannot impress upon you enough that this is a privileged meeting and that all discussion pertaining to it should be carefully guarded."[2] The remnants of the "keep quiet" policy remained in her comments, but they were fraying and thin as old lace curtains.

Averell "the Crocodile" Harriman persisted in holding fast with his reptilian jaws to the old ways, despite the advent of a new presidential administration. Even now, he was convinced that his quiet diplomacy would work. But now, in 1969, the wives and even the staff within the government were realizing that Harriman's approach had become a form of appeasement.

Harriman had heard rumors of the new administration's plans to "go public" about the POW/MIA plight. Before he left office (he would be replaced by Undersecretary of State Elliot Richardson on February 4), the crusty grandee called Melvin Laird, Nixon's secretary of defense, to warn him off this idea.[3] Laird listened to Harriman rant, but he would not reveal what he planned to do. He decided to do more research before he took any action.[4]

Laird selected a young man from the publishing business named Richard "Dick" Capen for a data-collecting mission. Capen had worked for Copley Press, a newspaper publisher in San Diego, and was used to taking the pulse of those in the news. Laird asked his aide to apply his listening and observational skills to the POW/MIA wives and families. Capen would go to San Diego in March and take the temperature of the POW and MIA wives, parents, and families.[5] Laird would be shocked at what Capen soon found out.

The atmosphere in the Miramar Officers' Club was electric. Buzzing with angry POW and MIA wives and parents, it was a hornet's nest of resentment erupting with repressed feelings and emotions. Years of accumulated government doubletalk had demoralized the group. But now they had a chance to express their concerns to a captive audience. This time the captives were the bureaucrats themselves.

Capen was only thirty-four, still a young man but confident of his skills and background. Frank Sieverts, special assistant to the deputy secretary of state and a POW from the Korean War, accompanied him. They had all arrived at Miramar to reassure the San Diego–area wives and families about the government's position on the POW/MIA issue. If Capen, Sieverts, and company had expected a warm welcome, they were speedily disabused of this notion.

The POW/MIA wives and families had had enough of the previous administration's vague directives and lack of response to their situation. By now many of the women had been single parents for three to four years. They were the heads of their households by default. Many had struggled financially, and all had suffered emotionally since their husbands' shoot-downs.

The white gloves were off, and nothing would have pleased the group more than to throttle the slick government reps who seemed to think they knew it all. "The Washington Road Show," as the wives cynically referred to these representatives sent to them from the State and Defense Departments, had five hundred angry and frustrated Navy wives from the San Diego area, as well as Air Force and Marine wives from the Los Angeles area, to answer to tonight. The lions were about to be unleashed upon the government's unsuspecting gladiators.

An Air Force wife named Pat Burns was among the first to get up at the meeting, unveiling a framed painting she had created that she said represented the lack of empathy from the top Air Force officials. Based on her own experience with the military, Pat declared that the motto "The Air Force takes care of its own" was a joke. She slammed the painting on the floor in front of the astonished visitors, scream-ing, "Take it back to D.C. and give it to the generals running the war!" With that, she promptly stomped out of the room. (No description remains of this painting, but the artist's conduct indicated its theme quite clearly.) After a stunned silence, wife after wife forced the repre-sentatives to confront the truth: the military's "keep quiet" policy was a failure. It was only further endangering the POWs and MIAs by shrouding their situation in secrecy.[6]

Sybil added her voice to those of the other women at the Miramar meeting, stating her deep reservations concerning the "keep quiet" pol-icy, noting that the longer the Vietnamese held the men, tortured them, starved them, and denied them medical treatment, the more likely they were to die in prison. If the American government planned to bring the men back alive, they had better publicize their plight to the world.[7]

Sybil spoke about her own negative experience with the "keep quiet" policy, noting that there had been no mail from the POWs since Oc-tober. She confronted Capen, saying, "We need a change of policy by our Government. Things are getting worse instead of better. There is less mail instead of more. We want our Government leaders to stand up and criticize the North Vietnamese for not abiding by the Geneva Convention."[8] Due to their secret coding and undercover work with Boroughs, Sybil and many of the women present that night knew far more than anyone from the Road Show about what was going on in the North Vietnamese prison camps.

While confronting the Nixon administration's delegates, Sybil and Karen were also tape-recording them. Their accomplice? Bob Boroughs, from Naval Intelligence. The maverick intelligence officer had rigged the two ladies up with tape recorders and speakers, which Sybil and Karen cleverly pinned to their bras. The government departments all distrusted one another, so the only way for the Navy to get an accurate report was to spy on the meeting. (Boroughs probably did this on his own without authorization.) Since the government was so clueless, Boroughs and the women he worked with decided it was time to do whatever it took to get the full picture. Sybil and Karen didn't hesitate to comply with his taping request.

After Sybil spoke, she noticed that Capen kept staring at her. She started to worry about the tape recorder bulge in her bra—was it obvious? She also realized that her tape and Karen's were running out. Ever resourceful, Sybil held up a printed sign that read, WE NEED A RESTROOM BREAK, and Capen promptly declared an intermission.[9]

The two women ran to the bathroom together, most likely giggling nervously, and flipped their tapes over to record the second half of the meeting. Other wives and parents got up and yelled some more. The delegates, by now speechless, must have known that if they wanted to make it out of the meeting alive, they had better relay the wives' message back to D.C., pronto.

Capen vividly remembered the women's anger that day: "It was therapeutic and we owed it to them. They needed to vent."[10] But what he had witnessed was far more than just venting. The women knew the American prisoners' situation was deteriorating rapidly—their "venting" was a desperate cry for help before it was too late.

The young State Department bureaucrat returned to Washington with his attitude duly adjusted. He continued his research on the issue and was horrified by what he found out. On a Department of Defense weekend retreat in early May, he presented his findings to his boss, Laird. After reviewing the evidence, Capen learned what some of the POW wives already knew: that the men were being tortured and denied proper medical treatment, food, clothing, and mail privileges. They were often not even identified as being POWs. "When he heard Capen's findings at the conference, Laird bellowed, 'By God, we're going to go public.'"[11] Capen made sure to vet the idea with the military head honchos, especially Admiral John S. McCain Jr., whose son John remained a prisoner of the North Vietnamese. "Whatever you feel is right, do it," he replied. Now they had the blank check they needed to move forward.[12]

Capen and Laird made it their joint mission to encourage and sustain the Nixon administration's focus on the POW/MIA issue while National Security Adviser Henry Kissinger simultaneously juggled delicate negotiations with the North Vietnamese. The POW/MIA wives and families whom Capen had gone to placate in March had taught him and Laird what they needed to know on that issue. Now the women had gained the national platform they needed to amplify their message.

Despite this breakthrough, the POW situation remained urgent. The women's tape recorders were not the only things running out of time.

On April 5, Sybil wrote a very frank letter to Admiral Moorer's executive assistant, admitting that at home she did not always display the self-control she did when in public. "At home I rant, rave, cry, throw dishes and hurl invectives at both Washington and Hanoi." Sybil also mentioned her "spies at the Pentagon" and her desire—indeed, requirement—that she meet with Nixon soon.[13]

Sybil was clearly letting the Navy and the government know that she had power, influence, and the ear of the POW and MIA families. Her thinly veiled references in her letter indicated that she and others might blow the whistle further if the government did not move quickly on the POW/MIA issue. She now had high-profile allies in the Pentagon in Laird, Capen, and Sieverts. Sybil received a speedy reply assuring her that things were indeed moving in the direction she desired. And then she got a message that she could not have imagined possible even a year earlier under LBJ.

Early on Monday morning, May 19, Dick Capen and Frank Sieverts phoned Sybil. Capen did most of the talking, in an excited manner. "Before you leave for school this morning, we wanted you to know that here in Washington, in just a few minutes, the secretary of defense is going to do the thing you've been wanting him to do for so long. He's going to publicly denounce the North Vietnamese for their treatment of the American prisoners and for their violation of the Geneva Convention."[14] All the POW and MIA wives' hard work was finally beginning to pay off. It was unbelievable that the government was finally listening, Sybil thought. "That was a real switch . . . The administration was publicly abandoning the 'keep quiet' policy as its predecessors should have done years before."[15]

In his press release that day and in his televised address, Laird broke the government's silence: "The North Vietnamese have claimed that they are treating our men humanely. I am distressed by the fact that there is clear evidence that this is not the case . . . The United States Government has urged that the enemy respect the requirements of the Geneva Convention. This they have refused to do." Laird continued to tick through the list of North Vietnamese war crimes, including its leaders' refusal to: provide a list of imprisoned and missing men; treat and release the sick and injured Americans; allow the free exchange of mail between prisoners and their families; and allow the inspection of the prisoner camps by an impartial organization such as the Red Cross.

Even more affecting were the graphic photos of prisoners that Capen distributed to the press that day. Obtained on the black market in North Vietnam, the pictures showed prisoners with injured and atrophied limbs, and men in solitary confinement. It was all out there now for the world to judge. It made only a minor splash in the American media at first, but the ripple effect in the wider world would be significant. In honor of July 4, the North Vietnamese decided to release three POWs. These men would prove to be perhaps the most valuable intelligence asset the Americans obtained during the course of the war.[16]

As she drove down the sunny California highway to her teaching job, Sybil suddenly realized that today (May 19) just happened to be North Vietnamese leader Ho Chi Minh's birthday. She must have smiled to herself, thinking that the Laird press conference was the perfect gift for "Uncle Ho."[17]

As Sybil readied for her annual sojourn to Sunset Beach, Connecticut, she got a call from her friend and fellow POW wife Karen Butler. Karen's sister had a contact with the West Coast editor of *Look* magazine in L.A., and she arranged an appointment for Sybil and Karen on June 20. *Look* was a slightly more literate version of today's *People* magazine, featuring short articles and lots of color photos. The covers in 1969 featured John Lennon and Yoko Ono, Mia Farrow, and the Smothers Brothers.[18]

When they arrived in L.A., both women were impressed by the luxurious *Look* offices, with their giant glass windows offering panoramic views of the city. Karen and Sybil spent more than an hour talking to *Look*'s editor about the POW mistreatment. He seemed empathetic but a bit bored. This was clearly not a story he thought would work for his magazine. Sybil was distraught: all this time and effort, and no one seemed to care about the men's plight. As she and Karen gathered their things to leave, the editor asked where he might get in touch with them on the off chance the magazine decided to run something. Both the women said to contact the secretary for the League of Wives in San Diego.

Flying home to San Diego that evening, Sybil and Karen had an epiphany. Sybil wrote in her diary: "We reasoned that we needed a national organization if we were going to get national publicity." They had already worked together with women all over the country for the telegraph-ins to the new president as well as to the Vietnamese embassy in Paris. Letter-writing campaigns were taking place all over the country, too, coordinated by POW and MIA wives to raise awareness of the situation. Now, Sybil felt, "all we really needed was a name. On the airplane that day we decided to call ourselves 'THE NATIONAL LEAGUE OF FAMILIES OF AMERICAN PRISONERS IN SOUTHEAST ASIA.' We felt the MIAs were implicit in this group, and Karen and I agreed I would be the National Coordinator."[19]

Later in July, Karen received a call from the editor, declining to do an article on the POWs or even the San Diego League. The POWs had been adequately covered in *Look* and *Life* magazines already, he explained. And the regional League might be better covered by a newspaper article. Karen's heart sank, but then she remembered the new angle she and Sybil had conceived on the plane ride home from L.A. in June. She "casually mentioned the National League. This was followed by a noticeable increase of interest in his voice. He asked if I would call him when the organization was completed."[20] The women had found the key that unlocked their all-access press pass.

The National League, just an idea in the two POW wives' minds a few weeks earlier, quickly became a reality. Sybil later recalled, "Never was an organization launched more efficiently. The fact that we paid our own expenses and didn't know the first thing about the rules of organizing were a saving grace."[21]

The POW/MIA wives, led by Sybil, took heart as they gained power first with their new government platform and next through their media contacts. Soon they would see themselves in *Look, Reader's Digest, The New York Times,* and *Good Housekeeping,* as well as their local newspapers. Television interviews followed. All forms of media were finally picking up the story.[22]

It didn't hurt the wives that they represented the late-sixties traditional feminine ideal so well. *The New York Times'* "Food, Fashion, Family, Furnishings" reporter certainly took note of this—they were an easy sell to the American public. "The wives, for the most part, are slender, gracious and attractive. One man who met several of them described them as 'pretty—like airline stewardesses.' Some of them *were* stewardesses; Mrs. Tschudy, for example, flew for American Airlines for 10 months before she was married."[23] This favorable confluence of events finally began to push the POW and MIA wives forward, out of the shadows and into the media spotlight. Now the ladies were ready for their close-up.

In June of 1969, Louise Mulligan was the first POW/MIA wife on the East Coast to go public, in the Norfolk *Ledger-Star*. Before she did so, she sat her six boys (ages seven to eighteen at this point) down and warned them that their lives were about to change. Her decision would affect them all and put them all into the same media spotlight the wives were stepping into. She worried about her sons and about her husband's reaction to her public fight when he returned. But the passing years without her husband had driven her to push the very buttons the State Department had originally warned Jane Denton *not* to mess with.

Louise also had a temperament that was well suited to speaking out. Like Sybil, Louise was convinced that this was the one and only way to rescue their husbands from a terrible fate. Jane Denton, Janie Tschudy, Dot McDaniel, Phyllis Galanti, and other Virginia POW and MIA wives admired her for this, even if some of them were not as strident in their approach. The women needed everyone's talents, and all different kinds of personalities, to make their organization a success.[24]

That same August, Phyllis received a warm letter from Louise, explaining that she was the new National League's area representative. She also related to Phyllis that she, Jane Denton, and another POW wife, Martha Doss, had all gotten letters brought back by Rennie Davis, the antiwar activist and top lieutenant for the New Mobilization Committee to End the War in Vietnam. While no one was happy about who was relaying this information, any communication from the men was treasured. Louise noted of her letter from Jim, "Mine was dated July 7th and sounded good. Says he's gaining weight, hope so." She went on to say that several of the women from her area had been in Washington and had lunch with a newly released Navy POW, Lieutenant Robert Frishman, who gave them encouraging news. "He said that morale was tremendously high and felt that we were worrying more than the men."[25]

Rennie Davis himself had brought Frishman, Navy petty officer second class Douglas Hegdahl, and Air Force captain Wesley Rumble back along with the mail. The men had not sought early release, but Rumble and Frishman were both seriously injured and thus deemed by their Communist captors as good candidates for early release. The North Vietnamese considered Hegdahl "the incredibly stupid one," but he was, in the words of fellow POW Gerald "Jerry" Coffee, "dumb like a fox."[26] Once he was released, Hegdahl "turned out to be a gold mine of information. To the tune of 'Old MacDonald Had a Farm,' he had memorized the names of more than two hundred prisoners."[27]

For his part, Frishman confirmed at a press conference on September 2 that Hanoi was indeed lying about providing "humane" treatment to the prisoners. He began by "refuting that claim by listing the abuse he and others had endured: the withholding of mail and lack of medical care, long periods of solitary confinement, torture, and forced confessions."[28] Later, when Rumble, the most seriously injured returnee, recovered, he was also able to give his debriefers his own list of prisoners, which was cross-checked with Hegdahl's original one.[29] This was part of the ripple effect of going public—a huge break for military intelligence, the wives, and the POWs and MIAs themselves.

The antiwar and peace activists, like Davis, Cora Weiss, and many others, seemed to have swallowed whole the North Vietnamese line that the prisoners were being treated well, perhaps to support their personal political agenda. Despite so much evidence to the contrary, Weiss still questioned Frishman and Hegdahl's account, and she was highly skeptical of their torture reports. "Weiss flippantly dismissed Frishman's arm injury with the comment that 'since he was captured as a "war criminal," he was lucky to have an arm at all.'"[30] Weiss and her crew continued to be blind to the facts and to live in a fictional world where prisoners of war were treated as honored guests by their North Vietnamese hosts. It was clear by now that nothing could be further from the truth. The motives of the most radical antiwar groups, who wanted to stop the war at any cost, were mixed at best, self-serving at worst.

Between the POW/MIA wives' going public in 1968 and '69, the formation of a National League, Laird and Capen's "go public" efforts, and new intelligence, the more radical antiwar groups appeared to be North Vietnamese sympathizers. Still, they remained the most reliable and consistent source of mail and packages for the POWs. Their work continued, and many POW wives remained trapped in this uneasy but necessary alliance. Phyllis Galanti, among many others, publicly acknowledged the growing dependence of POW wives upon antiwar activists. "Let's face it," she said, "it's too valuable a source to dismiss. It's the only way I'm getting mail."[31]

While Louise, Jane, and others had recently received news about their husbands, MIA wife Helene Knapp remained in the dark regarding her husband's fate. In an interview with the Sunday *Denver Post,* Helene described the limbo of not knowing the truth about her husband's disappearance. "It's like I lived until two-and-a-half years ago [when Herman was shot down] and then my life stopped," she revealed. "It's been such a lonely wait. And, each morning I think maybe today I'll know for sure."

Helene's home remained full of mementos of her husband, like the bronze plaque inscribed with the words FLY HIGH, FLY TRUE, FLY PROUD, a gift Herman had sent to his son, Robbie, on his third birthday. The plaque, a bronzed copy of Herman's favorite poem, "High Flight," by John Gillespie Magee, and his picture were displayed on a wall near the front door of the Knapp home. Helene placed these precious items there because "this is his home. I don't want that forgotten." It was still possible, Helene must have thought, that Herm might walk through the door one day and scoop up her, Robbie, and Cindy in his arms.

Like Sybil, Helene was not one to sit around and wait for things to happen to her. She was by nature a worker bee, full of energy and curiosity. Helene and her fellow Colorado Springs MIA wife Mary Dodge had recently gone to D.C. to support the passage of a congressional resolution demanding humane treatment for all American POWs as well as a full accounting of all the prisoners. Both Helene and Mary were members of Sybil's National League of Families and among the first members of the Colorado branch of the League. Mary was currently serving as the League regional coordinator for five states: Colorado, Wyoming, Utah, Montana, and Idaho.[32]

Another military wife had joined the fight in the Springs. Joan Pollard, whose husband, Air Force captain Benjamin Pollard, had been shot down on May 15, 1967, had just moved back to town in September of 1970, after three and a half years living in Shelbyville, Kentucky, her husband's hometown. While everyone there was solicitous and supportive of her, she felt isolated and alone as an MIA wife there.

Joan eventually heard about MIA and POW wives in other states. This sorority's members began to reach out to one another across state lines. Sybil's informal newsletters also found their way into Joan's hands. "Sybil knew more than anybody else did" at that time, Joan recalled. She felt less alone, more part of a group, because of this. There were others like her who "got it" and understood her position of not knowing if her husband was alive or dead. Joan knew Ben was alive somehow. But no one really believed her in Shelbyville.

Joan and Ben had been an integral part of the Air Force Academy community when he was recruited to teach there in the mid-sixties. He was part of the nascent astronautics program there, as well as a professor of aeronautics. He and Joan were a popular young couple, and she was soon elected president of the wives' club. Through this position, she and Ben met many prominent and well-known people from all across the state and the country at Air Force social events, and she still had many friends among the Air Force Academy faculty. Joan decided that was where she and her two children, twelve-year-old Mark and seven-year-old Ginny, needed to be. There she would be part of the Air Force community and perhaps help with the POW/MIA problem. She enrolled Mark at Washington Irving Junior High and Ginny at Longfellow Elementary, in Colorado Springs.

Joan had been in the Springs scarcely two weeks when she attended an evening meeting at Peterson Air Force Base and was volunteered to help with the local POW/MIA situation by the Air Force chaplain, Chris Martin. She barely knew what she was getting into, but she didn't hesitate to join the cause. Joan soon meet Helene through their joint advocacy. The two women had very different personalities and might never have met under other circumstances. But they shared a common cause and began working together in the Springs.

Joan would talk to anyone and was a skilled public speaker with great contacts. "I'd speak anywhere anybody asked me to," she said. She was the first woman ever to speak at one local men's club and later could still recall the utter silence when she began her speech.

One dark and rainy night, she showed up at the famous Broadmoor resort to tell her story. Only four men sat at the bar, and, while they invited her to join them for a beer, she felt they were all more interested in the baseball game on TV than the POWs and MIAs. "You win some, you lose some," she thought as she braved terrible weather to get home.

The next day, she got a call from one of the men who she thought had been only mildly interested in her plight. "Call me anytime," he said, "anything you need, I will help you." A prominent local businessman, he would become one of the local POW/MIA group's staunchest supporters.[33]

In tandem with Joan, Helene was becoming more and more involved with the POW/MIA movement, but she was still struggling with her new status. Though she'd had a gut feeling that Herman might be dead when she was first told that he was missing, now she wasn't so sure. Aside from the terrible grief she felt, she was also experiencing a loss of her former identity and sense of self. Like other women who had become POW and MIA wives before her, she didn't fit into any neat category as she had before, as the wife of an Air Force pilot and a mom. Just like her new friend Joan, she was both mother and father, homemaker and activist, the glue that held her family together despite the gnawing sense of grief that threatened to tear her apart. She had no concrete answer for the question so many in her situation were asking themselves: was she a wife or a widow?

That same September, Sybil, as the new National League coordinator, and a delegation of five other National League members went to Paris to meet with the North Vietnamese representatives. The trip was undertaken without any sponsorship by the U.S. government. Sybil wrote to government officials before the trip, to reassure them but also to put them on notice as to the group's intent: "Our trip should in no way be interpreted as reflecting discredit on our own government. However, we are going independently, and without government sponsorship."

Though the government was helping some behind the scenes, the League deliberately occupied a humanitarian, nonpolitical perch. This stance would prove both strategic and wise on the League's part. As they had found out over the years, any tinge of overt government control could quickly taint the group in the media's eyes and in the eyes of the American public. A neutral humanitarian approach was the correct play.

Fortunately, the League members had found financial sponsors in an aviation company, Fairchild Hiller, and *Reader's Digest*. The group left for Paris on Sunday, September 28, and would meet with the North Vietnamese delegation in Paris regarding both the American prisoners and the missing in Vietnam.[34]

The League delegation's composition reflected its multiple viewpoints. Members of the group represented each branch of the armed forces and both enlisted men and officers. The six individuals included one missing-in-action father, Thomas "Tom" Swain, and five wives: Mary Ann "Pat" Mearns, Nancy Perisho, Candy Parish, Andrea Rander, and Sybil. Andrea was the only black member of the delegation. Though African Americans formed a huge percentage of combat troops in Vietnam by 1967 (23 percent), only 2 percent of blacks were officers in the Air Force, Navy, or Marine Corps. Since most of the POWs were officers, a similarly small percentage of those POWs were black.[35] Donald Rander was among that small percentage of POWs who were both African American and Army.

Andrea recalled that she had received the call to go to Paris while she was at work one day. To this day, she is not sure who the call was from, but it may have come from the same Air Force wife who had called Sybil to join the group.[36] The person on the other end of the line asked her to go to Paris without many details. The first thing the POW wife wanted to know was: Why? When the purpose of the trip was explained to her—that the group would be going to try to obtain information about their missing and imprisoned men—Andrea was intrigued, but she explained that she would have to find childcare for her two daughters before committing. Government officials and trip organizers almost always forgot that most of the POW and MIA wives had children at home and were basically single mothers. They couldn't just leave the kids alone at a moment's notice. Thank goodness Andrea had a great babysitter, just four doors down, who could help, as well as family members on the East Coast.[37]

She was used to running things on her own and juggling a busy schedule. She also knew a thing or two about managing tough situations, thanks to her day job monitoring the crisis hotline at work. All these management and coping skills would serve her well on her mission to Paris. Andrea used her savings and borrowed funds from relatives to make the trip, leaving her two daughters, seven year old Lysa and two-year-old Donna Page, with her neighbor and grandmother, respectively.[38] This trip to Paris would mark the beginning of her activism.

The big issue on Andrea's mind when she made this trip was rank, not race. She recalled, "My experiences growing up in NYC allowed me to be very flexible and open about the race issue. So when it got to the point where I'm with the women to go to Paris . . . I felt a little twinge because I was not the rank that the other women were. The race part did not enter my mind." As the wife of an enlisted Army man, Andrea was briefly intimidated to be among older, more senior wives from other branches of the military. But it didn't take long for the ranks and the branch differences to vanish. "It wasn't as distinct as it could have been . . . because we knew what our goal was. The common goal was that we were seeking information about our husbands. This became more important than anything else as this trip developed."[39]

Once in Paris, the group checked into the InterContinental Hotel, a luxurious spot chosen for its superior phone service and its proximity to the American embassy. The hotel was in one of the most fashionable neighborhoods in Paris, not too far from the chic shops on the Rue de Rivoli and near the Champs-Élysées, but these pleasures were of little consequence to the dispirited visitors. Exhausted from both nerves and their transatlantic flight, the delegates dumped their bags in the plush lobby and began to plot strategy for the week.

By now, Sybil and Jim were deep into their covert communications work with Bob Boroughs at the State Department. Though blessed with a strong constitution and a calm demeanor, Sybil was terrified that the North Vietnamese were on to her. She thanked God for the Seconal sleeping pills she had brought with her to get her through the long nights of waiting.

The League delegation met each morning to review plans as the tension mounted and minor quibbles erupted. But still, they decided to stick it out until the Vietnamese agreed to see them. Sybil called each day for an appointment, and each day she was put off. After a week of tense waiting, the group was finally granted an audience at the North Vietnamese embassy on Saturday, October 4. Sybil was so nervous that day that "three times I went into the bathroom and had dry heaves as never before in my life. My whole digestive system seemed to be pushing itself way up into my throat." The only plus from this unpleasant experience was that Sybil was so worn out that she felt a sense of calm when she finally entered the embassy. She wore a favorite bright-pink wool suit, bought in 1965 for her husband's last change-of-command ceremony. Perhaps, she thought, it would bring her luck.[40]

Sybil's blood ran cold as Xuan Oanh, the head of the North Vietnamese delegation, greeted her with "We know all about you, Mrs. Stockdale," holding up a photo of her on the steps of the U.S. Capitol. "We know you are the organizer." *Well, thank God,* Sybil thought with relief. *At least they don't know any more than that!*[41]

To her colleagues, Sybil seemed cool and unflappable. Andrea noted later, "I remember her being so calm and I thought, 'How is she doing this?'" The Army POW wife had deep faith in Sybil and her leadership abilities. "I looked at her as a teacher, trainer, reader and writer—

she was keeping all the notes for us." During the meeting, Andrea kept reassuring herself, *Sybil's going to get us out of this. We're going to walk out of here and these men are going to be free!* "I was being unrealistic," Andrea recalled, "but I was thinking this was going to end—not the war, necessarily, but the situation with the men."[42]

Sybil, Andrea, and each member of her delegation then demanded information about their POW and MIA family members. They also delivered hundreds of letters of inquiry they had brought with them from POW/MIA families at home. Andrea specifically carried letters for the men (her husband among them) believed to be held in South Vietnam.[43] In between, they drank gallons of tea and ate Vietnamese candies and French crackers, not daring to offend their hosts by refusing the refreshments.

Andrea recalled the two-and-a-half-hour meeting as one long propaganda fest. "The women were questioned about their husbands, shown movies of napalm bombing, and urged to participate in peace movements." The North Vietnamese representatives promised Andrea that every effort would be made to arrange an interview for her with Madame Nguyen Thi Binh, the foreign minister and chief negotiator for the National Liberation Front (NLF).[44]

Before the group finally parted from their hosts, the mood had lightened somewhat. Sybil recalled: "We got the recipe for the candy, exchanged American cigarettes for Vietnamese cigarettes, and even took souvenir toilet paper from their bathroom."[45] Andrea remembered thinking that the whole place must be bugged.[46]

The Vietnamese gave them no information of substance or real promises to help. Andrea never did get to see Madame Binh. What the delegation did receive from the enemy was unintended: the publicity generated by the visit shone the world spotlight on the POW/MIA plight once again.

While the American women didn't get exactly what they wanted, the worldwide media portrayed the Vietnamese as heartless and cruel—exactly the opposite of the image they wished to show to the world. The ladies hoped that because the Vietnamese Communist regime had been placed in the public eye, the court of world opinion would unite against them and trigger the POWs' eventual group release and an accurate accounting of the MIAs. They returned home exhausted but triumphant in the knowledge that their mission impossible had once again put them—and the POW/MIA issue—in the spotlight.

That same October, the antiwar movement, led by the New Mobilization Committee ("the New Mobe"), led a peaceful national protest, dubbed the October Moratorium. On October 15, hundreds of thousands of Americans protested the war in churches, in schools, in local meetings. "From the White House that night, the staff could see thousands of candles flickering across the Mall." Though the protests were mostly peaceful, Nixon was desperately worried.[47] He decided he needed to comfort the country and tamp down some of the antiwar rhetoric. Out of that dark night, a landmark speech was born.

On Monday, November 3, at 9:30 p.m., President Nixon addressed the country in a televised address. He reached out to his core supporters, famously dubbing them the "silent majority." Nixon also outlined his "Vietnamization" strategy. This was Laird's term for the plan to withdraw American troops from the country while simultaneously training the South Vietnamese to defend themselves against not just the Viet Cong rebels in the South but also the North Vietnamese Army.[48]

After the speech, former ambassador and Nixon nemesis Averell Harriman appeared on ABC News "as a scoffing commentator—the same Harriman who had announced, 'I will not break bread with that man [Nixon]' . . . after the 1950 Senate campaign."[49] Harriman's long-standing antipathy toward Nixon coupled with the fact that Nixon had not asked him to stay on as part of his new administration generated the former diplomat's negative take on the speech. According to Nixon biographer Evan Thomas, Nixon had also "shifted the public perception, aligned himself with the patriots and identified the antiwar movement with the bombers and flag burners."[50]

Despite Harriman's sour grapes and the outrage of antiwar advo-cates, the speech was a resounding success: a Gallup poll found that 77 percent of Americans supported Nixon's view of the war.[51]

Though firmly in his "silent majority" camp, Sybil fired off a tele-gram to President Nixon after the speech, rebuking him for "not men-tioning the plight of the prisoners in your message to the nation on November 3rd. I personally can understand the difficulty which men-tioning them imposed for you. Many, however, cannot understand the deletion of their loved ones' desperate plight from your message and have expressed their deep concern to me about not being able to meet with you personally."[52] She did not realize it then, but her tele-gram would have its intended impact.

On Thursday, November 13, some incredible news came for Joan Pollard. After more than three and a half years with no word from Ben, she had received a ninety-word letter from North Vietnam. Joan had the letter in hand in Colorado Springs just after 3 p.m. the next day.

He was alive and was a prisoner of war in North Vietnam!

She could not believe it—and did not dare *let* herself believe it at first. Cora Weiss had gone over to North Vietnam and returned with a letter from her husband. Weiss had dropped the letter in the regular mail, with no special delivery. As Joan remembered vividly, "She didn't call me, she called the press." Soon the media was clamoring to speak to her: ABC, NBC, and CBS all contacted her (but not the govern-ment, which found out about Ben *after* the media did).[53]

The potent brew of media exposure from the League trip, Sybil's tele-gram to Nixon after his "silent majority" speech, and Laird and Cap-en's sustained pressure on Nixon to prioritize the POW issue finally provided the POW/MIA wives and mothers with the ultimate entrée.[54] In December, Sybil, Andrea, and twenty-odd other POW and MIA wives and mothers were invited to Washington for a reception, coffee, and press conference with the president. Their husbands, the American

POWs and MIAs, represented their own kind of silent majority—a forgotten majority,[55] one that the women now stood for. They would speak for those whose voices could not be heard.

The scene at the officers' club reception on the evening of December 11 was dazzling. All the heads of the U.S. government agencies were present. "These included the Chiefs and Secretaries of all the Armed Services as well as the Secretary of Defense, Secretary of State, and several of their assistants. Someone said it was the only time in Washington all these men were gathered in the same room."[56] (Capen and Sieverts, the "Washington Road Show" alums in attendance that night, must have warned their bosses and the military men that they had better show up if they didn't want to face the women's wrath.)

The next day, December 12, President Nixon spoke at a press conference in the White House. He and his wife, Pat, had spent the day with the twenty-six women (twenty-one wives and five mothers), feted at the previous evening's reception. These ladies represented the approximately fifteen hundred women, mothers, and wives of American POWs and MIAs in Vietnam. They represented all the military branches as well.

Of these women, only five were invited to stand with the president for the press conference photo call: Sybil Stockdale, Carole Hanson, Louise Mulligan, Andrea Rander, and Pat Mearns. All these women were National League members. Sybil was asked to take over as the spokesperson for the press conference when the president was done speaking. The government officials and even Nixon himself probably realized that she knew more than he did about POW/MIA issues.

Nixon would begin his speech to the press with these wives clustered around him like a phalanx of Amazon warriors:

"I have the very great honor to present in this room today five of the most courageous women I have had the privilege to meet in my life."[57] Sybil stood next to him, nodding in approval, dressed again in her favorite bright-pink wool suit. There was no doubt in her mind that she had gotten her money's worth out of that outfit.[58]

Twelve

DON'T MESS WITH TEXAS

IN LATE DECEMBER OF 1969, uber-wealthy Dallas businessman Ross Perot chartered two Braniff Boeing 707s in an attempt to deliver food, medicine, and Christmas gifts to American POWs held in Vietnam. In November, Perot had formed and funded the POW/MIA awareness group United We Stand. The organization supported the office of the president and spent $1 million on newspaper and television advertisements to promote awareness of the POW/MIA situation.[1]

Perot had recently begun to work with the Nixon White House, POW family organizations, and Congress to spotlight the POW/MIA issue.[2] The wiry, crew-cut Texan, president of Electronic Data Systems, took these actions as a private citizen, without official U.S. government backing but with Nixon and Kissinger's tacit approval. Perot had been recruited by Melvin Laird and Dick Capen to be part of Laird's POW Task Force and would prove to be "the sharpest burr . . . in the saddle of Hanoi."[3]

A 1957 graduate of the U.S. Naval Academy (the alma mater of so many downed airmen, like Jim Stockdale and Jerry Denton), Perot attributed much of his success to his Navy leadership and being a person of decisive action.[4] He was moved by the plight of the women and children left behind by the American servicemen taken prisoner and missing in action. Dallas-area POW/MIA wives had come to him seeking help.

One of these women, MIA wife Bonnie Singleton, had a son who had never met his father. She contacted Perot for assistance on behalf of the local POW/MIA wives. Sybil would later refer to Bonnie as "a real fireburner."[5] Bonnie's fellow POW/MIA wives in Texas respected her courage and outspokenness. Her friend and fellow Texas MIA wife Sallie Stratton remembered, "Bonnie was very active and I met her right away at the very first meeting of the area POW/MIA wives at Shirley Johnson's home. She was always very outspoken and at the time, more radical than I, but I admired her tremendously."[6]

Perot decided to deliver aid—Texas style. His first action under the United We Stand banner was to advertise the issue on a national scale. On November 9, which Nixon had declared a National Day of Prayer and Concern for the prisoners of war in Vietnam, Perot ran full-page ads in major newspapers across the country. These vivid images featured "two small children praying 'Bring our Daddy home safe, sound, and soon' . . . The ads demanded that the 'North Vietnamese and the Viet Cong . . . Release the prisoners now.'"[7]

Sybil must have jumped up and down for joy. Finally, *this* was the anti–North Vietnamese propaganda campaign she had been praying for. She had suggested this kind of effort years earlier to the Navy and the government, but to no avail. Because of his timing, money, and influence—and, no doubt, his being male—Perot was the one finally able to implement the anti-Communist campaign of Sybil's dreams. Soon she would be working more directly with the Dallas businessman. The ads were only the beginning of the Perot Pressure Plan.

On December 21, Perot's chartered Boeing 707 *Peace on Earth* was loaded up with fourteen hundred meals and other supplies to be transported to Hanoi for Vietnam POWs. The Braniff jet, sporting a gigantic red-ribbon decal, left Dallas Love Field that morning for Honolulu, Wake Island, Hong Kong, Bangkok, and finally Vientiane, in the country of Laos. The weary Perot entourage, accompanied by a stewardess/translator, finally met with a North Vietnamese representative and officials from the Pathet Lao at that group's headquarters, in Vientiane. Here they learned that the North Vietnamese would not let them land in Hanoi.

The rejected and dejected group returned to Bangkok via private plane to regroup and meet with North Vietnamese embassy officials. There, the group was informed that their delivery would have to be sent to Hanoi via Russia. "North Vietnam has said it would accept Perot's gifts, reportedly worth $400,000, only through the Soviet channel."[8]

Hanoi lay just three hundred miles to the northeast of Vientiane. A plane flight there would have taken just over an hour and twenty minutes.[9] Frustrated, the group next proceeded to Tokyo, then on to Anchorage, Alaska, where all the supplies had to be repackaged to fit Russian freight mail regulations. The entire local community pitched in: military, students, and other volunteers. Incredibly, the whole operation was completed in less than six hours. The flight ultimately landed in Copenhagen. After more meetings in Denmark at the Russian embassy, Perot realized that the delivery mission was futile. "The Russians were just as difficult as the NVA [the North Vietnamese Army] and Perot decided to scrub the mission completely."[10]

The Perot entourage returned to Dallas on New Year's Day 1970. They had not delivered any Christmas meals, but they had achieved something perhaps more valuable: they had served up a heaping helping of bad publicity for the North Vietnamese. The world had been watching the beribboned jet on television as it was shunted from one destination to the next, first by the North Vietnamese and then by the Russians. The fact that the generous Texas Santa and his jet sleigh were barred from delivering much-needed supplies to American prisoners rubbed the noses of the North Vietnamese and the Russians in another pile of negative publicity.

It was a calculated move on Perot's part, eliciting even more sympathy for the American prisoners. When he was interviewed upon his return to the States, the tech magnate drawled, "My new year's resolution is to quadruple my efforts to help the POWs."[11] More than a year later, Perot clarified the trip's primary objective: "The purpose of the Christmas trip was not to take packages to prisoners, but to put the North Vietnamese in the position where they had to talk. We wanted to create a pressure-cooker situation where they had to see us. They didn't have to love us, but they had to see us."[12] Perot historian Libby Craft affirmed, "The primary objective was to embarrass and try the North Vietnamese in the court of public opinion to get them to the 'table' to discuss the POW/MIA situation. The humanitarian objective was to do everything possible to improve the circumstances and secure the release of the men held in Southeast Asia."[13]

Like Sybil, Jane, Louise, Phyllis, Andrea, and many other POW and MIA wives, the businessman fully understood the value of publicity. He also had something in abundance that most military wives did not. As one reporter noted, the Christmas flights were a "diplomatic blitz with Perot supplying the most needed resource: money."[14] As MIA wife and later League coordinator Evelyn Grubb noted: "We're grateful to Ross Perot for his faith, his help, and his outreach with a strong hand and for putting his money where his mouth was!"[15]

Perot's support extended beyond the financial. Laird's second in command, Dick Capen, recalled that the Texan's greatest gift "was to give hope and support to the families when they badly needed it."[16] He would soon become the POW/MIA movement's most tireless private-sector champion.

On Christmas Day 1969, Perot had sent another Braniff jet to Paris for the latest round of the Paris peace talks. The spanking-new red Douglas DC-8 carried precious cargo: fifty-eight POW wives and ninety-four POW children. This time, the wives would attempt to plead with the North Vietnamese representatives in Paris for the American prisoners' release. MIA wife Kathleen Johnson, from Kansas, was on that flight, which she dubbed *The Spirit of Christmas*. Her husband, Army captain Bruce Johnson, was one of the early American advisers sent to Vietnam in July of 1964 after attending SERE school in California and undergoing extensive Vietnamese language training. His helicopter had been hit by enemy fire on June 10, 1965—just a month before he was due home from his Vietnam tour. Bruce had been listed as missing in action since that time.

Kathleen recalled that all the women, some with their children, had met up in New York to fly to Paris the next day. Kathleen took her three children, Bruce (ten), Bryan (eight), and Colleen (six), on the flight with her.[17]

The next day, every seat on the plane was filled. All the families on the flight were hopeful that their efforts might lead to a breakthrough. Bruce recalled, "By then, it had been four and a half years since Dad had been missing. We were still certain that our dad was alive and that we might have contact with him soon." The rules for this flight were much looser than those governing flights today. At a certain point, the kids were free to move around the cabin as they wished. Bruce decided to hang out around the cockpit. One of the pilots noticed him and beckoned for him to come inside. "Hey, you wanna fly this thing?" The pilot put Bruce in his seat and he even let him turn the dials. What kid would not love this? The pilot winked at Bruce: "Keep this under your hat!" Bruce nodded shyly, but he was bursting with excitement and had to tell his brother, Bryan, about it. To be noticed like that and made to feel special meant a lot to Bruce. He had felt immense pressure since his father left, but that pressure did not come from his mother. It was perhaps self-imposed. "Be the man of the house" was certainly something many military dads told their sons as they left for their tours of duty. As the oldest boy, Bruce felt responsible for his mom and his younger siblings. "I was focused on making Dad proud when he came back."

It was also a revelation for Bruce to meet other POW/MIA kids in a large group like this one. "It was the first time we had interacted with kids in the same situation." He realized he was not alone, not the only one in this nightmare scenario. Like their wives, the children found comfort in their shared experience. Bruce remembered meeting Andrea Rander and her two daughters, Lysa and Donna Page, on the flight. One of the girls had brought her baby doll with her for the trip. Bruce's sister, Colleen, had brought her own baby doll as well. He noted how kind Mrs. Rander was and how Andrea and his mother had an instant positive connection: the two women were not only both POW/MIA wives, but they were both Army wives.[18] There were few Army wives in the group or among the POWs and MIAs in general since the Air Force and the Navy accounted for most of the prisoners of war and missing during the Vietnam War. There were even fewer African American POWs and MIAs; Andrea was in a very small minority of African American POW wives and the only black woman on the Perot trip.

Under President Harry S. Truman, Executive Order 9981 officially desegregated the armed forces in 1948, but some units remained segregated until as late as 1954. The Vietnam War was the first major conflict to see a fully integrated military.[19] Vietnam War historian Marc Leepson noted, "Because of the draft, the racial composition of the Army during the Vietnam War—and to a lesser extent the Marine Corps—more or less reflected the racial composition of society in general. That was not true, though, in the Navy and Air Force, since those two services rarely had trouble filling their enlistment quotas, and African Americans served in those branches in much less representative numbers. And it was starkly different in the National Guard and Reserves."[20] Indeed, in 1969–70, "only about 1 percent of all [National] guardsmen were black."[21]

By 1969, when the Perot flight took place, African American servicemen made up 13.3 percent of all the personnel in the Army and the Marine Corps.[22] However, the Navy, Air Force, and Coast Guard tended to be much less diverse, mainly because those branches had enough volunteers and did not participate in the draft.[23] "While many draft-eligible men voluntarily enlisted in the Navy and Air Force—as those branches were perceived to be less dangerous—the draft itself conscripted men into the Army and, to a lesser extent, the Marines."[24]

During the flight, Kathleen was one of three women asked to be spokeswomen for the group. So was Andrea Rander. Both Andrea and Kathleen had attended the December 12 meeting at the White House for POW and MIA wives as representatives of Army families. Margaret Fisher, the wife of an Air Force pilot shot down over North Vietnam in 1967, was the third representative.[25] The women on board the

Paris flight felt that this was a purely humanitarian mission. "We didn't go for political reasons. We only went for our men," recalled Kathleen.

Indeed, Kathleen and many other wives felt that making public political statements could imperil not only the present expedition but also their husbands' military standing. "We never presented ourselves as hawks or doves," claimed Kathleen. "We were very mindful of our husbands' positions and our husbands' dignity."[26] Perot's aides on the flight offered to help her practice her statements in case the press asked her difficult questions. But Kathleen knew what she wanted to say and felt that rehearsing it would not be a good idea. "I felt it was better for me to answer spontaneously and be natural."[27]

When the group arrived at Orly Airport at 8 a.m. on Christmas morning, they were hustled onto a bus. It was a rainy, cold, and damp day. The bleak weather mirrored everyone's feelings that morning. Bruce remembered that "no one had slept on the flight. Everyone hit the ground rough." He had a sense of his mother, Kathleen, being pulled away from him and his brother and sister by the Perot organizers.

They immediately began phoning the North Vietnamese, trying to set up an appointment to meet that day, but the North Vietnamese refused to meet with the women and children. MIA wife Margaret Clark, a friend of Kathleen's who was also stationed in Kansas, then suggested that the women go to pray at the Cathedral of Notre Dame. Everyone agreed this was an excellent idea, much better than just going straight back to Orly.

Margaret's suggestion would profoundly change the course of events that day. The children and their mothers were bused to the church, the famous Gothic cathedral that pilgrims and tourists had admired since the Middle Ages. Its flying buttresses and rose windows were architectural marvels. But to ten-year-old Bruce, the cathedral seemed deeply mysterious. To him, it was a dark, damp cavern with gigantic candles burning everywhere and the kids all praying with their moms. The atmosphere was cold and foreboding. A feeling of dread washed over the boy. Bruce felt helpless, concerned for and protective of his mom.

What can I do to help her? he thought to himself.[28]

Suddenly, what some later considered a "Christmas miracle" occurred. Two French gendarmes arrived at the church and gently tapped the ladies on their shoulders. In the hushed atmosphere of the church, the police quietly informed the women "that the North Vietnamese delegation had relented—they would receive a small delegation of women."[29] The group all trooped back on the bus, to drop off a select group at the North Vietnamese embassy. Kathleen noticed the press trailing them. This was heartening: she knew by now what valuable allies they could be.

Wearing a leopard-print coat, Kathleen hopped off the bus. She, Andrea, and Margaret would go alone to speak to the North Vietnamese. No children or other wives were allowed. The three ladies didn't know exactly where the embassy was, but the local press gang did. They led the ladies there, walking backward while snapping their photos and filming for the television news. The press knew what sold papers: these women *were* the story. They could get the world's attention— and its sympathy—in ways that American ambassadors Lodge and Harriman never could.

The women were received cordially by the North Vietnamese. The embassy staff politely offered the women tea, but Kathleen and her companions quickly got to the point. They asked for information regarding their husbands' whereabouts and the prisoners of war and missing. The women represented themselves as part of a humanitarian mission, deliberately keeping politics out of the discussion. "We were never anyone's puppets," noted Kathleen.[30]

The North Vietnamese representatives were evasive, refusing to give the women any concrete details. "When will you tell us about the men?" asked the three POW/MIA wives, "When will the war be over?"

"Ask Nixon when the war will be over!" replied the North Vietnamese, almost in unison. Kathleen recalled dryly, "They never did share any information with us."[31] Andrea also kept trying to see Madame Binh—she had stacks of letters with her from other POW/MIA wives. She left some letters with Binh's staff, but she brought many more back home. Andrea later recalled that Binh was a hardcore

Communist, not sympathetic at all to their plight. "She did not want to see any wives from America."[32] The North Vietnamese wall could not be scaled. Not even by determined wives wearing leopard-print coats. Kathleen's son Bruce had hoped that the meeting "would result in an understanding about whether our father was alive or dead. That hope was not realized." But the fact that his mother, Andrea, and Margaret, with the help of the Perot organizers, obtained an audience with the North Vietnamese was a Christmas miracle in and of itself. Ross Perot was their hero, and their moms were their heroines. "It gave us a voice, too, just being part of it. It gave us a voice to be present."[33]

If the North Vietnamese wouldn't allow the wives of American POWs and MIAs into their confidence, what kind of Americans *would* they talk to?

The POW/MIA wives' frenemies Cora Weiss, Rennie Davis, David Dellinger, the two Berrigan brothers, and Tom Hayden fit the bill. They already had the ears and the trust of Hanoi. These activists were anti-Nixon, anti-government, and far left, which aligned them ideologically with the Communists. The North Vietnamese groomed these peace delegations when they visited North Vietnam, knowing that their propaganda would be disseminated through the best conduit of all: sympathetic Americans on the ground in the United States.

Jailers of the American POWs in Hanoi knew the plan well. Only three months after his September 1965 shoot-down, a senior North Vietnamese officer informed Jim Stockdale, "We will win the war on the streets of New York."[34] Propaganda, not guns, was the Communist's most deadly weapon. By association, radical antiwar groups soon became foot soldiers in that campaign.

Originally, the New Mobe, represented by radical civil rights lawyer William Kunstler, had offered to be a liaison group that would facilitate mail and communications between Hanoi and the POW/MIA families. Sybil learned of this plan while she was in Paris facing down the North Vietnamese in October of 1969. She was furious, and wrote that Kunstler was "an attorney who represented the leaders among the American pro-Communists. He was in close cahoots with David Dellinger, Rennard [Rennie] Davis, Tom Hayden, and other such Hanoi travelers, all trying to drag us and our husbands down into the muck where they survived."[35]

When the men's plan failed, Cora Weiss and the women of the left took over instead.

By mid-January of 1970, Weiss and David Dellinger, the self-proclaimed pacifist leader and founder of the left-wing magazine *Liberation,* had joined forces to officially found the Committee of Liaison with Families of Servicemen Detained in Vietnam (COLIAFAM). This organization had formed due to contacts between a North Vietnamese women's delegation and members of Women Strike for Peace (led by Cora Weiss) when the WSP visited Hanoi in the summer of 1969.

In December of 1969, Hanoi agreed to the forwarding of mail from the POWs to what would become COLIAFAM, and "North Vietnam also and for the first time agreed to answer questions on MIAs through the Committee of Liaison—a channel of communication that allowed North Vietnam to snub and bypass the Pentagon and the State Department."[36] Naturally, the U.S. government was wary of this alliance from the beginning, but it was hamstrung. POW and MIA families were demanding answers—and information that the government was unable to provide on its own.

COLIAFAM would quickly be characterized by newly formed National League members as "the most militant of all the peace groups."[37] The new organization began coordinating the travel of three Americans to Hanoi each month. Its mission, according to Weiss, was three-pronged: "Our purposes in going (to Hanoi) were: (1) to facilitate the mail, (2) to enable others to go as eyewitness reporters and to be citizen diplomats (technically illegal under the Logan Act), and (3) to see what was going on because so many times we didn't get any news in this country [the United States]."[38]

Later, COLIAFAM members would also repatriate POWs who chose to take early release. As early release violated the military Code of Conduct, most POWs derisively called these COLIAFAM missions "the Fink Release Program."[39]

Overtly political, COLIAFAM was the opposite of the growing League movement, which was staunchly humanitarian and mostly pro-Nixon. Sybil hated the group and feared using its courier service. But Bob Boroughs encouraged her to use any channels possible to get communication through to her husband. "I didn't want to send letters through them but Commander Boroughs said we had to in order to improve the chances of getting coded messages to and from [Jim]."[40] COLIAFAM didn't know it, but it was transmitting secret messages to the POWs through its own mail delivery. The alliance didn't last long.

Early in 1970, the U.S. government, realizing the security risk posed by COLIAFAM, rescinded its initial praise of the organization's POW/MIA efforts. The administration reversed its original stance, now advising POW families *not* to work with COLIAFAM.

When Cora Weiss, Ethel Taylor, and Madeline Duckles, founding members of COLIAFAM, returned from their December 1969 trip to Hanoi, the women claimed that the Nixon administration had now turned against them, and they urged National League members to protest at the White House: "It would be marvelous to see POW families walking up and down in front of the White House with signs saying—'Only you can bring our men home, Mr. Nixon—Set the Date!"[41] Taylor recalled that "families of POWs were asked to refrain from dealing with our Committee of Liaison, even though the transmission of mail and packages depended upon our committee."[42]

According to Weiss, the U.S. government told POW families not to send packages through COLIAFAM in New York, but instead to send their mail and packages to a post office box in Europe. "Whereupon," the peace activist later claimed, "some of the packages were opened and secret spying material was inserted. In Vietnam, we saw Colgate toothpaste tubes or wrappers of Wrigley's chewing gum with materials, parts and wires to put together radios and communications equipment." After this, the Vietnamese allowed only packages and mail that came through Weiss and Dellinger's organization.[43]

Of equal if not more importance to the POW/MIA wives and families, more complete POW and MIA lists were flowing primarily from the COLIAFAM mailing lists. Government channels were almost totally blocked. The only sure way to establish at least a partial list of POWs and MIAs was to rely on COLIAFAM. Sybil again recoiled at this arrangement: she did not think that antiwar groups should make POW/MIA lists public. "Something like this should go through the government."[44]

It was a Faustian deal, but many, like Louise Mulligan, Phyllis Galanti, Jane Denton, and even Sybil herself, realized they had to use COLIAFAM and other peace/antiwar emissaries like religious groups, Tom Hayden, Howard Zinn, and the Berrigan brothers to get communication through to their husbands. At the same time, the women were far from naive. Louise did not hesitate to call out antiwar activists on their rhetoric.

In a November 23, 1969, letter to WSP/COLIAFAM founding member Ethel Taylor, Louise questioned the organization's motives: "You speak of credibility in your letter to me—how we are to believe anything that the North Vietnamese government promises when most of our wives and mothers aren't even given the simple request of whether their husband or son is alive?" Louise went on to request that Taylor take a letter for her on her next trip to Vietnam, where she hoped she would press for impartial POW camp inspections. "I believe this should be a rather simple request IF the men are being treated humanely as they would have the world believe."[45]

Sybil echoed this attitude in her own letter to Madeline Duckles: "We . . . are under no illusions about the cruel treatment our loved ones have been receiving for years nor about the propaganda Hanoi hopes to gain from granting you visas to enter their country." She continued: "The world realizes that dissemination of information about our loved ones through other than a government or established humanitarian organization is an exploitation of our helplessness."[46]

On the other side of the world, Louise's POW husband, Jim, had directly experienced the impact of Women Strike for Peace and, later, COLIAFAM. He would later tell a congressional committee that these "peace delegations had begun visiting the POW camps as early as 1966." Jim testified that "many Americans, myself, were heavily pressured, heavily threatened . . . some men were even physically forced and tortured to visit with these delegations." These forced visits "did not contribute at all to our morale, except to lower it. The Vietnamese were able to exploit this as much as possible and tried to use the delegations to divide us."[47]

As another POW, Ted Sienicki, bluntly put it, "The world saw communism as 'on the march.' Professors taught that it was the inevitable future. We knew they [the North Vietnamese] were murderers of the highest degree. So we saw the antiwar people . . . as aiding the murderers."[48]

Many MIA and POW wives were upset when Cora Weiss and Madeleine Duckles returned from Hanoi in December of 1969 with a list of what they claimed were American pilots who were "Known Dead." The wives didn't know who or what to believe at this point. The list was not an "official" government list, and the deaths could not be confirmed or denied by the American government due to the North Vietnamese lack of compliance with Geneva Conventions rules regarding dead or missing servicemen. And, of course, there was the questionable politics of their source.

Pat Mearns's husband, Major Arthur Mearns of the Air Force, had been shot down in 1966 and not heard from since. Now Weiss claimed that he and four others were dead. As Pat recalled, "The Air Force did not change my husband's status and stated 'it was impossible to check the story.' This word added further to my three years of torture and caused a very unhappy Christmas for two small girls who believe their Daddy is still alive."[49]

Sandy Dennison, one of the founding members of the Coronado-based League of Wives under Sybil, was another of the unfortunate wives who received this communication from Weiss. Sybil noted this in her diary, commenting, "You can know just how insincere they were about wanting to help the families, just one or two days before Christmas, they contacted five wives and told them the North Vietnamese said their husbands were dead. They hadn't asked the circumstances, they said . . . Not such a nice Christmas present for these families. One was our own Sandy Dennison in San Diego."[50]

By June of 1970, COLIAFAM had released a 335-name list of POWs given to them by Hanoi. The North Vietnamese told Weiss and her delegates that this was their official and complete list of American prisoners in North Vietnam.

The U.S. government said otherwise: "The Pentagon said it had identified at least 40 other prisoners in North Vietnam through propaganda films, photographs released by Hanoi, Radio Hanoi broadcasts and statements made by nine men who were released earlier." No reference was made to U.S. prisoners who might be held in South Vietnam and Laos. A U.S. government official echoed Pat Mearns's sentiments: "The release of an 'incomplete' list causes grief to families of those not mentioned."[51]

MIA wife Marie Estocin, a founding member of the San Diego League of Wives, vividly remembered her own grief when she received word of her husband, Navy pilot Lieutenant Commander Michael J. Estocin, through a letter from Cora Weiss and COLIAFAM. Mike had been shot down on April 26, 1967, and not heard from since. Weiss's letter claimed that Mike had never been held in North Vietnam. "I was so upset, I cried for days. I thought that information told me my husband was dead." Contrary to this claim, the U.S. government had labeled him a POW, based on intelligence received through a letter from POW Richard Allen "Dick" Stratton, a good friend of Mike and Marie's. Marie would not find out for years what the truth of the matter really was. Mike would receive a posthumous Congressional Medal of Honor, but he would never return.

The COLIAFAM information could not be confirmed and was a source of agony to Marie for this reason. She was plunged into a purgatory even worse than the POW hell she had been consigned to previously.[52]

Whose account could the POW and MIA wives believe? What information should they tell their children and other family members? And just who had authorized Cora Weiss and her organization to broadcast such information without verification? The American government seemed to have abandoned ship, leaving the antiwar activists in charge. There was an information vacuum, and the peace groups had jumped in to fill it. As new National League member Evie Grubb, no fan of Cora Weiss's, grudgingly admitted, the peace groups "had gone to Hanoi, and they had returned with released prisoners . . . That was more than our government had accomplished in all the years since the first American was captured."[53]

Evie would be traumatized later when Cora Weiss announced that Evie's husband, Newk, was dead, a year after Pat had received the same pronouncement. Evie had gotten a heads-up from the State Department right before the announcement was made to the American press. "After five years of anxiety and fear, we received the ultimate blow from a stranger named Cora Weiss, who had not even had the decency to inform the wives and families of these men before publicly disseminating such life-shattering news."[54]

This was COLIAFAM's MO. They did not meet with the POW/MIA wives personally but instead tended to announce their casualty and missing lists during press conferences. While this might have maximized publicity for their group, to POW/MIA wives like Pat, Marie, and Evie, COLIAFAM's handling of the situation was harmful and disrespectful, and, above all, they disseminated questionable information. It added to their anguish, and the "what-ifs" tortured them far more than any official government report of death would have. An official confirmation they could have accepted, but this was a half-baked assumption of death without documentation—something required by the Geneva Conventions in order for the claim to be valid.

As if these public pronouncements were not enough, antiwar activists often gave out the POW and MIA wives' phone numbers and mailing addresses to various peace and antiwar groups demonstrating in Washington. This led to a deluge of unwanted propaganda. Louise and the other wives who used COLIAFAM services were also sent a barrage of antiwar materials, "pressure letters" about the war, and even doctored missives that deleted facts about the war to make their arguments stick.[55]

POW and MIA wives were forced to consume propaganda from the North Vietnamese strained through COLIAFAM's antiwar/"peace" filter. Peace didn't really mean peace: instead it meant pro-Communist rhetoric. Like the North Vietnamese pig-fat soup their husbands had to eat to survive, the POW wives were force-fed an antiwar propaganda diet. They had to accept this if they wanted their letters to go through. Those who refused, like Navy POW Edwin "Ned" Shuman's wife, Eleanor Sue Allen Shuman, were punished by having their mail cut off. Sue would later tell a Congressional Hearing Committee of her near nervous breakdown during that time.[56]

By early 1970, a great number of the POW/MIA wives appeared to be playing by the COLIAFAM rules. But these women had learned quite a bit under the LBJ regime about underground resistance and managing difficult people. The women had taken on their own government and had made critical progress. They had helped reject one ineffective administration, and now they were being given more attention under a new president whose goals meshed more favorably with their own. Next, they would use the peace activists to further their communications with their husbands and to help with accounting for the missing, accepting (but not buying) peace propaganda as a price to be paid.

While the peace activists might be the power brokers in Hanoi, the POW wives were on their way to becoming an even more powerful lobby in Washington. Sybil, Jane, Phyllis, Andrea, Louise, Helene, and hundreds of other wives were about to have a showdown in the nation's capital, supported by a posse of patriots: their new champion, Texas cowboy Ross Perot; Kansas senator and decorated World War II veteran Bob Dole; American astronauts like Apollo 13 commander James A. Lovell (many astronauts of the era were former test pilots and sometime drinking buddies of certain POWs); and even the Duke, western movie star John Wayne. The cavalry was coming, if the wives could hold the fort down just a bit longer.

An aerial view of Naval Amphibious
Base Coronado circa 1944.
Coronado would become the Navy's
training base on the West Coast.
(Courtesy of Coronado Public Library)

President Franklin Delano Roosevelt issued an executive order
that cleared Coronado of its Army presence and claimed North
Island for the Navy. Here, the president visits the base circa 1944.
(Courtesy of Coronado Public Library)

ANNE BRISCOE PYE
& NANCY SHEA

THE
NAVY
WIFE

Revised by BARBARA NAYLOR

What she ought to know about the customs of the Service and the management of a Navy household

The Navy Wife by Anne Briscoe Pye and Nancy Shea was a government-approved guide to Navy rules and etiquette. Each branch of American military service had a similar protocol manual for wives to follow. *(Robert J. Dole Institute of Politics 1965 Edition, Harper & Row)*

Jim and Sybil Stockdale as a young married couple. *(Courtesy of the Stockdale Family Collection)*

Sybil dancing with Beatle wig–wearing Navy fighter pilot Bud Collicott at an "old time aviator party" hosted at the Stockdale home 547, A Avenue in Coronado in December, 1964. *(Courtesy of the Stockdale Family Collection)*

Navy pilot Jeremiah "Jerry" Denton and his wife, Jane, in the late 1950s in the South of France (with their friends Navy doctor Ralph Beatty and his wife, Doris). *(Courtesy of the Denton Family Collection)*

Jane Denton as a young Navy wife in a portrait made just prior to Jerry's departure for Vietnam in 1965. *(Courtesy of the Denton Family Collection)*

Herman and Helene Knapp on their wedding day, June 21, 1952. Herman, an Air Force pilot, would become MIA during the Vietnam War. *(Helene Knapp scrapbook/Colorado Springs Pioneers Museum)*

Helene Knapp, now a Colorado Springs Air Force wife, would become a fierce advocate for the MIAs and eventually National Coordinator of the National League of Families from 1972–1973. *(Helene Knapp scrapbook/Colorado Springs Pioneers Museum)*

Secretary of State Dean Rusk, President Lyndon B. Johnson, and Secretary of Defense Robert McNamara meeting in the Cabinet Room of the White House on February 9, 1968. The Vietnam War would haunt them all and prove to be Johnson's political undoing. *(Yoichi Robert Okamoto/WHPO)*

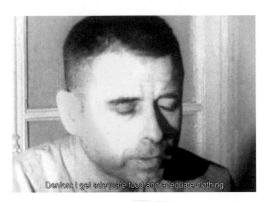

May 6, 1966. As a prisoner at the "Hanoi Hilton," Jerry had been brutally tortured. By blinking "T-O-R-T-U-R-E" in Morse Code during a filmed television interview, he was able to signal the abuse to Naval Intelligence. *(Still created from National Archives; Records of the Central Intelligence Agency [263.2589])*

The Hanoi March, July 6, 1966. The American POWs were marched through the streets of Hanoi and attacked by angry mobs of North Vietnamese. Front row (L-R): Richard Kiern and Kile Berg; second row Robert Shumaker and "Smitty" Harris; third row Ronald Byrne and Lawrence Guarino. *(U.S.A.F. photo)*

On September 9, 1965, Stockdale, the forty-year-old Commanding Officer, VF51 and Carrier Air Group Commander (CAG-16), flew his final mission. After returning from the target area, his A-4 Skyhawk was hit by antiaircraft fire. Stockdale would soon end up in the "Hanoi Hilton" along with his former Naval Academy classmate Jerry Denton and hundreds of other American prisoners of war. *(Courtesy of the DPMO, United States Department of Defense)*

Naval Commander Robert S. "Bob" Boroughs became the Navy POW wives contact in the Office of Naval Intelligence. Fortunately for the women, he didn't always play by the government's rules. *(Courtesy of the Boroughs Family Collection)*

LBJ shaking hands with Sybil and other POW wives on North Island, 1967. The president was keen for photo ops like these with the POW and MIA wives, but he would not speak to the women privately or in groups about their concerns. *(Courtesy of the Hoover Institute)*

National Security Advisor Dr. Henry Kissinger at the
Paris peace talks which began in May of 1968. The
negotiations to end the war dragged on for years.
(Courtesy of the Nixon Library and Archive)

LBJ's POW MIA Ambassador Averell Harriman and
his wife, Pamela, disembarking from an airplane in
Washington on January 20, 1969. Harriman knew for
years about the torture of American POWs in Vietnam
but was unwilling to reveal this fact to the American
public. *(Courtesy of the Nixon Library and Archive)*

Cora Weiss, formerly of Women Strike for Peace, became the
cofounder of COLIAFAM (The Committee of Liaison with Families
of Servicemen Detained in Vietnam) and public enemy number
one in the eyes of many POW MIA wives. Here, Cora is shown
with COLIAFAM cofounder David Dellinger and peace activist
Reverend William Sloane Coffin. *(Photo by Vic DeLucia/New York
Post Archives/©NYP Holdings, Inc. via Getty Images)*

Sybil, the one (and only) founder and first national coordinator of the National League of Families for Prisoners and Missing in Southeast Asia. She is shown here with roses. They became an important symbol in her coded letters to her imprisoned husband. *(Courtesy of the Stockdale Family Collection)*

POW MIA wives (L-R): Ruth Ann Perisho, Candy Parish, Andrea Rander, Sybil Stockdale, and Pat Mearns leaving the North Vietnamese delegation building after meeting with North Vietnamese representatives on October 4, 1969. *(UPI/Bettmann Archive/Getty Images)*

Army POW wife Andrea Rander was a full time working mom and the only African-American woman on the founding Board of the National League of Families. *(Courtesy of the* Baltimore Sun*)*

Andrea at home with her two daughters, Page (three and a half) on the left, and Lysa, (nine) on October 9, 1969. *(Courtesy of the Baltimore Sun)*

Secretary of Defense Melvin Laird with key members of the National League (L-R): Louise Mulligan, Jane Denton, Sybil Stockdale, Laird, Mary Winn, and Iris Powers. *(Courtesy of the Denton Family Collection)*

Evie Grubb (right), National Coordinator of the League of Families from 1971–1972, presents the flag of the National League of Families of POWs and MIAs to Secretary of Defense Melvin Laird, center, as Jan Ray, left, looks on in Washington. The POW MIA flag would become an enduring and instantly recognizable symbol of American prisoners of war and missing. *(Courtesy of the Denton Family Collection)*

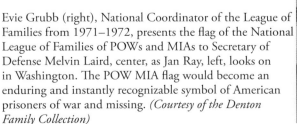

Kansas Senator Robert J. "Bob" Dole as a World War II Army officer. Dole's experiences as a gravely wounded military veteran made him sympathetic to the POW/MIA cause. He was instrumental in helping to successfully launch the National League of Families in May of 1970. *(Courtesy of the Robert J. Dole Archive and Special Collections)*

White House press conference with the National League of Families members on December 12, 1969. (L-R): Carole Hanson, Louise Mulligan, Sybil Stockdale, President Nixon, Andrea Rander, and Pat Mearns. President Richard Nixon became a strong supporter to the POW and MIA wives and their cause. *(The Richard Nixon Presidential Library and Museum, WHPO-2620-14A)*

Fellow POW wives and best friends Janie Tschudy, left, wife of Navy Lt. William L. Tschudy, and Jane Denton, at home in Virginia Beach, Dec. 19, 1969. *(AP Photo/Charles Kelly)*

Texas business mogul Ross Perot was a fervent supporter of the POW/MIA cause, of the Dallas-area POW/MIA wives, and later, of Sybil Stockdale and her National League of Families. Here, Perot is shown embarking on his "Peace on Earth" flight to Paris. December 21, 1969. Accompanying Perot on the flight were (L-R): Mrs. Bob Jeffrey, Mrs. Greggf Harkness, Mrs. Bonnie Singleton, all of Dallas, and Mrs. Michael McElhanon of Fort Worth. At right in doorway of plane is Murphy Martin of WFAA-TV, director of special projects. Boy at left is unidentified. *(Dallas Morning News/Associated Press)*

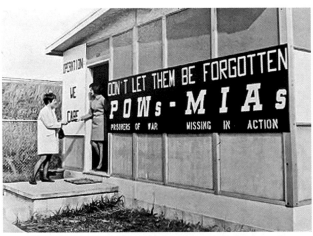

Navy POW wives Dot McDaniel and Janie Tschudy at the opening of the Virginia Beach "Operation We Care" office, October 22, 1970. This became headquarters for the Virginia Beach POW/MIA wives' efforts.

Volunteers are shown working in Richmond, Virginia, at the "Write Hanoi" office. Phyllis Galanti and her friends Connie Richeson, Judi Clifford, and office manager Gwen Mansini worked tirelessly at the office, along with dozens of other local volunteers to publicize the plight of the prisoners and missing. *(Courtesy of the Virginia Historical Society)*

Kathleen Johnson and her son Bryan and Andrea Rander and her daughter Lysa are pictured here arriving at Orly airport in Paris on Christmas Day, 1969. Kathleen, Andrea, and their children were among the fifty-eight wives and ninety-three children flown by Ross Perot to Paris on his "Spirit of Christmas" flight to seek news of their POW/MIA husbands and to raise awareness of the issue. *(Bettmann Archive/Getty Images)*

Louise Mulligan, a forceful New Englander, would be the first East Coast Navy wife to speak to the press. Her "May Day" speech on May 1, 1970, would be a galvanizing event for the POW/MIA cause. *(Courtesy of the Louise Mulligan Collection)*

Sybil Stockdale with Margot and Ross Perot and Senator Bob Dole at the press conference for the International Appeal to Justice/May Day events. May 1, 1970. *(Courtesy of the Robert and Elizabeth Dole Archive and Special Collections, University of Kansas)*

Now known as "Fearless Phyllis," Phyllis Galanti gives a speech to the combined houses of the Virginia General Assembly in Richmond on February 9, 1971. *(Courtesy of the Virginia Historical Society)*

Assistant Secretary for Defense for Public Affairs, two-star Air Force General Daniel "Chappie" James became the assistant secretary for defense for public affairs and the POW/MIA liaison under Nixon. *(Courtesy of the Hoover Institution Archives)*

Colorado Springs Vice-Mayor Larry Ochs in Paris protesting on behalf of American POWs and MIAs in Vietnam. December 16, 1970. *(Courtesy of the Colorado Springs Pioneers Museum/Helene Knapp Collection)*

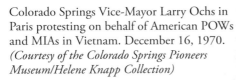

March 8, 1971: Phyllis Galanti on the back of the "Write Hanoi" truck. Hundreds of thousands of letters protesting the treatment of the POWs and the missing would soon be on their way to the North Vietnamese embassy in Sweden. *(Courtesy of the Virginia Museum of History)*

French Communist reporter Madeleine Riffaud meeting with Phyllis Galanti in Paris in February of 1972. Madeleine had interviewed Phyllis's POW husband, Paul, in Vietnam soon after his shoot down. *(Courtesy of the Virginia Museum of History)*

January 26, 1973. (L-R): Phyllis Galanti, Helene Knapp, and Darlene Sadler meeting with Nixon at the White House in their capacity as leaders of the National League of Families. *(Courtesy of the Richard Nixon Library and Museum)*

Sybil, Jim Jr., Stanford, and Taylor tackle Jim on the tarmac upon his return home February 15, 1973. *(Courtesy of the Stockdale Family Collection)*

The Stockdale boys made this banner to welcome their Dad home to 547 A Avenue in Coronado. *(Courtesy of the Stockdale Family Collection)*

Jane Denton, Louise Mulligan, and Phyllis Galanti and their families await the return of Jerry, Jim, and Paul on February 15, 1973, at Naval Station Norfolk. *(Courtesy of the Denton Family Collection)*

Jerry Denton is hugged by his wife, Jane, and children after arriving at the Norfolk Naval Air Station on February 15, 1973. *(AP Photo/Charles Kelly)*

Phyllis and Paul Galanti reunited at last. A shot of their reunion would make the February 26, 1973, cover of *Newsweek* with the headline: "Home at Last!" *(P.A. Gormus, Jr./Richmond* Times-Dispatch*)*

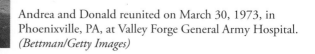

Andrea and Donald reunited on March 30, 1973, in Phoenixville, PA, at Valley Forge General Army Hospital. *(Bettman/Getty Images)*

Operation Homecoming press conference photo of (L-R): Louise Mulligan, Jane Denton, and Phyllis Galanti at the Portsmouth Naval Hospital in Norfolk, Virginia. February 17, 1973. *(Denton family photos)*

Returned Navy POW John McCain was still on crutches due to injuries and torture sustained during his captivity when attending the May 24, 1973, Nixon Gala at the White House. *(Courtesy of the Richard Nixon Presidential Foundation)*

The May 24, 1973, POW Return Nixon Gala was held on the White House lawn and is still the largest dinner party ever given to date at the White House. Here, President Nixon is shown with Sybil and Jim Stockdale. Jerry Denton is visible on the far left of the photo standing next to Pat Nixon *(Courtesy of the Richard Nixon Presidential Library and Museum (NARA LP-RN))*

Thirteen

MAY DAY DEBUT

As 1970 DAWNED, ATTITUDES were only just beginning to change for the better for minorities. Women's rights lagged even further behind. Shirley Chisholm, the first black woman elected to Congress, in 1968, would confirm this, declaring, "Of my two 'handicaps,' being female put many more obstacles in my path than being black."[1] She was not the only one who had lost her patience with the sexism so prevalent in American society. Women of all races, colors, and creeds were pushing back and organizing themselves into feminist groups. These groups were not composed of just intellectuals and students; housewives were also jumping into the fray. One female journalist reporting on the burgeoning feminist movement ominously warned her male readers, "They [feminists] were all pretty mad . . . You guys better watch out. They're coming to get you."[2]

This same all-points bulletin should have gone out to members of the State Department, the Pentagon, and the U.S. military who dared stand in the way of Sybil and her League of Wives. The POW/MIA wives did not identify as feminists, but they were facing many of the same problems as their more radical sisters. Most of these military wives chose to ignore these gender issues and move forward instead with their own agenda. As Louise Mulligan put it, "A woman can do anything she puts her mind to."[3] Feminism, in the minds of most conservative military wives, was associated with the left and Communism. Furthermore, their fight was focused on their husbands' plight, not on their own status, which they selflessly deemed a much less pressing issue at the time. Andrea recalled, "It was now starting to build by 1970, now we're getting up to Capitol Hill. We're going to do whatever we have to do, say whatever we have to say to get those guys home."[4]

Unlike most of his government colleagues, Republican senator Bob Dole had gotten the League's all-points bulletin. His strong, independent mother, Bina, had raised him to respect feminine force. Dole understood exactly what Louise was saying: a woman could do anything she set her mind to. The savvy politician knew better than to stand in the League's way.

Dole was born in rural Russell, Kansas, on July 22, 1923. His father, Doran Ray Dole, ran an egg and cream distribution station and, later, a grain elevator. Doran missed only one day of work in forty years and taught all his children that in life, "there were doers and there are stewers."[5] Bina was a traveling saleswoman, selling Singer sewing machines and vacuum cleaners. Bina reportedly "was not afraid of confrontation and lived by the practical slogan: 'Can't never did anything.'"[6] These independent, hardworking parents would pass their deep-rooted work ethic on to their son.

The young Dole grew into an outstanding student and popular athlete. He possessed leading-man good looks, a wry, midwestern sense of humor, and an easy rapport with both men and women. As with so many men of his generation, Dole's college career at the University of Kansas and his dreams of becoming a doctor were interrupted by World War II. After his military training, he deployed to Italy in 1943 as second lieutenant in the Army's 10th Mountain Division, quickly distinguishing himself with his courage under fire. The young serviceman was seriously wounded in April of 1945 just three weeks before the war ended while attempting to save a fellow soldier during combat. Enemy fire caught him in the right shoulder and back, resulting in permanent physical disabilities. The wounded serviceman then spent a total of thirty-nine months in military hospitals.

Dole was awarded two Purple Hearts and a Bronze Star with an oak leaf cluster for his heroism. Now a decorated war veteran, the young man began taking classes toward his bachelor's degree at the University of Arizona and returned to his home state, where he completed undergraduate degrees in history and law at Washburn Municipal University (later Washburn University), in Topeka, in 1952.[7]

The young veteran's career in public service began at the age of twenty-six: he served one term in the Kansas legislature, then went on to serve four terms as the Russell County attorney. In 1960, he was elected to the U.S. House of Representatives, and in 1968 he became a member of the U.S. Senate.[8]

When Bob Dole first arrived in Washington, in 1961, he knew he wasn't, as Dorothy said in *The Wizard of Oz,* in Kansas anymore. By 1969, when he moved into his Senate position, he knew well how to navigate the corridors of power in Washington. But the lack of attention to imprisoned and missing servicemen embroiled in the Vietnam War seemed inexplicable.

He had a determination to represent his country, with a focus on veterans and the disabled, given his own war experiences. The former soldier had already proved he possessed courage, and he was shocked by the division he saw within the government. The new senator was even more discouraged by the ignorance some of his political colleagues displayed regarding the Vietnam War, now playing out on television and wreaking havoc on families across the country. Sons, fathers, and brothers were being swallowed up by a jungle country thousands of miles away. In 1970, many politicians in Washington still seemed almost oblivious to their plight.

Senator Dole was stunned to find that in both the House of Representatives and the Senate, even at this late date, "no one knew what a POW or an MIA even *was.*"[9] He vowed to change that, out of a deep sense of empathy for the American prisoners of war, some of whom had been trapped for as long as six years in filthy, crumbling Vietnamese prisons. He stood nearly alone in his concern for the POWs and MIAs at this time, without much popular or political support.

The new senator must have thought, *Hadn't Americans lived through the Korean War and World War II?* Perhaps it was just blatant denial of an unpopular conflict. Regardless of the "why," the midwestern politician was determined to raise awareness of the POW/MIA issue, making this cause one of his first missions. He soon teamed up with Charles A. Moser, chairman of the Freedom Rally Committee (FRC). Moser held the FRC gathering in D.C.'s Constitution Hall on February 21, 1970, the weekend of Washington's Birthday. Dole was a part of a bipartisan slate of speakers that also included Thomas Downing, a Democratic congressman from Virginia; Dr. Walter Judd, a former Republican congressman from Minnesota; and film and TV actress Arlene Dahl. But Moser's real star was Louise Mulligan, the outspoken POW/MIA advocate and League area coordinator from Virginia Beach.[10]

Louise did not mince words at the Freedom Rally.

She forcefully pointed out that the League's Paris trip in September and early October of 1969 had produced no tangible results, save bad publicity for the North Vietnamese. "To date, they [the North Vietnamese] refuse to even let the wives and mothers know if their husbands or sons are in fact prisoners. They later stated that if the families were to come to Paris, they would tell them what they wanted to know. They went to Paris, at considerable expense and inconvenience. Upon arriving in Paris, they met with delaying tactics and frustration. Calls to the North Vietnamese compound were met with replies such as: 'There is no one here who can help you!' or 'We do not understand.' And always met with laughter in the background." Louise further noted that even when Sybil, Andrea, and the other wives finally gained an interview at the embassy, they received no information on their husbands and sons. "The wives and mothers were shown propaganda films and pictures . . . They were told to go home and demonstrate, join peace groups. I question how peaceful these peace groups are!"[11]

Only three hundred guests turned up for the rally. After all the publicity, this was a disappointing and demoralizingly low turnout. By comparison, antiwar rallies in Washington led by the New Mobe and others were generating hundreds of thousands of protesters. The October 15 Moratorium had drawn 250,000 protesters in D.C. and two million nationwide. The November 15 Moratorium March on Washington, a month later, had been even more massive—the largest antiwar protest of the era, with as many as half a million attending.[12] The POW/MIA movement had to change its tactics fast to try to capture public interest—and support.

On Friday, March 20, Senator Dole's office issued a proclamation on behalf of Louise, Sybil, and all the POW/MIA wives and families. This time, it was not simply a request for help, but instead a call to arms. On the Senate floor, Dole said he was "shocked that only 300 persons attended the rally in Constitution Hall," in February. (The hall seats 3,811 people.) Dole said, "It was then resolved that 'Constitution Hall would be filled within 90 days in a resounding demonstration of support.'" The Appeal for International Justice, scheduled for May 1, would show the POW/MIA wives and families that America *did* care about the plight of their loved ones, and it would show the North Vietnamese and Viet Cong that their behavior was not acceptable.[13]

Like Moser, Dole enlisted the aid of a bipartisan committee. Comprising six senators and six representatives, the group was evenly split between Democrats and Republicans. The Kansas senator emphasized that "while some Senate and House Members have differing views about the conduct of the Vietnam war, all agree that American prisoners in Vietnam have not been treated in accord with the 1949 Geneva Convention." This seemed to be the one issue of the war that almost everyone on both sides could agree on.[14]

Determined to rally the nation around this cause, Dole rounded up heavy-hitter support for the League. Well-known public figures and politicians like astronaut James A. Lovell, the Apollo 13 commander, Arizona senator Barry Goldwater, and even Vice President Spiro Agnew were invited to be part of the May 1 program, as was Texas mogul Ross Perot.[15]

These men all lent connections, political star power, or money to the cause. However, the workhorses who would really deliver the goods—the bodies needed to "fill the hall"—were the women. One of Dole's first calls when he began organizing the May Day event was to Sybil. She recalled the 11 p.m. phone call she received in late February from the senator. Her job? "It was to get as many families there as possible. This required getting government transportation, which we were able to do, but it all required tremendous time and effort."[16]

Sybil and Louise thus became the super-organizers of the POW/MIA wives and families for the event. With the help of Washington-area military wives and other active supporters like Jane Denton and Phyllis Galanti, Louise and Sybil delivered what the well-intentioned Moser could not: bodies in seats.[17] Parents, wives, and children all came to D.C. to support the cause. The Air National Guard airlifted seven hundred POW/MIA family members, at the government's expense, for the meetings on May 1 and 2.[18]

Sybil, Louise, Jane, and many other POW/MIA wives and family members arrived early in Washington for a series of hearings of the House Committee on Foreign Affairs Subcommittee on National Security Policy and Scientific Developments, with Wisconsin congressman Clement Zablocki in charge. Zablocki was a liberal Democrat, a strong anti-Communist, and a supporter of the Vietnam War. That Wednesday, hundreds listened as MIA wife Kathleen Johnson, just back from an April trip to Paris (Kathleen had also been on Perot's "Spirit of Christmas" flight in December of 1969), testified in front of the committee, along with Senator Dole and Congressman L. Mendel Rivers.

On Friday, even more families and wives had arrived in the nation's capital. The audience at the hearings swelled. POW wives Sybil, Jane Denton, and Valerie Kushner—a POW/MIA activist and wife of Captain Hal "Spanky" Kushner, a prominent figure in the 2017 Ken Burns series *The Vietnam War*—were among those who told their stories to the committee. Ross Perot testified, lending his powerful voice to the proceedings.[19] The Texas wives came out in force for Perot, with Bonnie Singleton lined up to speak at the May 1 evening program. Sandy McElhanon and Paula Harkness also attended with their children.

The Texas wives would also be strongly supported by their congressman Olin Earl "Tiger" Teague, a Democrat and the longtime whip in the House. The World War II veteran had just returned from a trip to South Vietnam, where he had watched pilots take off from aircraft carriers for bombing runs, many never to return.[20] Like Senator Dole, Teague was a leader on veterans' issues. He was not about to let his Lone Star State ladies down on May Day. He would also be a speaker at the evening event.

Both Teague and Dole would give these women full credit for their fierce dedication to the May Day rally and the POW/MIA cause. Speaking specifically of the League ladies, Dole declared, with a wink, "You turn a bunch of women loose on a project, they're gonna either get it done or kill everyone in their wake."[21] Unlike so many government officials before them, both Dole and Teague had the smarts to give the women the platform they needed and to then get the hell out of the way.

Constitution Hall, the site of the February Freedom Rally and of May's Appeal for International Justice, is a beautiful neoclassical building designed by architect John Russell Pope. Situated near the White House, it is smack in the middle of the nation's capital.

Built in 1929 by the Daughters of the American Revolution, Constitution Hall is perhaps best known as the building where singer Marian Anderson was banned from performing in 1939. Anderson biographer Allan Keiler noted that the Daughters of the American Revolution (DAR) "refused to allow her use of the hall because she was black and because there was a white-artist-only clause printed in every contract issued by the DAR." At that time, the hall was segregated. First Lady Eleanor Roosevelt later resigned from the DAR in protest.[22] But by May 1, 1970, thirty-one years after the Marian Anderson debacle, segregation was gone. The new National League was born fully integrated: it included the wives, parents, and family members of prisoners of war and missing from every branch of the American military, regardless of race.

This gathering of military wives and their families, supported by high-level politicians, entertainers, and astronauts, had a common goal: to let the world know about human rights injustices.

Another relic that was blown away (at least temporarily) by the prisoner and missing issue was military hierarchy among the women. The rank order of the men, which by association was conferred onto their wives, melted away, becoming unimportant. Working hard and collaboratively was what defined the wives now. This old-fashioned caste system, at least for the time being, was rejected by the group. Bob Boroughs's son Tom later recalled that his father had been a strong proponent of this approach, urging the women "to get rid of the military wife hierarchy and work together to get the men out . . . Of all the things my dad did, that was the thing he was most proud of."[23]

Senator Dole opened the May 1 Appeal for International Justice/ National League evening as the master of ceremonies promptly at 8 p.m. After the Air Force Band played and the Reverend Edward Elson, chaplain of the U.S. Senate, gave the invocation, Senator Dole gave his remarks, in line with the international justice theme. "Today we say that justice will never come to Southeast Asia unless we who do not have loved ones missing or listed as prisoners start to become as indignant as those who do."[24] This was everyone's fight, whether for or against the war.

Dole emphasized the legal violations of the North Vietnamese: they had refused to honor the Geneva Conventions, to identify American prisoners, to allow prisoners to receive mail from their families, or to give them adequate food or medical care. This was not a partisan cause: "It is a cause of humanity." Dole ended his impassioned speech by circling back to the League ladies who had confronted the North Vietnamese on the men's behalf. "We sense the anguish of these families in the repetition of the wives' question to the North Vietnamese in Paris, 'Am I a wife or a widow?'"[25]

Sybil, as the coordinator of the National League, stepped up to bat next. She must have looked out over the crowd with satisfaction. She and Louise, Dole, Perot, and their many supporters had indeed filled the hall to capacity. She began her speech by addressing the government's "keep quiet" policy head-on, noting that only after years of silence and the accumulation of evidence about prisoner torture and maltreatment did the government finally start listening to the families. "We began to speak out in 1968 and were grateful when the U.S. government publicly expressed concern for our men in 1969."[26]

Sybil was careful to emphasize the League's independence from the government as well, assuring the audience that "we have often asked the U.S. government officials for counsel and advice, but we have then made our own decisions independently."[27] The ladies refused to be government puppets—they knew better after their years of "keep quiet" under LBJ. They were determined to run the show from here on out.

Popular singer Jack Jones followed Sybil, singing "The Impossible Dream," which would become a theme song for the POW and MIA wives.

After Sybil, Kathleen Johnson spoke about her missing husband, Army major Bruce Johnson. Only a few days before, the Army MIA wife had flown back to the States from Paris. She had journeyed for the second time (this time without her three children) to try to get information about her missing husband. After eleven days of pleading for an audience with Madame Binh of the NLF, Kathleen had returned home discouraged and empty-handed.[28] She was followed at the podium by Bonnie Singleton, the Dallas POW wife whose little son had never met his father. Both women's stories were heart-wrenching and compelling. But the real fireworks came from Louise Mulligan. She would electrify the room with her speech.

"We beg of you to hear our call—May Day! May Day! Do not turn your back on the hundreds of mothers who want their sons returned, do not ignore the children who cry out for the love and guidance of their fathers and the hundreds of wives who have grieved for years, some for husbands who will never return! Hear our call of distress and the cry from within the walls of the prison camps—May Day! May

Day!!! HELP. PLEASE HELP."[29] With the pilot's international distress call ("Mayday" comes from the French *M'aidez*—"Help me"), the Virginia Beach activist got everyone's attention. The POW and MIA families finally felt like someone had connected with them on a visceral level and had been willing to verbalize their pain. Louise demonstrated to the crowd that no one needed to suffer in silence or "keep quiet" anymore. She had helped break the sound barrier set up by her own government.

The evening was a triumph, a successful coming-out party for the National League. But despite the women's success, a plot to take over the League was already incubating in D.C. Sybil did not have a chance to even drink a celebratory glass of champagne before she had to gird for battle again.

The next morning, May 2, the League of Families hosted its inaugural meeting in the auditorium of the Interior Department. The wives and families, still euphoric from the night before, plunged into their packed agenda. But they soon encountered counterforces attempting to take over the nascent League.

A group of retired Air Force officers from the Washington area wanted to take control of the organization and set themselves up as its paid officials and administrators. The ladies would be reduced to licking stamps and stuffing envelopes while the men ran the show. Bob Boroughs warned Sybil that she could not let this happen. "If you let them get on that stage, they will convince the families they should be in charge. You can't let that happen, Sybil!"[30]

When the men appeared at the May 2 League meeting, Sybil ignored them, letting the group's extensive agenda and swift decision to incorporate push them out. The men left, furious, but Sybil had prevented the takeover. Like Boroughs, Sybil knew that if individuals outside the League were in charge, it would lose the one thing that made it unique: the requirement that you had to be the family member of a POW or MIA to belong. She also had learned another important lesson from all of her activism: "The slightest taint of Washington slickness was the surest turn-off for the media, who were our strongest allies."[31]

Real progress on behalf of the POWs and MIAs was being made thanks to the Appeal for International Justice and National League events of May 1 and 2. The National League of Families of American Prisoners and Missing in Southeast Asia was incorporated on May 28, 1970, in D.C. The League's new founding board met in August. It included Iris Powers, Joan Vinson, Muriel Egan, Edwin Brinckmann, Carole Hanson, Jane Denton, Kathleen Johnson, Eileen Cormier, Irene Davis, Shirley Johnson, Carol North, Nancy Perisho, and Andrea Rander.[32]

Andrea had to overcome family opposition to her involvement in the League. Don's mother, Andrea's mother-in-law, did not support her activism at first. "She felt I should be at work or with the children, not out in public being an activist." Her mother-in-law saw the League as political, not as a humanitarian group, and Andrea felt she was at a crossroads. "I was scared. Am I taking on something bigger than me?" she thought. Then she decided the objective was to help Donald. She soon found that "the League gave me the strength to do what I had to do." She also felt included. The other wives were "so welcoming to me. It was good for me and my kids."

The fact that Andrea was African American seemed to be of minimal importance to the group. "I didn't feel I was any less than them." She had found, when she began her work with the League, that rank was more of an issue than race. "Rank bothered me more than my color." Over time, Andrea and many other wives found that this barrier had begun to melt away also.

Senator Dole attested to a distinct change of tone he was seeing on the Senate floor. "In the Senate, a different Senator is making a speech every day on the prisoner of war situation. Some of those on my committee . . . have differing views of the war. But they all agree that our prisoners are not being treated humanely. And this is the thrust, or at least the hope that we can attract attention nationwide and worldwide to these facts."[33]

Meanwhile, Phyllis finally was making progress with the media at home in Richmond. She had been trying hard to get the *Richmond Times-Dispatch* interested in the POW/MIA issue. Unbelievably, the staff was still telling her that the POWs were not enough of a story yet. Fortunately for Phyllis, the *Times-Dispatch* was not the only paper in town.

The Richmond News Leader was the afternoon rival of the morning *Times-Dispatch*. In 1969, a young conservative, Ross Mackenzie, had been named editor of the editorial page. He was fascinated by the POW/MIA issue—an issue that had not yet received the broad exposure he felt it deserved. Mackenzie recalled, "I was casting about for a local gal to feature on the editorial page." Then he learned about Phyllis.

Mackenzie phoned Phyllis and set up an interview with her, her two supportive friends Judi Clifford and Connie Richeson, and Petersburg, Virginia, MIA wife and League member Evie Grubb. Mackenzie played the interview across two pages as a November 11, 1970, Veterans Day feature on Phyllis and the plight of the POWs.[34]

The very next day, Phyllis excitedly wrote back to Mackenzie, thrilled with the coverage and the fact that the Associated Press had picked up the piece. "Again, thank you from the bottom of my heart for the wonderful spread about the prisoners of war and missing in action in last night's paper! It was really more than I could have hoped for." At the end of the letter, Phyllis noted that Mackenzie and his staff "had performed a fine service for our men. We are on the way to showing that they have not been forgotten."[35]

Nearly all the Richmond newspaper coverage of Phyllis from this point on was in the *News Leader:* Mackenzie had seen what others could not: a compelling saga about the women. That interview and its companion pieces quickly snowballed and helped lead to "the groundswell of support she had locally," as well as to a ripple effect in the press, both regionally and nationally. Years later, Phyllis would tell Mackenzie, "Ross—You really did change it all for me that day you had Connie, Judi, and me into your office. At last someone would know about our MIAs and POWs."[36] Phyllis found a powerful ally in the *News Leader,* soon becoming one of the most widely known women in Virginia. On February 9, 1971, Phyllis would give a rare speech to the combined houses of the Virginia General Assembly, helping to generate even more publicity for the POW/MIA cause.[37]

Innovative partnerships and publicity campaigns for the POWs also blossomed during this time. In 1969, two college students from Los Angeles, Carol Bates and Kay Hunter, started a POW/MIA Bracelet Campaign, under the auspices of Voices in Vital America (VIVA), a conservative collegiate activist organization. Hunter later dropped out of the organization, but she was soon replaced by fellow student Steve Frank. Adult adviser Gloria Coppin, a wealthy L.A. housewife married to a military aviation specialist, facilitated the organization's entrée into the California political scene.[38]

In 1970, Los Angeles conservative TV personality Bob Dornan introduced Carol and her VIVA colleagues to three wives of missing pilots, Jane Denton among them. The students and wives began to think of ways to draw attention to the plight of the POWs and MIAs and support U.S. soldiers without becoming embroiled in the political controversy. Jane, Phyllis, and Dot McDaniel were skeptical of the idea at first, thinking that the bracelets "didn't fit in with our dignified white-gloves-and-pearls approach."[39] But the times were changing, and the gloves and pearls were quickly coming off.

The VIVA students decided to have simple bracelets made in nickel and copper, with each imprisoned or missing man's name, rank, and date of loss inscribed on them. Gloria Coppin's husband donated enough copper and brass to make the initial twelve hundred bracelets.[40] On Veterans Day, November 11, 1970, VIVA officially kicked off the bracelet program. Despite the reservations of some of the POW wives, the bracelets quickly became a massive hit. "With production costs of thirty cents per piece for bracelets that sold for $2.50 to $3.50 each, the bracelet was the goose that laid the golden egg."[41] Through the bracelet sales, VIVA raised tens of thousands of dollars for all kinds of POW/MIA awareness-building programs, from bumper stickers and newspaper ads to matchbooks, buttons, and brochures.

Hollywood stars Bob Hope and Martha Raye signed on as honorary co-chairs of the organization. Notable figures such as Princess Grace of Monaco, singer Johnny Cash, and evangelist Billy Graham all wore the bracelet in support of American prisoners and missing in Vietnam.[42] VIVA developed a close partnership with the League, donating large amounts of money to the organization. These shiny, malleable bracelets became the most recognizable symbol of the POWs and MIAs from the Vietnam War.[43] By 1976, when VIVA closed its doors for good, the organization had sold more than five million bracelets.[44]

When the war finally ended, many families would find creative uses for bracelets returned to them in the mail by former bracelet wearers. POW wife Marty Halyburton, former southeast regional coordinator of the National League, would recycle fourteen pounds' worth of POW bracelets with her husband, Porter's, name on them by turning them into a chandelier for her breakfast room.[45]

Things had taken off for the League and the POW/MIA movement. At this point, Henry Kissinger emphasized, "The POWs were an absolute top priority in our mind."[46] A tremendous shift in attitudes had taken place, thanks in large part to the efforts of the POW and MIA wives. But both Sybil and Louise were exhausted by the demands placed on them in their dual roles as the West and East Coast's most visible activists and as full-time moms. Sybil had been working day and night to keep up with her TV appearances, White House meetings, interviews, and public speaking engagements.

As the National League's coordinator, she had been on the *Today* show in New York in January, with Barbara Walters and Hugh Downs. The appearance was arranged by *Good Housekeeping* magazine as part of its publicity for a major article on Sybil and the League that would appear in the February 1970 issue. Wearing a heather-blue knitted wool dress, her hair and makeup done by the *Today* show makeup artists, Sybil worried about Barbara Walters and her reputation as "abrasive." She was pleasantly surprised to find that Walters "was as sympathetic and cooperative as she could be and asked all the questions she could to let me explain my point of view."

The League's national coordinator also continued coding letters to her POW husband, Jim, under the supervision of Bob Boroughs. Though she had grown prolific and skilled in this work—she was Boroughs's best student—her missives caused her severe emotional stress. Her communications had to be done exactly right: the consequences of a botched job were too horrible for her to contemplate. Sybil later reflected, "I seemed to be motivated by the psychology that the harder I worked and the faster I ran the sooner the problem would be solved."[47]

On the East Coast, Louise was also stretched too thin. Raising her six boys alone while overseeing Virginia Beach–area League operations out of her bedroom was beginning to take its toll. After the exhilaration of finally being heard at the May Day League events, she had tried her best to spend the summer focusing on her boys. But she could never forget about her husband's ongoing plight: "You feel torn in many directions . . . You are trying to be a mother and a father to your children and you feel that you have to do everything you possibly can for your husband."[48]

How much more could the women endure?

Fourteen

HERE COMES YOUR NINETEENTH NERVOUS BREAKDOWN

AFTER THE HUGELY SUCCESSFUL League May Day convention, the wives opened their National League office at 1 Constitution Avenue on June 30. The Reserve Officers Association donated free office space[1] and the White House donated a free long-distance WATS telephone service.[2] Sybil, Jane, Andrea, Phyllis, and Kathleen could not believe they finally had a legitimate office in the nation's capital. It was a long way from the League's humble beginnings at Sybil's dining room table in Coronado. Clearly, they had been heard by the current administration. Henry Kissinger later recalled that the League's advocacy had a great "effect on the President, on me, and on Laird."[3]

Now that the League had a physical headquarters, bylaws were quickly established and formulated around the two major principles under which the group had operated since the very beginning. First, the League was nonpolitical and nonpartisan. Second, the organization should be composed solely of family members of missing or captured Americans in Southeast Asia.[4] Dot McDaniel succinctly articulated the difficult perch the League occupied: "The task of the National League of Families now was to pressure Hanoi publicly while privately pressuring Washington, a hard balance to maintain and a tightrope we had to walk."[5]

After the May 1 and 2 events, Sybil needed a break from her own high-wire act between the government and the POW/MIA families. Like magic, Deborah Szekely, the owner of the famed Golden Door Spa, in Escondido, California, called and invited Sybil to spend a week at the spa as her guest. Sybil had mentioned to a D.C. female reporter she knew that "it was one of my suppressed desires" to go, but it cost $100 a day—way out of Sybil's price range. Having a free week at a fabulous spa was a dream come true for the exhausted POW wife. The offer could not have come at a better time. Sybil promptly arranged for childcare for the boys and packed her bags. When she arrived at the spa, she found, to her delight, that the movie star Kim Novak was in her class of twenty. Each day, the women were issued a fresh pink sweatshirt with their breakfast tray. The meal consisted of coffee, half a grapefruit, the newspaper, and a rose served privately to guests in their rooms. Her daily schedule was packed with exercise, massage, and healthy eating. Sybil must have felt like Kim Novak herself, wearing long, elaborate gowns (borrowed from friends) for cocktails and dinner each evening. The only downside was that the "cocktails" the ladies were served were really "mocktails" of grapefruit juice, and the food was sparse. Sybil lost three pounds that week, as well as a good amount of pent-up stress. And, best of all, "I did look lots better for my trip to Washington the next week."[6]

Refreshed from her week at the Golden Door, Sybil helped to formalize the incorporation of the League and install a new national coordinator, Air Force MIA wife Joan Vinson, who already lived in Washington. Sybil was elected chairman of the National League board and, along with the staff, she helped to devise a more formal organizational structure that divided the country into five regions, each with its own coordinator. Each state had its own coordinator as well. This served to increase the awareness of what was going on across the country as each regional and state coordinator submitted periodic reports on League activities, fundraising, and publicity in their sphere of influence.[7]

Sybil later remembered the initial tension at the League office as they settled in: "There was lots of dissension among the different factions and Joan and Iris and others in the office (all volunteers, remember) were often at odds with each other."[8] Trouble was still coming from outside forces as well. With the help of the League's new attorney, Charlie Havens, Sybil managed to fend off one last coup attempt by an outside Air Force retiree.[9]

Unlike the LBJ regime, the Nixon administration realized it needed to cultivate good relations with the League and support the POW/MIA cause. Dan Henkin, the assistant secretary of defense for public affairs, at the time told Sybil: "We knew you were going to mop the floor with us . . . if we didn't join you."[10]

Henkin's recently named deputy assistant secretary of defense for public affairs, Air Force brigadier general Daniel "Chappie" James, would soon become the Pentagon's most recognizable "face" of the POW/MIA issue. Like Sybil, he had to walk a tightrope between the government and the families with finesse. Otherwise he would be thrown to the lions. This didn't faze the general, who had battled other seemingly insurmountable obstacles and enemies in the past and won.

James was born in 1920 in Pensacola, Florida. An African American, he grew up in the segregated South. As a boy, he was drawn to the Pensacola airfield, and the speed, dash, and daring of the fighter pilots he encountered there. There was no doubt in his mind that he wanted that kind of life. He attended Tuskegee Institute, in Alabama, where he joined the famed all-black military corps of Tuskegee Airmen. He enlisted in the Army Air Corps in 1943 and completed his fighter pilot training that same year. He would serve as a fighter pilot in World War II.

In 1957, he graduated from the Air Command and Staff College at Otis Air Force Base, in Massachusetts. He flew 101 combat missions in the Korean War, earning the nickname "Black Panther" (the symbol was even painted on to his flight helmet). He also served in the Vietnam War, flying seventy-eight combat missions. James's biggest Air Force claim to fame during the war was his steady command of the Operation Bolo MiG sweep, which destroyed seven Communist MiG-21s—the highest total kill of any mission during that war.[11]

By 1970, James was a legend. The hulking former football tackle had gravitas and the respect of his peers, both black and white. But there was one more battleground where he would have to prove himself, one loaded with potential minefields. This time, a reporter of the era noted, "the battleground is public opinion, and no one is more at home there than Chappie James."[12]

A staunch Nixon supporter, James gave no quarter to antiwar protesters, peace groups, or draft dodgers. The general's response to those who opposed the American government? "And to those who say they'll change the government or burn it down, I say 'like hell you will.'"[13]

James would become a powerful and useful ally of the National League families. But his entry into his new position and into the League infrastructure was not without friction. Sybil and the West Coast wives had already thrashed the government's Washington Road Show reps in March of 1969. When they met with Henkin and James in the spring of 1970, at a country club in San Diego, relations between the POW/MIA families and the government were still mistrustful and volatile. Sybil recalled how the Navy wives from Coronado, the Air Force wives from Apple Valley in the Mojave Desert, and the Marine wives from El Toro in Orange County all gathered to hear the latest report from Washington. This time there was not even a pretense of politesse.

"Dan and Chappy [sic] had gotten up and finished telling us all how everything was okay and pretty soon one Air Force wife got up and she said something like; I've been in this situation for 4 years and haven't done anything and so on. She took a glass that she had—it was like a martini glass and she threw it against the wall and smashed it and left the room." Sybil observed: "They were really rattled because by then we had become extremely outspoken."[14]

Fortunately for James, most of the League members immediately liked him. He was a fighter pilot, like their husbands. He had seen repeated combat in Vietnam as well as in the previous two American wars. He was an inspirational speaker and could be a huge asset to the POW/MIA cause. League board member Sallie Stratton was a fan: "He was so supportive, so wonderful and genuine. He really cared and listened and was more forthcoming on information than most government staff."[15] The general did receive criticism from some of the wives at the outset of his new job for favoring the Air Force and for neglecting to mention the MIAs and POWs held outside of North Vietnam: those thought to be in captive in South Vietnam, Laos, Cambodia, and the People's Republic of China. Henry Kissinger took James to task for this omission; it did not happen again.[16]

Even a towering Air Force brigadier general still had to fall in line behind the civilian leaders of this fight—the women, with Sybil at the helm.

Ross Perot also continued his efforts to support the League. On June 4, Speaker of the House John McCormack was featured in a televised address inaugurating Perot's prisoner-of-war display at the U.S. Capitol. The diorama (which looked like something a visitor would see in the Museum of Natural History in the 1960s or '70s) was designed to shock. At the center of the exhibit were two lifelike figures representing the American POWs. Historian H. Bruce Franklin later described it: "One sits in the corner of a bare cell, staring bleakly at an empty bowl and chopsticks on which a huge cockroach is perched. On the floor are other cockroaches and a large rat. The other figure lies in a bamboo cage, ankles shackled." Replicas of this display would soon pop up at state capitol buildings all over the United States.[17] Eventually such dioramas would become a common sight at shopping centers throughout America.[18] The words "POW" and "MIA" were finally becoming part of the American vernacular.

Senator Bob Dole continued to watch the POW/MIA issue carefully, and he soon saw another opportunity for the cause. Dole and Phyllis Galanti had been in contact often. He was impressed with Phyllis, her businesslike manner and, most of all, the influence she had among her peers. Like Phyllis, Connie, Judi, Sybil, and many others, the young senator had also been thinking about Sweden's stance as a neutral country. He decided to appeal directly to Sweden's prime minister,

Olof Palme, suggesting the relocation of American POWs from Vietnam to his country.

Sweden had a long history of neutrality during wartime. In 1834, King Gustav began this long tradition by royal proclamation. From this time on, the Swedish refused to take sides in times of conflict. During World War II, the Scandinavian country simultaneously harbored both Nazis and Nazi refugees. After the war, Sweden opted to continue its tradition of noninvolvement.

Over the postwar years, anti-American feeling grew in Sweden to the point that LBJ recalled the American ambassador to Sweden in 1968. The United States did not have an ambassadorial presence in Sweden for the following fifteen months. President Nixon decided to change tack, sending U.S. ambassador Jerome H. Holland (only the second African American to be chosen as a U.S. ambassador) to Sweden in April of 1970 to fill this gap.[19]

Because of its neutral stance, Sweden was the only Western nation that recognized the North Vietnamese Communist government. While Prime Minister Palme was visiting Washington in June of 1970, Senator Dole sent him a telegram suggesting that "the Swedish Government, in accordance with the 1949 Geneva Convention, offer to intern within Sweden, United States personnel held prisoners of war by the Democratic Republic of Vietnam until agreement can be reached on the release of all the prisoners. Internment within Sweden would assure these Americans of the treatment to which they are entitled by the law of nations and concepts of civilized society."[20]

Palme, in an attempt to cultivate good relations with the United States, flew to D.C. to give a talk at the National Press Club on Monday, June 8. After his talk, thirteen National League members, led by Sybil, met with Palme at the Mayflower Hotel. The ladies presented the prime minister with a list of POWs and MIAs in Southeast Asia. Palme accepted the list. Sybil knew she had to take advantage of this opportunity, so she arranged a press conference, using the occasion "as a vehicle to press the Swedes for help in the press."[21] On the surface, things finally seemed to be moving in the right direction. Heartened

by Dole's suggestion and Palme's willingness to meet with League representatives, Phyllis wrote excitedly to the senator:

"Thank you so very much for sending me a copy of the wire you
sent Prime Minister Olof Palme of Sweden during his recent visit to
the United States. I was very pleased at your suggestion that American Prisoners of War be interned in Sweden. It is a very novel solution, and one which I think should be pursued. I have my passport all
ready and could easily make a trip to Sweden!"[22]

The seed had been planted, but a Sweden trip for Phyllis was still
far from certain. She had more work to do to make this idea a reality.
They needed currency, something to bargain with. Coming to Sweden empty-handed was not going to produce an audience with the
North Vietnamese. Senator Dole was trying his best to help them, but
the POW/MIA situation was just one of many items on the Nixon administration's Vietnam priority list. Phyllis, accordingly, switched into
high gear, with her good friends Connie and Judi as her wingwomen.
This was one opportunity that she was not going to let slip through
her fingers.

On June 17, 1970, Phyllis arrived home from her job at Reynolds Metals Company. It had been a long and depressing day. She was pain-
fully aware that today was the fourth anniversary of Paul's capture by
the North Vietnamese. If her life had gone as planned, she probably
would have been home like Judi and Connie, caring for a baby or even
a young toddler, waiting for her husband to get home from his own
job. Instead her life revolved around her job, her POW activism, and
her friends. She was becoming more and more self-assured and independent. A few weeks before, she had done something she never
imagined she could do: she gave an impassioned speech about her husband and his perilous situation. She had been a featured speaker at a
POW rally in Richmond, along with Jeff Grubb, the son of Evie Grubb,
from Petersburg, and her MIA husband, Newk.

A recently released POW, Major Norris Overly, had spoken at
that same rally. Overly had helped nurse POW John McCain back

to health and had witnessed firsthand the brutal torture going on at the Hanoi Hilton, where he and Paul Galanti were both incarcerated. By Overly's own admission, the Richmond POW rally was a "fizzle."[23]

Summer had arrived in Richmond, in all its sticky, humid glory. Children were out of school, playing outside, enjoying the sunny weather, splashing happily at the pool with their parents and families. But this was not what Phyllis saw. What she saw instead was the years slipping by, and fleeting images of phantom children she and Paul might have had by then. They might never arrive, she mused, if the war didn't end soon. Although she rarely pitied herself or thought *Why me?* she was becoming increasingly frustrated. Not depressed, but angry.

The long day did bring one bright spot she had not expected.

There was a letter from Paul waiting for her when she went out to get her mail. Her heart pounded as she opened it to find that he was alive and well, despite being imprisoned in the Hanoi Hilton. It "couldn't have come at a better time," but the bearer of the letter was not a member of her own government. It did not arrive through official channels. It was brought instead from members of COLIAFAM who recently visited North Vietnam.[24] Like Jane, Sybil, Louise, and so many others, Phyllis would work all sides of the political realm to obtain communication with her imprisoned husband.

She continued to work for Reynolds in Richmond. They had been flexible with her work schedule, giving her large chunks of time off to pursue her POW/MIA activism. Her close friends Judi and Connie and their families had become like her own family. They were all part of the security net she had woven to keep her sanity intact. Phyllis was an introvert, quiet and self-effacing. But Paul's situation had forced her to be out and about, to be social.

She was the very definition of a military wife: calm, reserved, and diplomatic. Having grown up in a military family herself, she knew the rules of the game in a way that some military wives did not. She innately avoided conflict, and the frustration she was experiencing almost drove her mad. She could no longer tolerate the situation as it was. She knew she was going to have to do something bold and unexpected to make herself heard on behalf of those, like Paul, whose voices been silenced. The personality of shy, retiring Phyllis was transforming itself from introvert to extrovert in order to battle the enemy.

In September, a local businessman gave the Virginia Beach POW/MIA wives an empty prefab building near the Virginia Beach–Norfolk Expressway at 500 First Colonial Road to use for their POW/MIA volunteer efforts. Dot McDaniel remembered that, on September 17, "we opened our headquarters with a big red and white banner reading 'Don't Let Them Be Forgotten!' Now we would have a place for our volunteers to work. We could combine our assorted POW/MIA files and mailing lists, and use our headquarters as a backdrop when we kicked off our big campaign to send the delegation to Paris."[25]

That same week, a peace group and the Black Panthers had both brought letters back from Hanoi.[26] In October, Jane would meet with pacifist Quakers at the American Friends Service Committee headquarters. The group would give the women advice on the North Vietnamese embassies in Paris and Sweden—possible diplomatic channels with the POWs.[27] While Jane and many of her League friends would continue to work both sides of the political aisle to communicate with their POW husbands and to help account for the missing men, the Navy was realizing more and more how insidious COLIAFAM really was. On April 6, Jane and other POW wives received a letter from the vice admiral of the Navy cautioning the families about working with COLIAFAM. "I reiterate my previously expressed attitude on organizations such as the Committee of Liaison. The action of the North Vietnamese in dealing through such groups, rather than at any official government level, is a propaganda ploy designed to promote the credibility of those who oppose the United States position in Vietnam. Such actions perpetrated at your expense on such an obviously humanitarian issue speaks poorly of those involved." However, the admiral stopped short of disallowing mail from dissident sources: "We will take no action which might impede the flow of mail from your loved ones." Since the government had nothing to offer regarding communications with the POWs, how could it forbid it coming from outside groups?[28]

The offices at 500 First Colonial became an oasis for these wives, a place to meet, plan, and work for their burgeoning cause. Jane and her other POW/MIA wife friends, like Janie and Dot, found comfort and purpose in their escalating involvement with the movement. Instead of working out of their bedrooms and on their kitchen tables, the ladies had a "real" office to use. Jane and Jerry's son Jerry III remembered that this period was when his mother finally "got her gumption back."[29] That fall Jane was so busy she didn't have time to brood. Her diary entries consequently became much more like business memos—shorter and more of a daily journal than the ruminations of prior years. Her language was more direct and confident. Questions were now directed toward the government and the military. She didn't second-guess her instincts now. In early October, she attended the first National League convention in Washington and was elected vice chair of the League board.[30] After the convention, she worked hard with Dot, Janie, and the other Virginia Beach POW/MIA families to raise money to send a League-sponsored delegation to the Paris peace talks. And all the while, she continued to work with Bob Boroughs, writing her letters to Jerry.[31]

In October, the League launched "Operation We Care" at its headquarters, with the local press covering the event. The campaign volunteers wrote petitions on behalf of the POWs to the North Vietnamese and circulated them everywhere in the local community: at grocery stores and shopping centers, in parking lots, and on street corners. You couldn't escape these Virginia Beach POW/MIA wives even if you tried.[32]

That same fall of 1970, Sybil decided to move to Washington, D.C., to be closer to the action. She had only one free move with the Navy, but as League board chair, Sybil convinced herself that she could help Jim and the POWs more if she lived in the nation's capital. She could become more of an "insider" this way, she reasoned. Stan also needed vision therapy, and she thought Washington might have better doctors. The older boys, Jim and Sid, were off at college and boarding school. Sybil hired a young woman they knew from Coronado named Kitty Collins to come along and be the younger boys' live-in nanny.[33]

Sybil's good friend from Coronado and fellow POW wife Patsy Crayton also decided to move to D.C. to help in the League office. Patsy was young and had no children at home to care for. Sybil offered to move Patsy's furniture with hers to Washington. To Patsy, this sounded like a great idea and an adventure. She could help her husband and enjoy some time in D.C. while supporting Sybil. A win-win, she thought as she packed her bags.[34]

As Sybil and the younger boys waved a tearful goodbye to 547 A Avenue and its rose-covered walls, she wondered, was she really making the right move, for the right reasons? The move to an unfamiliar place, with young children and little support, soon became draining to Sybil, physically and emotionally. The debates between League members about organizational policy, though necessary, set her nerves on edge.[35]

By October, the League had moved to a larger office on K Street in downtown D.C. Public and governmental support for the group was more forthcoming: a red "Bat Phone" was installed with a direct line to Henry Kissinger, Nixon's national security adviser. Patsy, who was working in the League office, said, only half-jokingly, "The White House probably bugged everything!"[36] The ladies also gained a regular audience with Kissinger, meeting with him every two months about the POW/MIA situation.[37] Like the Virginia Beach wives, the D.C. wives found comfort in being with others in their situation. They also consolidated mailing lists, made copies, fielded outside calls from POW/MIA family members and the press, and organized League board meetings, which took place very six weeks. And drank lots and lots of coffee.

Patsy found herself in charge of planning the League trip to Europe that Jane Denton and others were fundraising for. League members, 174 of them, would fly to Paris together and then fan out into thirteen different European countries to raise awareness and try to gain audiences with the North Vietnamese representatives at their embassies and consulates. At the end of the trip, the group would meet up in Geneva again. The trip would not take place until the next summer, but it required most of Patsy's time and attention during the fall of 1970.[38]

Unlike Patsy and the younger, more unencumbered wives, Sybil felt trapped and depressed in D.C. She would often go home after dropping the boys at school and crawl back into bed, debilitated with anxiety. *Thank God for Kitty,* she often thought. She wasn't sure how she would be able to function alone. "Moving had wiped out my last drops of energy and willpower. I'd get up and force myself to see you boys off to school," she wrote in her diary, addressing her sons, "forcing an optimism and cheerfulness I was far from feeling. As soon as you were out the door, I'd go back up to bed, covering my head with a pillow, trying to shut the world out of my life." When Stan and Taylor came home in the afternoon, Sybil would pull it together and force herself to become the smiling, happy mother they all wanted her to be.[39]

Sybil soon realized that the government wanted her help—but only if she was a safe three thousand miles away from the nation's capital. Her presence in D.C. was apparently too close for comfort for government staffers who worried that she might become too emotional if they dealt with her in close quarters. In addition, the cost of living in Washington was crushing. She agonized over how she would be able to manage it all alone.[40] Sybil soon withdrew from her day-to-day League duties. Despite being worn out and sick at heart, she continued to serve as the League's board chair. Still, one can't help hearing the Rolling Stones' 1966 lyric "Here comes your nineteenth nervous breakdown" when imagining Sybil spiraling into depression—a delayed reaction, perhaps, to circumstances that would have knocked out those with less fortitude years before.

Karen Butler heard through the wives' grapevine about Sybil's depression and flew to D.C. in October, along with another friend of Sybil's,

Margie Kopfman. Karen remembered that when she arrived, Sybil was in bed, medicated with one or possibly two drugs. Karen, a trained nurse, recognized one of them as Mellaril, commonly prescribed at the time for psychosis.[41]

Sybil confessed to her friends that she was terrified and anxious—so much so that she had not paid her bills that month. Karen and Margie immediately took over, with Margie writing checks and having Sybil sign them. With her friend's affairs now in order, Karen insisted that Sybil get psychiatric help immediately, and she did. Sybil recalled, "I decided I didn't care whether it was weak or not. I couldn't go on feeling the way I did."[42]

A month later, Jane noticed that Sybil was on edge at the League's November board meeting. After the group adjourned, the board members all went out to dinner. Jane recalled, "Sybil—desperately angry, militant, and in the mood for revenge—wants at gov't just to 'even the score' . . . said she was tired of being constructive."[43] Who could blame her? After the massive amounts of work Sybil and the women had done, she still felt like an outsider in Washington. And she was fighting another, internal battle to keep calm and carry on in an alien environment.

Sybil knew that the League had made huge strides, and she was proud of what they had been able to accomplish despite so much opposition. But years of battles, big and small, with the government and the military had pushed her to the brink. After reading an article in *Time* magazine that the Vietnam War could last for five more years, she had decided that was her limit. "Mentally, I thought well, okay, I can hold out for 5 years if I have to. It is very interesting because as soon as that five-year mark past [*sic*] I went right down into a deep clinical depression."[44] Thankfully, Sybil found the right psychiatrist. Dr. Robert Moran helped her see that she was not weak for seeking mental health care—she was smart. He pointed out to her that most anyone would have been depressed and anxious in her situation. He called her "Stockdale" and made her laugh and listened to her problems. He even, inappropriately, flirted with her a bit. Just seeing him regularly, talking things out, and getting her mind off her problems boosted her morale.[45]

The Son Tay raid, on November 21, buoyed her spirits even more. Secretary of Defense Laird had ordered American Green Berets to raid the Son Tay prison camp, in North Vietnam, in hopes of liberating its prisoners. Their intel proved dated: the prisoners had already been moved to another camp. But the effort showed the enemy that the United States was serious about rescuing its soldiers held in violation of the Geneva Conventions. "Although the Son Tay raiders did not free any prisoners, the U.S. government had publicly demonstrated to Hanoi and to an increasingly skeptical public that America had not forgotten her captured servicemen." When the American POWs finally heard of the rescue attempt, failed though it was, their morale, like Sybil's, soared.[46]

In December, Sybil was invited by Admiral Moorer, chairman of the Joint Chiefs of Staff, to his home for a fancy Christmas party. In anticipation of the event, she had bought a red velvet evening gown that she could not wait to wear. (All her life, Sybil loved dressing up.) Another obstacle loomed unexpectedly, however.

Sybil's OB-GYN, Dr. William Cooper, had noticed some cellular changes that could indicate cervical cancer. He sent her to the hospital, without delay, for more testing. "Instead of wearing the red velvet dress on December 17, I was wearing a hospital gown at Sibley Memorial Hospital and having further tests made." The powerful board chair of the National League had been so terrified all fall, she decided she had used up her anxiety. She also credited Dr. Cooper and Dr. Moran for keeping her calm during the testing phase.[47] While she did not have cancer, her doctors recommended she have a hysterectomy, "to be on the safe side of the cancer threat."[48]

While Sybil was wrapped in her hospital gown, a group of delegates from Colorado Springs was in Paris, demanding action on the POW/MIA issue. They had also wrapped up boxes of "presents" for the North Vietnamese: 125,000 letters to dump at their embassy door and other embassy doors all across the City of Light. The missives were all written by Colorado Springs and Pike's Peak area residents and addressed to the North Vietnamese representatives in Paris. This letter campaign, like the one Phyllis had directed in the Richmond area, fell under the National "Write Hanoi" umbrella.

On December 16, the Colorado Springs for Prisoners of War group that was affiliated with the National League protested in front of the North Vietnamese embassy, in the Eighteenth Arrondissement, with the express intent of getting arrested. The four Springs picketers knew that, following the 1968 Paris student riots, any gathering of more than three on the streets of Paris was illegal. All the better, as they planned to embarrass the Communists in front of the world. On international television! A bespectacled, smiling Larry Ochs, vice mayor of Colorado Springs, carried a placard reading, MAI VAN BO WHY WON'T YOU SEE US? (Mai Van Bo was the North Vietnamese chief negotiator in Paris.)[49]

As John Herzog, the PR man for the group, recalled, the French gendarmes essentially winked at them. They let the American protesters do their thing and eventually asked them to disperse, but they did not arrest them. The Colorado Springs delegation got the international publicity they sought without spending a single minute in a French jail cell.[50]

By January of 1971, Sybil's psychotherapy was beginning to pay off. Despite concerns about her physical health, her confidence and strength seemed to be returning. She and other representatives from the National League scheduled a meeting with Henry Kissinger. He had to cancel at the last minute. In his place he sent a young general, Alexander Haig, to meet with them.

When Sybil and other League members, including Jane Denton, Kathleen Johnson, and Andrea Rander, received word of the canceled meeting, Sybil recalled, "we were stunned with disappointment, which rapidly turned to anger. We were tired of seeing assistants to assistants. Weren't our men important enough?" The wives almost canceled the meeting with Haig, but they decided to go and blow him up. When they arrived, Haig was ill-prepared for the ladies' urgent questions about their husbands. The general announced that it would be another two months before the women could see Kissinger again. Sybil's eyes narrowed and she hissed:

"We don't want to wait two months to see Dr. Kissinger, General Haig. We want to see him in two days. We'll still be here on Monday and if he cares about our men, he'll somehow make the time to see us. We're tired of being put off. Do you understand what we are saying? Are we communicating with you?" A nervous, sweaty Haig replied, "I can assure you, you are communicating with me very well—so well, in fact, that I have worked a hole in the pocket of my pants and my change has fallen out all over the floor!" With that, the tension broke. Having made their point and been assured of a Monday meeting with Kissinger, the ladies politely put their coats back on and left.

Kissinger promptly met with the POW/MIA wives the following Monday. With a smile, he asked what the ladies had done to rattle Haig so badly. He assured the women that Haig was so shaken by the meeting that he had left the building that day to escape a second encounter. He then promised to be as honest and open as he could possibly be with them without compromising national security. But he painted a dark picture of the future.[51]

Kissinger was still making little progress toward peace with the Vietnamese, who continued their stonewalling tactics. He feared that the war might drag on indefinitely. Nixon's top negotiator later recalled that the North Vietnamese "were cold-blooded bastards. They were manipulating us." The lengthy negotiations were, in Kissinger's view, deliberate and strategic; he would later state that the North Vietnamese had "tried to break our spirit, they tried to keep it [the war] going until we would make concessions." He communicated the essence of this situation, though not any details, to the women that day.[52]

Down and discouraged, the entire group departed. The League members might be able to gain important meetings with top American government officials now and scare the hell out of Alexander Haig, but the North Vietnamese were still in control of their husbands' fates.[53]

Fifteen

WRITE HANOI
AND SILENT NIGHTS

ON JANUARY 31, 1971, the world watched as America's space cowboys made yet another triumphant lunar landing. Astronaut Alan Shepard led the third successful landing on the moon with the Apollo 14 mission.[1] It seemed as though almost anything was possible for the Americans—except ending the war in Vietnam. That same month, Phyllis had redoubled her efforts to raise POW/MIA awareness. Under the auspices of the National League's "Write Hanoi" letter campaign, Phyllis and her volunteers kicked off a Richmond-based "Bring Paul Home" letter-writing campaign in January. This effort urged those from all over the state to write the North Vietnamese government in support of the tenets of the Geneva Conventions regarding prisoners of war.

Bring Paul Home letters from concerned Richmonders demanded proper food, shelter, and medical care for the POWs, mail privileges, and the free flow of information regarding both POW and MIAs. Form letters were made available all over the state through Richmond's TV station WWBT and its Bring Paul Home letter-writing office. Judi, Connie, and Phyllis all worked there night and day with their dedicated volunteer office manager Gwen Mansini to manage the letter collection.[2]

Judi recalled that the Write Hanoi "office" was really a large trailer on the property of WWBT-TV, under the station's tall antennas. WWBT had generously donated the space for the local POW/MIA effort. "We had three phones, large tables for desks, posters on the wall of Paul in jail, and American flags everywhere." The women were surrounded by boxes of "Write Hanoi" materials, dozens of volunteers, and phones that never stopped ringing.[3] On January 22, 1971, the campaign got a publicity boost when Ross Perot arrived in Richmond for a Write Hanoi luncheon at the Hotel John Marshall. Phyllis and the Texas maverick millionaire appeared together later that day on local TV.[4]

On February 12, shy Phyllis faced yet another test of her mettle. This time, she addressed the Virginia Senate in a televised press conference. This appearance would kick off a larger, area-wide effort for the Bring Paul Home campaign. The former housewife who just wanted to stay home instead spoke out forcefully on the POW/MIA issue, making a not so subtle jab at her own government during her speech: "Paul is a very patient, very easygoing person. But I know he must be wondering why the greatest country in the world can't get him out of that rathole he's been in for four and one half years." While she was not advocating for early prisoner release, Phyllis was demanding that the world *listen,* that it rebuke the North Vietnamese for their inhumane treatment and force the Communists to improve the prisoners' living conditions immediately.[5]

Richmonders and Virginians statewide responded in force to the appeal in ways they had not before. Schoolchildren, military veterans, firefighters, teachers, policemen, college students—everyone seemed to unite on this issue. *Don't stand by and let this happen,* Phyllis and her friends pleaded. The women knew how concerned the North Vietnamese were about their public image. If they continued to chip away at this, one day, they reasoned, their defenses might finally be breached.[6]

Former POW Norris Overly was back in Richmond to speak with Phyllis on February 12 in front of the Virginia Senate. He saw a seismic shift in Richmonders' attitudes since the June POW rally at the state capitol. "The difference that I noted is that there is more support by people who are not directly involved in the POW issue." People like

Judi, Connie, and their families who saw a need and responded to it. Overly pointed out that, unlike Virginia Beach, with its "colony of wives," Richmond had only six men among the possible prisoners.[7] Jane Denton, Janie Tschudy, Louise Mulligan, and others in Virginia Beach had a tight-knit group of women all in the same situation, with a military base at its core. But Phyllis had no family to support her, and few other military wives in her situation in her adopted city.

Instead, Phyllis got by with a little help from her friends.

The result was a truckload of 750,000 letters: 450,000 from Richmond and 300,000 from Northern Virginia.[8] Now Phyllis, a former "shrinking violet," and her allies had the currency they needed to bargain their way into the North Vietnamese embassy in Stockholm. They didn't fight their way in like traditional soldiers—they *wrote* their way in. In the case of the POW/MIA wives, the pen would prove mightier than the sword.

Phyllis made her long-awaited trip to Stockholm on March 8, 1971, armed with an eighteen-wheeler truck—covered in WRITE HANOI bumper stickers—that contained 750,000 letters demanding the ultimate release of the POWs as a group and adherence to the tenets of the Geneva Convention in the meantime. Accompanying her was a diverse group of nine others, including Judi and Connie, who had left their children at home with their husbands.

As Judi later related, the team of supporters the women put together was carefully planned. "The choice of these people was imperative." Phyllis's colleague Cliff Ellison, personnel director at Reynolds Metals Company, was selected in large part because of his Swedish background: his parents were both Swedes, and he spoke the language fluently. His linguistic skills would be crucial in Stockholm. Gwen Mansini, the women's dedicated office manager, was a skilled organizer who helped keep things running smoothly. Prominent Richmond businessman Joe Antonelli and local banker H. L. "Ted" Baynes signed on to show the support of the city's business community for the POW issue. High school student Don Smith, head of the Young Republicans at his high school, rounded out the entourage. "We tried to get a cross section of the population involved," noted Judi.[9]

But Phyllis's most important allies came from the Richmond media.

WWBT-TV Channel 12 newscaster Ed McLaughlin and manager Jim Babb were Phyllis's secret weapons. The media coverage they would generate and the injustices they would document were exactly what the POW/MIAs needed.[10]

The Richmond Write Hanoi delegation arrived on a cold, gray Tuesday afternoon. The Swedish press immediately mobbed the group: journalists from four newspapers and a television station and AP and UPI reporters all sought interviews. The next morning, March 10, the story was all over the news, and it was time to act. The group had set up their own appointments, and they met first with American ambassador Jerome Holland and his embassy staff.

While sympathetic and helpful to Phyllis and her entourage, Holland and his people had faced a steep uphill battle as they attempted to combat the Communist propaganda coming out of Hanoi. Most of the media in Sweden came from left-leaning sources that tended to paint the American soldiers in Vietnam as ruthless and combative warriors.[11] The Write Hanoi delegates next had a fruitless meeting with the head of the International Red Cross. Judi remembered indignantly, "He was awful, definitely a Communist. He said, 'We will not help you, period.' He never even asked us to sit down!"[12]

Phyllis would later tell Frank Sieverts, deputy assistant secretary of state for POW/MIA matters—and member of the original "Washington Road Show" team at Miramar—that both the Red Cross and the Swedish government were "non-committal" and that neither were willing to intervene much in POW affairs.[13]

The most important development of the day came from a spontaneous, unannounced visit to the North Vietnamese embassy. Phyllis, Ted, and Joe went there on foot and asked a Swedish woman working at the embassy for an appointment. This time, cordiality was tossed out the window. Phyllis sweetly explained to her, "If we are not granted an audience, then we would come back with all of the press and our

750,000 letters that we had with us." Her gambit had the desired effect: Phyllis was told to call back that afternoon for an appointment.[14]

Phyllis kept calling the North Vietnamese embassy, but the staff refused to return her calls. She continued to slowly and calmly repeat what she would do if they refused to speak to her. The North Vietnamese representatives finally agreed to see her, accompanied by two men from her party. No other women from her party would be allowed into the embassy. "Women had absolutely no value" in that culture at that time, noted Judi.[15] Phyllis prepared to meet with them the next day and spent a restless night in her hotel, worrying.

The next morning, Judi and Connie fussed over Phyllis and her outfit, advising her on what to wear. They all knew the power of image. This ensemble needed to be simple and unadorned, but it had to have some punch to it. That way, Phyllis could make a statement about her position, her loyalty, and her mission without having to say a word. The embassy had told her to leave her "Nixon propaganda" at home, as well as the letters—and the media.[16]

With her two best friends' approval, Phyllis chose a simple navy-blue dress with tall boots and navy stockings. She wore no jewelry except for her wedding ring. But her Hermès silk scarf, a gift from Judi's mother, sent a clear message: it was red, white, and blue.[17] Judi and Connie nodded with satisfaction as Phyllis departed for her appointment: her friends knew her well enough to know that she would somehow get the job done. She had gotten further than they ever expected she would by boldly demanding an audience with the North Vietnamese, using her literal ton of letters as a bargaining chip.

Phyllis arrived at the embassy with Ted and Joe in tow at 10:30 a.m. sharp. The embassy was a villa in the suburbs of Stockholm. Ted and Joe later recalled that the structure resembled the infamous Bates Motel, from the Hitchcock thriller *Psycho*. It was not exactly a welcoming place. The Americans were served various refreshments, which Joe and Ted later compared to "Styrofoam potato chips."[18]

The Americans were told where to sit, and to speak in English. Monsieur G. Viet, the North Vietnamese chargé d'affaires, and his assistant interspersed their English with French, which was the diplomatic language and the language they would use to communicate that day between themselves in front of their visitors. Their assumption that the Americans spoke only English would prove to be a serious strategic mistake.

Phyllis took the lead, surprising the North Vietnamese, who did not expect a woman to lead the discussion. "I want to know how my husband, Paul, is—what is his physical condition?" The men took down her mailing address, and Phyllis was shown his name on a list of POWs sent from Hanoi. They refused all information and letters she had brought with her, but one of the men did read a letter from a seven-year-old American child asking for the POWs' safe return. Phyllis then asked the men, "Would it would be possible to bring the American POWs to Sweden for internment?" referring to Prime Minister Palme's offer to accept the American prisoners. The men stubbornly continued to insist that they had no knowledge of this offer.

When Monsieur G. Viet and his cohort spoke about her in French, assuming she did not speak the language, college French major Phyllis stopped them, letting them know she understood exactly what they were saying about her. When they claimed they had no way to communicate with Hanoi, she called their bluff, noting the obvious antennas and communications equipment attached to the top of their building. At every turn, Phyllis showed herself much cleverer than the diplomats charged with keeping her at bay.

After an hour and twenty minutes, the conversation began to disintegrate. The North Vietnamese soon asked Phyllis, Ted, and Joe to leave. Viet and his staffer did not stand up; this was a subtle dismissal and a knowing disregard for diplomatic politesse. They hoped to put this sassy American woman in a place of submission this way. But Phyllis knew how to handle them.

She got up and left without being officially dismissed, leaving her letters for Paul on the table. She later would tell Judi and Connie about the scene at the embassy. They were totally astonished that shy Phyllis had made such a bold move. "She was controlling them and the situation. I don't know how she knew to do that, but she did!" noted Judi proudly.[19]

The story of Phyllis and her entourage and her success in gaining entry to the North Vietnamese embassy helped generate fresh interest in the POW/MIA story—an ongoing goal for the National League and all the families of POWs and MIAs. Too often, the ladies knew, the POW/MIA story took a backseat to issues of far less importance. The country kept forgetting about its captured and missing men and needed to be constantly reminded of them. Phyllis and the other POW and MIA wives refused to let them fall off the radar.

During that same trip, under-the-radar efforts were also made to meet secretly with Prime Minister Palme. Judi remembered, "It seemed there was no hope of getting to Palme. Then 'a man' from the U.S. State Department contacted her under 'utmost secrecy' with phone numbers to use." After a flurry of calls from Phyllis, Judi, and Connie, an appointment was set. But only the three women were to attend. None of the men from their entourage were invited. Judi noted, "We were to tell absolutely no one including those traveling with us and especially no other POW wives. The officials didn't want a steady flow of POW wives there."

Judi vividly recollected the Stockholm secret meeting: "We went out several days later saying we were going shopping. A man met us and took us to a small hotel nearby. He walked with Phyllis and talked to her the whole time in excellent English though he was Swedish. At the Hotel café, we were told that 'because of high security risks' we would not see Palme. But this man would take our material and photos. He gave us gold brooches with the seal of Sweden on them from Palme, he said. He stressed again secrecy. . . . We felt he was very sincere."

But nothing happened. Phyllis and her friends were very disappointed with this outcome. Had they come this far only to leave empty-handed? "Phyllis asked again why we had to keep the meeting a secret since we hadn't met with him. The man said he was doing a favor for 'an important American friend.' So we agreed." The mysterious man looked through all of Phyllis's materials and asked her questions for ninety minutes. After the episode, the man disappeared. "Phyllis was very firm that we never speak of it."[20]

Unbeknownst to the women, Deputy Assistant Secretary of Defense Dick Capen had also tried, through secret channels, to work with the Swedish government on interning the American POWs. Like Senator Dole, Sybil, and Phyllis, he saw the Swedish solution as a real possibility.

Before Capen came on board at the Defense Department, he had worked in the newspaper business, and he had developed a friendly relationship with a newsprint supplier based in Sweden. This colleague's family owned a shipping line that included two ships named the *Gripsholm* and the *Drottningholm*. These two ships had a unique history: both had been employed during World War II to transport prisoners of war to neutral countries.

Capen remembered: "I led a secret, small mission to Sweden to meet with my friend the chairman of this line who readily agreed to donate two ships for a proposed move of POWs from Hanoi and South Vietnam to Sweden or another neutral site. The Geneva Conventions encourage such internment in neutral countries. My contact went to Olof Palme, a strong ally of NVN. He in turn met with the NVN and made this proposal. It all was set up in such a way that Palme would get full credit for his humanitarian gesture. My plan was to raise the funds secretly to underwrite the costs. I felt quite confident that this could be done."

But in the end, Palme showed his true allegiance: "Palme thought this would be seen as a gesture of support for the USA so he backed off." Capen had known all along that the secret plan was a long shot, but, like Phyllis and Sybil, he was willing to pursue all leads, try anything he could to help rescue the men.[21]

Once again, the Americans had hit the North Vietnamese wall— impossible to scale and unyielding.

After her return from Sweden, shy Phyllis was well on her way to becoming Fearless Phyllis, as she would later be known. She was becoming increasingly outspoken and more critical of the Nixon government. In a letter to her friend Ross Perot on April 6, 1971, she vented her frustration and her willingness to go further in League efforts to obtain the release of the POWs and an accounting of the MIAs. Phyllis noted that while she was in Sweden, the Swedes kept asking her, "Why doesn't your government do something?" She found she could not convincingly answer that question.

Phyllis also noted the shift she was seeing among her League friends and within herself. The women had avoided becoming political, consistently choosing the humanitarian path instead. While this approach had been highly effective in the past, it still was not enough. "It is now becoming very apparent that everyone else is using our men politically, both the North Vietnamese and the United States government. I don't think it will be very long before the families begin taking a political stand, because we are not getting the results we want . . . Why should I have to travel halfway around the world to try to get help for our men who were sent to war by their own government?"

Phyllis ended her letter to Perot with a declaration of intent. Something was changing, she sensed, among her friends in the League and within herself. It was not just their policies that were transforming, but the way the women saw themselves and their roles. Phyllis would never be a feminist. But she was becoming a human rights activist and one who would never quit until the POW rescue was complete. And she was finding that the National League was evolving along with her: things needed to be clearer, stronger, louder.

"We do not want to become a group of loud, boisterous, pushy women . . . But the lives of our husbands are at stake. If we have to take a more political stand to achieve this end, many of us are willing to do it."[22] The personal was about to finally become political.

By May, the U.S. government was finally beginning to realize the level of frustration the National League and its officers, like Phyllis, were experiencing. As Sybil had told the men in Washington years earlier, the wives of POWs needed to be treated like their own wives—you couldn't just say you loved them on your wedding day and then forget about them.

On May 27, Sweden announced its support for the Viet Cong, sending the group $550,000 in medical aid.[23] This must have been a crushing blow for Phyllis, after all of her efforts—and the publicity coup—in Sweden. As in World War II, the Swedish government refused to commit to one side or the other during wartime. In June, an editorial in *Newsday* punctured the hopes of POW wives everywhere. It bluntly stated, "Sweden, the only Western nation recognizing North Vietnam, plainly doesn't want to offend the Hanoi government in any way. It doesn't need Sweden, but Swedish Prime Minister Olof Palme's Social Democratic Party needs Hanoi to keep its left wing happy."[24] By refusing to take sides, Sweden *had* taken sides—with the Communists in Hanoi. They refused the role they could have taken as a Good Samaritan host country. It became disappointingly clear to the U.S. government and the POW/MIA wives that Sweden had chosen not to stay neutral.

Air Force general James Donald "Don" Hughes, one of Nixon's military assistants, wrote to Senator Dole on May 19, 1971, telling him he had contacted Phyllis. The U.S. government had identified her as a key influencer regarding POW/MIA issues. The men knew they had to be careful, as she had a direct line of communication with military families. If women like Phyllis, Sybil, Jane, and Helene weren't "handled" properly, the U.S. government might just have a full-on rebellion on their hands. Regarding Phyllis, the condescending Hughes wrote that "she, like so many others feels the ever-increasing pressures of frustration and anxiety and need to be reassured periodically." He was relieved that she was already pro-Nixon, and he felt that "she will influence the other girls in her area as best she can."[25]

Dole agreed with Hughes in his response: "Certainly understand the feelings these girls have occasionally of the need to be reassured, and appreciate your giving her a call."[26] However, it wasn't just "the girls" who needed reassurance at this point. Other family members were also showing their displeasure with the American government and the seemingly endless war. Senator Dole received hundreds of letters from POW/MIA family members attesting to this.

One particularly poignant letter Dole received came from Paul Galanti's father, Philip Galanti. The June 15, 1971, letter begged the Kansas senator to work within the government to set a withdrawal date from Vietnam for all U.S. troops, provided the prisoners were released within thirty days. He deemed the war and Nixon's "Vietnamization" policy "tiresome, worn-out, meaningless, and trite."

Time was running out. Like his daughter-in-law, Philip was not willing to wait and be patient anymore. He knew what the outcome would be for Paul and his fellow POWs if the war continued for much longer. All the blood, treasure, and time spent by the United States would end up being for naught. "If some dramatic positive action is not taken soon," Philip wrote, "the prisoner problem will go away since they will probably all be dead."[27]

The League trip to Europe that Patsy Crayton had labored over in the League office for months, and which Jane, Dot, and many other POW/MIA wives had fundraised so tirelessly to support, would also take place in May. Sybil would not be on that trip. She decided she still needed some distance from the organization. "I just wanted to be occupied elsewhere," she later recalled.[28]

In contrast, Helene was beginning to ramp up her own activity with the League in Colorado Springs. She and her friend and fellow Air Force MIA wife Mary Dodge were among the 174 participants in the League's trip abroad. Along with other area POW and MIA wives and some family members, they left on May 19 from Peterson Field, in Colorado Springs. Their first objective: to meet and influence delegates to the Geneva Conventions meeting on May 24, which was being held under the auspices of the International Red Cross. The title of the conference was "Government Experts on the Reaffirmation and Development of International Humanitarian Law Applicable in Armed Conflicts." The meeting was limited to legal experts from thirty countries, all of whom had signed and agreed to the tenets of the Geneva Conventions.[29]

The goal of the League delegates was to contact and try to influence the legal experts present to help and support the POW/MIA cause. They soon found that the side conversations and the relationships developed outside the closed conference walls made a difference. Joan Vinson, the League's national coordinator at that time, stated, "We hope to express our concern for all prisoners of war, and all those affected by the conflict in Vietnam. We hope that the countries represented at the meeting will resolve to demand impartial inspection of all POW camps, a complete account of prisoners and the missing, immediate release of the sick and wounded, and that mail flow be in accordance with provisions of the Geneva Conventions."[30]

Helene and Mary were assigned to cover Switzerland, Sweden, and London at the Paris peace talks. They were particularly horrified by the Swedish delegation: the Swedes gave them a bulletin with a photo of happy, smiling, well-fed American "POWs." Clearly this was a propaganda piece sent by Hanoi, the channel through which Sweden got most of its news of the war.[31] Like Phyllis had found before, Sweden was not really a neutral country. It was the job of Helene, Mary, and the other National League members on this trip to call out these images as false representations of what was going on in the prison camps.

In Paris, the women encountered delegates who were both hostile to and sympathetic to their cause. One English-speaking man at the conference refused to talk to Helene about the American POWs and MIAs, instead asking, "Did you bring the wives of the Vietnamese men missing in action with you?" Despite this attitude, Helene followed him and continued trying to reason with him. "I didn't come to this conference to talk to the likes of you," the man snapped. "I have no time for you."[32]

The League group had its supporters, too. Helene and Mary were most impressed by Philip Habib, whom they met on May 28 in Paris. The chief assistant to U.S. envoy David K. E. Bruce, Habib spent hours with the group and answered every question they had directly. He assured the women that peace was coming and eventually all the POWs would be returned.[33] No one was too sure, however, about the MIAs, like Herman Knapp and Ward Dodge, husband of Mary Dodge.

But the League trip was successful in that it kept the POW/MIA issue in the world spotlight. The group visited thirty embassy offices in eleven cities that May.[34]

In June, Sybil and her boys moved back home to Coronado. As they made the cross-country trip, they became more and more excited. Sid had joined them and was pressed into service to drive, while Stan made tuna fish sandwiches in the backseat. No one wanted to stop for long. After the dreary D.C. days, the sunshine and palm trees of California could not have looked more appealing to Sybil. When they finally arrived at their destination, she "wanted to hug everyone I met on the streets of Coronado. Oh, how relieved I was to be back where I seemed to belong. Even the furniture seemed to heave a sigh of relief as it settled back into its familiar locations."[35]

On June 13, 1971, *The New York Times* published what would soon be known as the infamous Pentagon Papers, leaked by a former Marine, Defense Department staffer, and analyst for the RAND Corporation think tank, Daniel Ellsberg. This classified study was compiled on the orders of former secretary of defense Robert McNamara. The papers examined U.S. policy toward Vietnam from President Truman through the Johnson administration (1945–1967). The U.S. Justice Department under Nixon tried to stop publication of the papers, but the effort ultimately failed. Articles were published first in the *Times* and then in *The Washington Post*.

The damning conclusion? That the United States government had escalated the war all the while knowing that it was on the losing side of the equation. The report also confirmed that JFK's administration had helped to overthrow and assassinate Ngo Dinh Diem, the leader of the South Vietnamese government, which America supported. If our own government had no faith in our allies and our capabilities, then why the hell, readers of the *Times* and the *Post* wondered, were we still sending our men to be killed in Vietnam?[36]

Support for the war at home was eroding daily; the protests were increasing, with voices calling, louder and louder, for an end to the conflict. Rebellion was brewing even from within the "silent majority." Most of the POW/MIA wives had been in this camp for years. They had been trained to be strong government and military supporters, but they were now completely disgusted with Washington politics. Their suspicions about the war and those leading it were confirmed. Mc-Namara was now right up there with Cora Weiss as a target of their ire. They knew to be wary of antiwar figures, but McNamara? Wasn't he supposed to be on their side?

The Nixon administration was not implicated in the Pentagon Papers, though the president was incensed to see classified government reports leaked to the public. Instead of seeing the papers as a potential help, separating his administration's policy on Vietnam from those of JFK and LBJ, "the leak of the Pentagon Papers brought forth a profound paranoia in Richard Nixon . . . The ultimate manifestation of this drive was the White House Special Investigations Unit, informally referred to as the Plumbers, whose first assignment was to raid the office of Ellsberg's psychiatrist. Later, members of the group would carry out one final mission, the Watergate break-in, which ultimately cost Nixon the very thing he had sought to defend: his presidency."[37]

But in 1971, the Watergate scandal had not yet happened. The wives were more than curious to see what Nixon's next move would be regarding the war and their husbands' fates.

In September, Sybil, Jane, and many other POW and MIA wives and families returned to Washington for the second annual League conference, held at the Statler Hilton. Every September at the League convention, elections would be held for the new League national coordinator and board chair. For the 1971–72 year, the League had elected a new national coordinator, Evie Grubb, from Petersburg, Virginia. Carole Hanson served as the League's board chair.

Evie was tenacious and had a bulldog manner about her. Not everyone liked her, but she was a hard worker and got the job done.[38] Carole was extremely tall and looked like a fashion model, with a diplomatic manner that played well in the press. Her hope for the League? "We are probably the only organization in the country that is trying to put itself out of business" by bringing home the POWs and accounting for the missing men.[39] Only then could the League finally close its doors.

Sybil was in town to testify before Zablocki's congressional committee for a second time. This year, she noticed that her troops were restless. "There was seething unrest among the POW/MIA Families with some feeling that we should become a political rather than humanitarian organization." A political action committee was established, and Henry Kissinger was soon informed "about the possibility of a revolt against the Administration by our Organization."[40]

The Nixon administration was conducting its own high-wire act, negotiating with both the families and the North Vietnamese in Paris. They knew they couldn't afford to blow it with either group. The 1972 election was at stake. This time, the administration knew it had better send a high-level official to the League's banquet to placate the ladies—or suffer the political consequences. Even in an election year, LBJ would never have shown up.

Richard Nixon did show up. Unlike his predecessor, he *knew* he needed to be there.

Sybil recorded Nixon's words from that evening in her diary: "I have considered the problem of obtaining the release of our POWs and missing in action as being one that has Presidential priority. I can assure you that every negotiating channel—and now I say something here that I am sure all of you will understand—including many private channels that have not yet been disclosed, are being pursued."[41]

In his closing remarks, the president gave his word that he would continue working hard to end the war, get the POWs home and the MIAs accounted for, and gave credit where credit was due—to the women who surrounded him that night.

"I am just so proud of how great you have been and I am not going to let you down."[42]

The newly elected League leaders, Evie and Carole, were tireless in keeping up the League work that Sybil, Louise, Jane, and the others had begun. Carole vividly remembered, "As we held our board meetings in Washington, D.C., we all would 'walk the halls of Congress' at least once a month, spreading the word about our husbands and the length of time they had been incarcerated." The MIA wife emphasized the instructive role that the wives were still playing even in 1971: "We were, in fact, educating Congress in regards to this issue. Most did not know that there was no list provided by the North Vietnamese and very little mail received. Their lack of knowledge was frustrating, but slowly, congressmen and senators began to listen to us. At least, some of them."[43] Carole also instituted a hugely popular "Don't Let Them Be Forgotten" POW/MIA bumper sticker campaign that, like the POW/MIA bracelets, helped raise awareness for the movement and for the League.[44]

That same autumn of 1971, Helene Knapp was hard at work with her "Silent Nights" Christmas seals campaign. Three million seals, designed by Colorado Springs artist John Manson, a friend of Helene's, had been sold by early December. The POW/MIA office on East Kiowa Street was flooded with hundreds of orders waiting to be filled.

The seal featured white letters on a blue background, with the words SILENT NIGHTS and LEST WE FORGET: 1964–1971. The prisoner of war featured on the stamp was Lieutenant Commander Richard Allen Stratton. He was pictured sitting alone on a bench in solitary confinement, looking up at a "Christmas Star." Helene remembered, "To use today's vernacular, it went viral!"[45] This striking image and message ultimately generated $30,000, all of which was donated to the National League.[46]

Though the League's charter deemed it a humanitarian group, the formation of a political action committee within its ranks had changed the dynamics of the organization—and some of its members. Sybil herself noted the impact of this internal PAC with satisfaction and the savvy of an experienced political operator: "It didn't do any harm at all to have a radical fringe group as part of our organization." When some of the more outspoken wives asked Sybil what she thought of them picketing the White House, she told them it was their decision. "It didn't hurt to let the White House know our loyalty was wearing thin."[47]

Jane, too, was now willing to push the Nixon administration. In a letter to Phyllis on National League stationery, she urged League members to send a "barrage of mail to the President and to Congress during the Christmas season . . . to emphasize the importance of the prisoner of war–missing in action issue." She was becoming more and more impatient for resolution. Instead of sending letters to the North Vietnamese, the wives were now sending pleas on behalf of their husbands to their own government.

At the bottom of the holiday appeal, Jane added:

"This has <u>got</u> to be the New Year we've all been waiting for."[48]

Sixteen

IS PEACE AT HAND?

NEW YEAR'S 1972 CAME and went. Champagne glasses were emptied. Confetti and party hats lay crumpled on the floor. The ball dropped in Times Square. But still the POWs remained POWs. The MIAs stayed unaccounted for. Jane's wish that this year would be the year the men finally returned home already seemed like wishful thinking.

Although Sybil was no longer the coordinator of the League, she remained on the board and acted as a League watchdog on the POW/MIA issue. Though she was a Nixon supporter, the welfare of Jim and the other American prisoners and missing was her top priority. When Nixon neglected to mention the POW/MIA issue on a national telecast with Dan Rather in January of 1972, it was Sybil who called him out—by sending a telegram directly to Rather, pointing out the omission.

General Hughes, Nixon's chief military assistant, took Sybil to task for the Rather telegram. He was now going to get the Haig treatment from Sybil. "He didn't own me, and he better get that straight."[1] When he dared to tell Sybil, "I only have 28 days left on this job, and I'm going to see to it that nothing goes wrong," Sybil had the perfect comeback. "I said I wished I could know I only had 28 days left as a POW wife!"[2] Hughes later called and apologized, even offering Sybil a ride to D.C. on his government plane. She was still so angry with him, she declined the offer and took a commercial flight instead. No one could say the League's founder was in the pocket of the Nixon government.

After the League's January board meeting, Bonnie Singleton was given the task of gathering statements from congressional candidates regarding their stand on the POW/MIA issue. Sallie Stratton recalled that, despite POW/MIA "family dissatisfaction with the results of the current Vietnamization policy . . . the League as a unified body gave a qualified endorsement of our President's peace plan."[3] Mainstream members were on board with Nixon. But the League's "radical fringe group," as Sybil called it, was not on the same wavelength.

In early February, Jack Anderson, a popular *Washington Post* columnist, reported that President Nixon "has made overtures to Hanoi through every possible channel to find out who is being held and to negotiate for their release." As he had promised the ladies of the League at their banquet the previous fall, every lead was being followed and the prisoner release was a priority for the president. Henry Kissinger continued his negotiations, both public and private, in Paris, but progress was excruciatingly slow.

The National League was beginning to fracture, despite strong efforts by Carole Hanson and Evie Grubb to keep the group on a unified track. Dallas MIA wife and League board member Sallie Stratton recalled that League "families were just as split" as the country on the war.[4] Though many of the women felt that Nixon was doing the best he could, everyone was weary of war and the constant obstacles thrown up by the North Vietnamese negotiators in Paris. As a result, by early February of 1972, "the families at home were . . . as splintered as a broken windshield."[5]

Some of the League's best-spoken and most dedicated activists had left the League to join a more political group: POW/MIA Families for Immediate Release. Between 350 and 450 POW/MIA family members who had been part of the National League split off from the group and formed their own organization. Like the League, the group established a Washington office.[6] POW wife Valerie Kushner, for one, was ready to push harder and yell louder to get her husband, Captain

Hal Kushner, an Army flight surgeon, back. After five years of being a single parent and a tireless activist, she was done with the humanitarian approach of the League. Valerie not only joined POW/MIA Families for Immediate Release, but she also switched her political allegiance. The former League member seconded George McGovern's presidential nomination at the Democratic Convention, then hit the campaign trail to stump for her candidate.[7] Highly competent, independent, and articulate, Valerie would be missed by many of the League wives. "She was a spitfire," Kathleen Johnson recalled fondly.[8]

Louise Mulligan had left the League the previous May, when the organization refused to poll its members regarding whether or not to pressure the administration for withdrawal from Vietnam. Louise felt strongly at this point that "the leadership was no longer representative of the wishes of its members."[9] She had come close to the end of her rope. Her nerves were frayed, and her physician implored her to take a break. While she did not join POW/MIA Families for Immediate Release or stump for McGovern, she withdrew from League activities at this point. "The phone was ringing twenty hours a day. I had the phone company take the ringers off for my mental health."[10]

"After I left the League I did some interviews on my own and that's when I started using the word 'expendable.' Such as, 'If President Nixon continues to withdraw our troops from Vietnam, with no commitment for the release of our prisoners, he will be the first President who has labeled our men as expendable.' That's how frustrated I was!!!"[11] She had put her heart and soul into the fight, but, like Sybil, this prominent East Coast organizer and activist had reached the limit of what she could endure in terms of the daily grind of League activities. She desperately needed a break.

Although League members were becoming more divided on the home front, they still rallied together as Americans abroad. The latest group that planned to fly over to Paris in February of 1972 included three POW/MIA wives: Phyllis, Kathleen, and Sharon White. Conrad and

Carole Mikulic, a wealthy couple supportive of the group's efforts, and the League's lawyer, Charlie Havens, went with them. This time, the group decided, a new approach was required.[12] It was time to focus more on individual diplomacy and personal connections. Phyllis was "convinced that the time for the large and dramatic trip is past. In order to enter into substantive talks our delegations must be small and relatively quiet."[13]

The POW letter-writing campaigns like Write Hanoi had been formidable weapons and had provided the women with the leverage they needed to gain appointments at the North Vietnamese embassies in Paris and Stockholm, but, as time wore on, the letters began garnering some negative publicity for the Americans. The staff at the suburban post office in Choisy-le-Roi, site of the North Vietnamese delegation's headquarters, was overwhelmed by the enormous volume of letters that continued to be sent, pleading for the American POWs' release. U.S. news sources claimed that the North Vietnamese were now routinely rejecting the letters. (The North Vietnamese vehemently denied this.) The embassy spokesman instead accused the Americans of racism because they showed "more concern for a few hundred Americans than for hundreds of thousands of Vietnamese war victims."[14]

The League delegation arrived in Paris on February 10. On the eleventh, Phyllis, along with Charlie, Sharon, and Kathleen (now on her third trip to Paris), headed for Versailles, the site of the Paris World Assembly for the Peace and Independence of the Indochinese Peoples, on February 11–13. They hoped to be able to meet personally with representatives of the North Vietnamese government, the Viet Cong, and the Pathet Lao to plead for the men's release. To their dismay, conference organizers were informed that they could not be seated unless they identified themselves with the antiwar groups. This the League reps were not willing to do. "We said we could not speak for the League that way," reported Phyllis later. Though the League had been forced to work often with antiwar groups, the still nonpolitical group refused to ally directly with their strange bedfellows of the past.

However, Phyllis, Charlie, Kathleen, Sharon, and the Mikulecs all found out that the side conversations and personal chats they had in the lobby were well worth their time. "In the two and one-half hours of conversation that we had in the lobby we achieved more and had more varied contacts than if we had actually been seated," Phyllis wrote.[15]

One on one, some of the North Vietnamese representatives were kind and understanding. Kathleen had warm memories of an empathetic Vietnamese man who had been a teacher before the war. He was one of the delegates representing the Viet Cong. When she explained her situation as an MIA wife seeking any information she could find about her husband, Bruce, he responded that "as one human being to another, I will do everything in my power to learn about your husband." The delegate understood her pain all too well: he had not seen or heard from his own wife and children for many years.[16] Kathleen would never know whether her new friend was able to keep his promise.

The group then returned to Paris and attempted to visit the Vietnamese embassy on the Left Bank. Phyllis was told to call the next week. She did this repeatedly, to no avail. Reporters from UPI explained that the Communist representatives would probably never see Phyllis or anyone in the League entourage, for three reasons: the Tet Offensive, worries about Nixon's upcoming trip to China, and the cancellation of the Paris peace talks by American diplomats.[17]

Despite some progress with North Vietnamese individuals, the wall of the larger Communist government had risen yet again between the North Vietnamese and the American wives of the prisoners and missing. Phyllis wrote a letter in French from her home base at the InterContinental Hotel and dropped it in the mail slot of the North Vietnamese delegate general, Xuan Thuy. In this letter, Phyllis clearly tried to separate herself and the League from the Nixon administration. Her attempts to focus on the humanitarian issue—the POWs and MIAs—are clear:

"I am in Paris at the direction of my organization, the National League of Families. I represent all the families with men who are prisoners or missing in your country. No one wants peace more than the prisoners' families." Phyllis hoped the emphasis on family and peace, rather than policy, would grab the delegate general's attention.[18]

The lesson Sybil Stockdale had learned so early on after Jim's shoot-down, that there was no substitute for a personal visit, would also serve Phyllis well. On February 18, the night before she was supposed to leave to return home, she finally got the call she had been hoping for.

French Communist reporter Madeleine Riffaud returned Phyllis's calls from earlier in the week. Could she come over and see Phyllis right now? Phyllis was already in bed, but she immediately agreed, throwing her clothes on and dashing down to the hotel bar for their hastily arranged rendezvous She was not going to miss her chance to meet with Riffaud, who had met with Paul and interviewed him just a few months after his shoot-down in 1966.

Riffaud spoke no English, but Phyllis's excellent French allowed her to communicate easily with her. Phyllis didn't let Riffaud's Communist views stand in the way of obtaining information about Paul, either. She had dealt with many others like her before. Speaking with Riffaud was a breakthrough for Phyllis: the POW wife found that the French Communist reporter was much more open and less dogmatic than the American members of COLIAFAM. Bringing awareness to Paul's plight and ultimately getting him home was what mattered, and she was determined to speak to anyone who had information about him, no matter their politics.

Kathleen's photo of Phyllis and Riffaud from their evening chat in Paris shows the two young women seated with their heads close together.[19] Phyllis is blond and fair and looks like the all-American cheerleader. Riffaud looks quintessentially French, her dark hair in a long braid, sporting sleek leather pants and a skinny ribbed turtleneck. The women look like chic friends who know each other well. They could be meeting at a café to discuss the latest film by Claude Lelouch, or the futuristic fashions of André Courrèges.

Instead, the women's conversation was about life and death (and not in the abstract, à la existentialist writer Jean-Paul Sartre). Phyllis was trying yet again to establish a lifeline of communication to bring Paul home. She had learned that the only way to approach the Communists was as a humanitarian. Any association with the U.S. government was suspect. In her meeting with Riffaud, Phyllis "emphasized that our League was not sponsored by President Nixon and his administration and that we were asking the same questions of everyone who might help our men." The women on the trip were simply wives who wanted to get their husbands home safely.[20] It was the same message Phyllis had conveyed in French to Xuan Thuy earlier in the trip.

Phyllis's friend Judi Clifford recalled later that although Phyllis had a real rapport and connection with Riffaud, she could not help but be a bit jealous. After all, Riffaud had seen Paul more recently than she had. That fact rankled Phyllis.[21] Even so, she felt that meeting with Riffaud was "the most rewarding part of the trip for me. I feel we bridged a huge gap in our three and one-half-hour visit."[22]

Even prior to the trip, Phyllis had decided that being less dogmatic in her views and listening to others, even those with views that were opposite her own, was crucial. The personal contacts were what she felt were moving things toward reconciliation.[23]

March 26 through April 1 marked the National Week of Concern for Americans Who Are Prisoners of War or Missing in Action. The week was fully supported by the government, and the Department of Defense highlighted the week with a program at 10 a.m. on March 29 at the Pentagon. The Marine Corps band played, the chief chaplain for the U.S. Army gave the invocation. All the heavy hitters were present: Admiral Thomas Moorer of the U.S. Navy, the chairman of the Joint Chiefs; Melvin Laird, the secretary of defense; and Air Force brigadier general Daniel "Chappie" James, the deputy assistant secretary of defense for public affairs and the POW/MIA families' point man.

The U.S. Navy and Air Force pilots jetted overhead in the "missing man formation" flyover. The event displayed every bit of pomp and circumstance the government could muster. The current administration was wooing the women in no uncertain terms. Finally, the government was telling the women they loved them, that they understood their pain. In exchange for this show of devotion, the administration wanted their political support.[24]

Would the women accept Nixon's proposal or would they turn away? Pat Nixon had turned her future husband down many times before she accepted his marriage proposal, but his persistent pursuit finally paid off. Would this scenario repeat itself between the Nixon administration and the POW/MIA wives? The women had yet to make their final decision.

In May, the National League held a special meeting for members to discuss the organization's political position on the war (if any) and the presidential candidates for the 1972 election. Jane and Sybil were bowled over when they were invited to stay at the home of the chief of naval operations, Admiral Elmo Zumwalt, and his wife. This was a huge honor, accorded to them as the wives of two of the highest-ranking naval prisoners of war.[25]

By now, the government knew that the League was a force to be reckoned with. Back in March, Kissinger had asked the ladies to lend the administration their support.[26] MIA wife Sallie Stratton was also present at the Kissinger meeting and was heartened by his conversation with them: "I found Dr. Kissinger to be a charming, soft-spoken, very confident man. He assured us any agreement reached with the Vietnamese would be a package deal, including the men from Laos and Cambodia . . . I was duly impressed by his demeanor and trusted his promises."[27]

But some of the women were beginning to waver in their enthusiasm for the current administration. "Even Jane was torn between Nixon and McGovern at that point."[28] Jane had been particularly incensed by an April 1972 Nixon reelection campaign solicitation letter stating that the president deserved a second term because "he has brought us out of a devastating war and set us on the path to peace."[29]

What?! Jane must have thought. *Did I miss something here?*

The war was *not* over, the country was not yet on a path to peace. These misstatements (though rapidly corrected by the Nixon campaign office) reinforced an earlier decision Jane had made that surely would have shocked her ultraconservative husband. In an interview with the local newspaper, Jane stated that the letter "reinforced my earlier decision to attempt to become a member of the Virginia delegation to the Democratic National Convention in Miami,"[30] which would take place July 10–13, 1972. Jane ultimately would not become a delegate in Miami, but she had made her point and criticized the Nixon administration publicly.

For this reason, Jane must have avidly observed what transpired at the League's special May meeting. Representatives for both Nixon and McGovern were invited to speak at the League meeting. Neither was very impressive. "Mr. Dolf Droge, Nixon's rep, was an expert on the history and culture of Vietnam, but he was clearly lacking in terms of his explanations of U.S. military and diplomatic policy in Vietnam." Sybil recalled, "His representation of the President was a disaster."[31]

Sallie Stratton had a different reaction to the young hippie historian, who communicated much of the presentation through songs. She felt his analysis of Vietnamese culture was critical to understanding their foe. Droge explained how "all discussions have been from either a hawk or dove position, both of which are totally irrelevant, he told us. What is needed is the *owl position,* one based on an understanding of the Vietnamese people and their long history." Still, Sallie admitted that she was one of the few who enjoyed his talk. The League membership in general was not impressed.[32]

Jane and Sybil told Admiral Zumwalt at breakfast the next day about what they deemed the Droge fiasco. Zumwalt stormed into the League's press conference later that day and grabbed the mike. He had concluded that he must "go down and try to speak to the families to give them my own view that the President had remained steadfast in his intention not to ease the pressure on North Vietnam until the prisoners were released and the missing accounted for." Zumwalt was glad he had done so, later observing that the audience's questions "were good, hard and tough, and demonstrated that Sybil and Jane had not been amiss in their estimate that these long-suffering families needed some personal attention from the White House."

Energized by the positive reaction he received, Zumwalt decided to visit the White House and relay their reaction to Kissinger. "It was the only time I had ever dropped in on Henry unannounced. He came into the reception room, obviously perturbed at my arrival. I let him have it in no uncertain terms that I thought the White House had let down these families. Henry was infuriated and an acrimonious exchange took place."[33]

The admiral's appearance saved the day for those in the Nixon camp. Sybil wrote later that "I believe it was his appearance and being willing to lay his job on the line to represent the President and our political persuasions as individuals rather than a group" that allayed the fears of League members about the current administration's stance.[34]

The next day, May 8, the U.S. government announced the blockade and mining of Haiphong harbor, in North Vietnam. Known as Operation Linebacker I, the campaign began with the bombing of the harbor from the air, in addition to a honeycomb of mines detonated in the harbor itself. This decisive military action won over many POW/MIA wives, giving them hope that the current administration would do what it took to finally end the war. Many felt that the presence of the mines would give the U.S. military leverage over the North Vietnamese and perhaps force their hand regarding the American POWs and MIAs.[35]

Louise Mulligan, for one, was thrilled. She felt the offensive was long overdue. "I remember very well that morning. I put in a call to the White House and requested to speak to General [Brent] Scowcroft (who had replaced General Hughes as Nixon's military aide). I waited some time and the General came on the line. I asked him, 'Who ordered the bombing?' There was a pause and he said, 'Mrs. Mulligan, are you asking me who made the policy?' I said, 'I know exactly what I am asking you.' He said, 'I can't tell you that.' So I said to him, 'Are you going to continue the bombing?' He said, 'Yes, until they sue for peace!' and I replied, 'That's all I want to know!'"[36]

Roger E. Shields, then the thirty-two-year-old civilian in the Office of the Assistant secretary of defense for International Security affairs spearheaded the DoD task force for POW repatriation was convinced this action is what would ultimately bring the Communists to heel. "We knew we had an agreement, and that the men were going to come home."[37]

At the end of that week, Sybil and Phyllis both stayed at the Army and Navy Club, just off Connecticut Avenue and only a few blocks from the White House. The League office, in the American Legion building, was just around the corner. Phyllis and Sybil must have spent some time together plotting strategy. Phyllis's was surely humming her favorite song at the time, "I Am Woman," by Australian singer Helen Reddy, released that same month. Phyllis was no feminist, but she loved the song's line "I am invincible." She later wrote, "That's how I felt. I loved confrontation on the" POW/MIA issue. She "knew we couldn't be licked." This feeling of confidence and mastery of the issue led her to be more politically active within the parameters of the League. Phyllis was now acting as the Virginia committee chair for the League's Non-Partisan Political Action Committee and would attend the state and national conventions for both the Republican and Democratic Parties in 1972.[38]

With the November election rapidly approaching, the Nixon administration knew that if it lost Middle America, as LBJ had after the Tet Offensive, it was sunk. The ladies reflected this constituency. The government's next move had to reflect support for the POW/MIA issue or the ladies might throw their support to McGovern. Some, like Valerie Kushner, already had. Jane was totally on the fence and upset with the Nixon fundraising letter.

When Sybil, Phyllis, and Maureen Dunn—wife of Navy pilot Lieutenant Joseph P. Dunn, who went missing in 1968—requested a meeting with the president, they got it. The three women had been elected at the League's May 7 meeting specifically "to meet with President Nixon to reaffirm our extreme distress and our expectations that an immediate policy be adopted that would insure an accounting of our missing men and the release of our POWs, not just the withdrawal of combat troops. We wanted the Paris Peace Talks reconvened simultaneously with inspection of POW camps in South Vietnam, Laos, Cambodia and North Vietnam."[39]

On May 15, a press conference was held, with Sybil, Phyllis, and Maureen representing the National League. Sybil served as the spokeswoman for the group. The meeting illustrated the range of different viewpoints within the League membership and debunked the idea that the League was a puppet of the Nixon administration.

Dressed in a red, white, and blue outfit,[40] Sybil began by pointing out how critical she and the League had been of Senator J. William Fulbright, chair of the Senate Foreign Relations Committee, who had not held hearings on the POW/MIA issue during the entire eight years that Americans had been held in captivity. Sybil stated, "We consider the committee derelict in its responsibilities, and we said so. The point is, we don't play favorites, and we are considering what is best for our husbands and sons, their health, and in many cases, no doubt, their lives are at stake."[41]

Phyllis was clear that she had been "very very critical of the Administration in recent months, and I wanted to be convinced with all my heart that everything possible was being done. This mining [of the harbor] has given me that assurance, and this meeting has given me that assurance. I hope that the other families in our organization will be heartened by this also."[42] Maureen told the reporters gathered at the White House after the meeting with Nixon that "I am the only MIA wife here. Please be reassured that the President is encompassing all aspects of Southeast Asia. This includes Laos, South Vietnam, and Cambodia."[43]

Maureen, Phyllis, and Sybil felt comfortable enough with President Nixon to speak their minds with him and not hold back. Sybil even ventured to give her own tactical advice to the president during their meeting. "I told the President I would land the U.S. Marines in North Vietnam and claim it as U.S. territory." Her plan once the country was occupied? To keep it until the prisoners were released and accounted for. Nixon apparently laughed at the idea during the meeting. Though Sybil didn't tell the press this, she had noticed that Kissinger jotted a note down with her suggestion.[44]

Nixon assured the three ladies that the mining of Haiphong harbor meant the North Vietnamese would be out of oil in four months. He felt strongly that, after that, they would be forced to negotiate.[45] When Maureen still had questions toward the end of their time with the president, he invited the ladies to "stay here and ask me all the questions you have. You ladies come first."[46]

Maureen wanted assurance from Nixon that the MIAs would not be forgotten at the end of the war. He readily gave it, assuring her that they were on his radar as well.

Over the summer of 1972, movie actress turned political firebrand Jane Fonda would make her infamous visit to North Vietnam, where she was photographed sitting on a North Vietnamese antiaircraft gun. She had a full schedule while visiting North Vietnam, set up by her Communist hosts. It included tours, live and taped broadcasts to GIs through Radio Hanoi, and meetings with American POWs, sometimes against their will. When she returned to Los Angeles on July 31, she announced that she would be "abandoning her career" until after the November election, "in order to campaign against the Vietnam War." Over the years, she would receive the derogatory nickname "Hanoi Jane."

The POWs would never forgive Fonda for supporting the Communists and denying their mistreatment at the hands of the enemy,[47] despite the actress's repeated apologies many years later.

The POW and MIA wives, though, barely gave Jane Fonda a second thought. The women regarded COLIAFAM and Cora Weiss as far more dangerous. But ultimately, most POW/MIA wives believed that Fonda and others like her were simply Communist-leaning pawns in the larger chess game of Vietnam. The League leadership were determined to checkmate their opponents, and they would do so through their own anti-propaganda awareness campaigns.

During the third weekend in September, the League leadership had their regularly scheduled bimonthly meeting with Kissinger. Sybil recalled that "this was the first meeting when he told the group that he hoped that soon he would have an announcement to make which would bring our waiting to an end."[48] Instead of feeling elated, Sybil felt let down and depressed. "Still nothing definite," she wrote.

But on October 12, just before the League's 1972 convention, Kissinger returned from Paris extremely hopeful. Sustained U.S. military action had finally brought Le Duc Tho, the former Viet Minh leader negotiating on behalf of the North Vietnamese, back to the table. The two diplomats had "worked out a ceasefire to be followed within sixty days of a withdrawal of all U.S. forces and the release of all American POWs."[49] Though the war was not over yet, it seemed that progress was finally being made.

Just two days later, the League hosted its third annual convention at the Statler Hilton, in Washington. League membership continued to grow: the organization now numbered 2,983, in addition to a "Concerned Citizen" group of more than five hundred non–family members. Both presidential candidates were invited to speak at the gathering. Only Nixon showed up, and he was received warmly by the crowd. Recently released Navy POW Lieutenant Mark Gartley also attended and spoke about the strict censorship of mail and packages to the prisoners. He noted that prisoner treatment had been much improved in the past several years. The publicity generated for the POWs by the League surely had not hurt.[50]

The excitement over a potential peace agreement was pulsating through the air at the Statler Hilton. Consequently, perhaps the most important agenda item was the discussion of Kissinger's explanation of the agreements he had worked out with the North Vietnamese regarding the prisoners and the missing. League membership was parsing his every word on the matter carefully:

"There will be a return of all American prisoners, military or civilian, within 60 days after the agreement comes into force. North Vietnam has made itself responsible for an accounting of our prisoners and missing in action throughout Indochina, and for the repatriation of American prisoners throughout Indochina."[51] This clarification was especially important for the MIA families, who lived in constant fear that their loved ones (or their loved ones' remains) would be left behind when the war ended.

On October 15, Phyllis was nominated for the position of board chair and then elected by secret ballot. Louise Mulligan, who had never run for a League office before and had backed off from League efforts for months, ran for a board seat in a last-ditch effort to set a fire under the League. She did not win, but she was glad she had put her name forth.[52] After an interview with the League leadership in D.C., Helene was nominated for national coordinator and elected unanimously.[53] Though Evie Grubb would have liked to have stayed on as League coordinator, League leadership wanted new direction and fresh ideas. Helene's fundraising ability had already been noticed, and she had become friends with board chair Carole Hanson when Carole visited Colorado Springs to receive the $30,000 check generated by the Silent Nights Christmas seals campaign.[54]

Now the vivacious Colorado Springs MIA wife and the once shy but now fearless Phyllis joined forces. They would make a formidable team. Helene and her children, Cindy and Robbie, moved to D.C. for her one-year term. Phyllis would travel back and forth from her home base in Richmond and be in constant phone contact with Helene and the other League officers and board members. Though the two women were both seasoned Leaguers, they had inherited a frequently fractious group. Together, they deftly steered the League through sometimes treacherous political and emotional tides.

On October 26, not even two weeks after the League convention, Kissinger held a press conference, proclaiming, in his guttural German accent, "We have now heard from both Vietnams, and it is obvious that the war that has been raging for ten years is drawing to a conclusion, and that this is a traumatic experience for all of the participants . . .

We believe that peace is at hand. We believe an agreement is in sight."[55]

This declaration would soon be viewed as premature and would later haunt Nixon's national security adviser and top negotiator. Sybil's gut reaction was that Kissinger's declaration was just more of the same old blah-blah. She was sliding down into another depression due to the war and financial issues at home. "The fact that the Peace is at Hand statement didn't produce anything really was just further evidence to me that the war would probably go on forever."[56]

League board member and MIA wife Sallie Stratton was also disappointed. Her feelings were reflected in a statement the League itself had issued expressing its members' distress:

> *The Families of Americans who are missing and held captive in Southeast Asia had harbored desperate hopes that a peace treaty could be signed before Christmas and that at least some of our men, particularly the sick and injured and those men held for long years, would be quickly reunited with their families.*
>
> *We had expected that all other prisoners might be home by March and that identification and accounting would be taking place in the interim. Now we know that we must face another Christmas with no immediate peace in sight. It is a bitter prospect and the disappointments and frustrations are severe.*[57]

There were growing feelings of hopelessness among the League membership. Joan Vinson was the chairwoman of the League's Non-Partisan Political Action Committee, which sent out a voter appeal made clear on that the organization was not taking political sides in the election.

"We acclaim no one. We endorse no one. We are not on anyone's bandwagon. We want and need you all on ours." At the bottom of the appeal was this chilling slogan:

"The POW's ARE DYING TO VOTE!"[58]

The president was reelected on November 7 in one of the biggest election landslides in American history.[59] Many POW and MIA wives apparently still felt that if McGovern had prevailed, all would be lost for the POWs and MIAs. With Nixon remaining at the helm, Sybil, Phyllis, Sallie, and many others reasoned, perhaps the men still had a fighting chance.

For many of the wives, six or more years had passed since their husbands were shot down. Children born when their fathers left for Vietnam had never met their dads. Holidays, birthdays, weddings, and funerals came and went for these families while the men languished in prison or their whereabouts remained unknown. Many of the women were struggling to be full-time activists as well as both mother and father to their children. It was all becoming too much to bear.

Jim Stockdale Jr. graduated from Ohio Wesleyan University, and Sid, a crew star at South Kent Prep School, in Connecticut, was selected to row in the Junior Olympics in Milan. The children were all doing well, but financially Sybil was worried. She had invested in two condos at Mammoth Mountain, California, before realizing she could not afford them. She began to slip back into the fog of depression she had experienced in the fall of 1970 in Washington. She started seeing a civilian therapist and hired an attorney to help her sort out her finances. Jim might never come home, so she needed to prepare for the worst.[60]

On December 18, Nixon ordered the Air Force B-52s to bomb Hanoi. The offensive, which the government named Operation Linebacker II, soon became better known as the "Christmas bombing." Naturally, the action was unpopular with the antiwar lobby, both foreign and domestic. "The prime minister of Sweden [Olof Palme] compared the United States to Nazi Germany," wrote historian Geoffrey Ward. "James Reston, of *The New York Times,* pronounced the raids 'war by tantrum.'"[61]

The bombing was exactly what the prisoners in Hanoi and their families had been hoping for.

In the North Vietnamese prisons, the POWs cheered wildly when they heard the bombs. Prisoner John McCain painted a vivid scene of the reaction of the prisoners held with him in Hanoi: "Despite our proximity to the targets, we were jubilant. We hollered in near euphoria as the ground beneath us shook with the force of the blasts, exulting in our guards' fear as they scurried for shelter. We clapped each other on the back and joked about packing our bags for home. We shouted 'Thank you!' to the night sky."[62] Robbie Risner, one of the group of defiant POWs dubbed the "Alcatraz Eleven," reinforced McCain's account: "On the 18th of December—I think that was the first night of the B52 raids—there was never such joy seen in our camp before."[63]

The men hoped and prayed that the war might finally be coming to its conclusion. After eleven days of bombing Hanoi, the capital city was in shreds. Kissinger's take? "I think the Christmas bombing broke their back."[64]

After years of stalling subterfuge and fruitless exchanges at the Paris peace talks, the North Vietnamese finally came back to the negotiating table. (Perhaps Chiang Kai-shek had been right all along.) On December 29, the bombing stopped, and the Vietnam War was on its way to its final conclusion.

Seventeen

"WE CHOSE TO BE TOGETHER"

ON JANUARY 1, SYBIL REFLECTED on the new year in her diary. Like Jane, Phyllis, Helene, Andrea, Kathleen, and all the other POW and MIA wives, she could "not help but wonder, as always, if this will be the year Jim comes home. Time has never dragged before as it does now." Then she wrote out her New Year's resolutions:

1. Swim every day
2. Write in diary regularly
3. Keep positive attitude[1]

Seven years and four months had passed since Jim's capture. Jane had lost Jerry seven years and five months ago. Phyllis had waited for Paul for six and a half years now. Louise had waited for Jim for almost seven years. Andrea had waited for Donald for almost five years.

But those five women were more fortunate than some, in that they knew their husbands were alive. For the past six years, Helene had not known Herman's fate, and for seven and a half long years, Kathleen had received no word of Bruce. A seeming eternity had passed for all of these women, as well as for Janie, Dot, Joan, Sallie, Sandy, Bonnie, Karen, Jenny, Debby, Patsy, and hundreds more POW/MIA wives and family members, since their loved ones' capture or disappearance.

Some thought they could not take the waiting for even one day longer. But they had little choice but to continue their lonely vigil and pray that a resolution would finally come. Would Kissinger finalize his agreement with the North Vietnamese, or would this result in yet another crushing disappointment? Sybil's resolution to keep a positive attitude was surely the hardest one for her to implement.

POW/MIA families were on edge in January regarding the war's resolution. Congress was gearing up for a big fight when it reconvened on January 2. At issue: war funds. The Democratic Congress had announced it would cut off war funds if there was no settlement with the North Vietnamese by January 20, Inauguration Day.[2]

Though Louise was not elected to the League's 1972–73 board—perhaps she was considered too much of a firebrand—she wrote to Helene and Phyllis on January 9, thanking them for finally polling the membership. She admitted that she continued to harbor "very strong feelings about the running of the League," especially when it came to making public statements. She felt that both Helene and Phyllis had been chosen because of their good judgment and integrity, and that therefore the two women should be able to make statements to the press about the League without checking in constantly with the board and the membership. However, Louise continued to feel that the League should "take a purely non-political stance and NO statements should be issued either publicly or privately from ANY ELECTED OFFICIAL."[3] She still felt that the humanitarian stance of the League lent it a special status that no political group could match.

On January 22, the day before the Paris Peace Accords were initialed, former president Lyndon Johnson died of congestive heart failure at his ranch in Texas.[4] Most POW/MIA wives felt that his indecisive approach to the war had prolonged it. They now knew for a fact that his "keep quiet" policy had been damaging to their husbands' welfare and perhaps had even prolonged their captivity. It is doubtful that they shed many tears over Johnson's demise.

On January 23, Nixon addressed the nation in a televised address. During the broadcast, he announced that the peace treaty had been signed by Kissinger and Le Duc Tho in Paris at 12:30 p.m. local time.

A cease-fire would take effect on Saturday, January 27. All American troops would be withdrawn during the subsequent sixty days. All prisoners of war in Indochina were to be released, also within that sixty-day period. The fullest possible accounting of American MIAs in Indochina was also expected. Aid to South Vietnam would continue within the terms of the agreement.

During the address, Nixon made a special point of praising and mentioning the efforts of the POW/MIA wives and families. He described them as "some of the bravest people I have ever met: the wives, the children, the families of our prisoners of war and missing in action." He thanked this group for resisting antiwar activists and protesters calling for peace at any price. "When others called on us to settle on any terms, *you* had the courage to stand for the right kind of peace."

"Nothing means more to me," remarked the president, addressing the POW/MIA wives and families, "than the fact that your long vigil is coming to an end."[5]

After Laird, Capen, Reagan, and others convinced him it was vitally important to support the POW/MIA issue, the president had been consistent in his support for the women. As in most marriages—personal or political—there were bumps in the road, disagreements and quarrels. But overall, it seemed as though Nixon really had been "the One" for the POW/MIA wives and their families. The president who would finally bring the prisoners home.

Fortuitously, the League board and its members were in Washington for their regular January board meeting just after the big announcement. Knowing this, Pentagon officials arranged to tell League board members their individual news at the Army and Navy Club all at one time. Helene told *The Washington Post* the next day, "We chose to be together" to hear about their husbands' fates.

Helene and the Air Force wives met in one corner. The Navy wives, including Phyllis, huddled together in another area. And Iris Powers, the lone Army mother of a missing-in-action son, heard her news alone. Major General Verne Bowers told her that her son Lowell, missing in action since April 2, 1969, was not among the returning prisoners. Iris told the *Post*, "It hurts when you know it's hopeless . . . But I felt so sorry for the general—I thought if I cried he would, so I didn't."[6] Helene remembered it being "one of our most important and heart-wrenching meetings during my tenure as National Coordinator."[7]

After the peace treaty was finally signed, the slow-motion lives so many POW wives had all felt they were living suddenly hit warp speed. It was a blur of cleaning, organizing, calls, interviews, dress shopping, hair appointments, and house decorating. Flowers and gifts began to pour in to celebrate the men's return. Most of the wives were numb. Their hopes had been up and down for so long, they almost didn't allow themselves to believe that their long-awaited reunions with their husbands might finally occur. Sybil's reaction summed up how many of the women were feeling on January 23: "Just can't believe it. Can it really happen? Just can't believe Jim will really be home . . . Have optimistic but still skeptical attitude."[8] Phyllis was joyful but overwhelmed. In her diary on January 24, she noted, "Awoken by more calls! Kissinger had a 90-minute press conference giving specifics. Release could be soon . . . I'm a basket case."[9]

Ever meticulous and organized, Phyllis even kept a spiral-bound notebook record of all the gifts and who gave them to her, with the name of the gift giver and date received. This way she would remember to whom she owed a thank-you note. It felt like she and Paul were getting married all over again. One of the first gifts Phyllis received was an orchid corsage from Pat and Richard Nixon. She and Paul also received matching ski sweaters, champagne, bouquets of red, white, and blue flowers, a tennis club membership, and even a cartoon by Phyllis's friend Jeff MacNelly, a Pulitzer Prize–winning *Richmond News Leader* editorial cartoonist.[10]

When she was interviewed by *Life* magazine about her husband's impending return, Louise Mulligan jokingly mentioned that she had bought a new house with a lavender bedroom. She noted, "Well, there's no way Jim Mulligan is going to live with lavender. We painted the room but the drapes are still up, lavender with blue tassels. Every time one of the kids comes in, I hear, *Mother*, when are you going to get *rid* of them?"[11] In fact, the entire house had been *pink* when Louise purchased it, and the shades in the master bedroom were decorated with pink pom-poms. Louise and the boys had taken care of that immediately by repainting every room and jettisoning the offending shades.[12] Of course, house decor was not of any real concern to her. Louise's main fears were for her sons and how they would relate to their father after his long absence. "The group psychiatrist says the boys are all young men now and it will be between them and their father. It will have nothing to do with me. They'll have to make their own peace."[13]

Andrea Rander was excited to feed her POW husband, Donald. She had been practicing her cooking to get ready. "Donald loved to eat. I can't wait to fatten him up." But, like Louise, Andrea's more pressing issues concerning her husband's return were family-based. It had been almost five years since she last saw him, and she was worried about how this would affect their relationship. "I'm mentally trying to get us back together even before he gets here. We had a pretty good marriage, but I know we're going to have some problems. He's not just going to walk through that door and be the same man who left."[14] During Don's captivity, Andrea had relied on her strong Presbyterian faith and her church community for support. "My faith helped me cope and made me feel stronger during Don's absence." She and her children went to Sunday school and church almost every Sunday and prayed together at every meal. This religious belief that had sustained her for so long would continue to ground her during this stressful time.[15]

The MIA wives were operating in a less hopeful but similar mode. Knowing that the MIA lists were incomplete and inaccurate, Helene, Kathleen, and all the MIA wives hoped their husbands might somehow be among the returnees. Maybe, just maybe, Herman and Bruce would walk off one of those planes returning home. Kathleen felt like any day now Bruce would walk back into their home, saying, "I had you worried, didn't I, Bon?" (His nickname for her was Bonnie, or Bon.) She imagined she would lovingly scold him: "You could have called me, Bruce: I burned the roast!"[16]

None of these women were the play-by-the rules military wives their husbands had left behind. What would the men think of these newly empowered, outspoken, independent activists? Would they even recognize them? Would their long-anticipated reunions end harmoniously or acrimoniously? The wives' joyful anticipation was tinged with nervous worry, in part because of a military psychiatrist's dire warnings of possible sexual dysfunction, violent rages, and medical issues that the returnees could possibly face.[17] Though she acknowledged in interviews that she had gone from "bashful" to "independent," Phyllis worried that Paul might not like her new persona. She recalled that her husband did not appreciate women who were "too pushy or aggressive and he won't like it if he thinks I'm that way now."[18] The women would have to wait and see how things unfolded.

The homecoming was being meticulously planned to give the families of the returnees the best possible circumstances for a successful reunion. Under Secretary of Defense Melvin Laird, the Department of Defense had set up a task force in the spring of 1971, in anticipation of such a return. The task force was placed under the supervision of Roger Shields, special assistant in international security affairs assistant secretariat, and Rear Admiral Horace H. Epes Jr.[19] The original name, Operation Egress Recap, was "a bit of Pentagonese even the Pentagon now declares it can't translate."[20] Secretary Laird agreed. On January 8, just weeks before he left office, he scrapped the enigmatic "Egress" title, swapping it out for one that would strike a more human chord with the public: Operation Homecoming.[21]

Changing the title of the operation was the easy part. Its implementation was a massive proposition. This daunting job fell to Shields, described by *Life* magazine as a "young, bulky, crew-cut Ph.D. in economics."[22] Shields had worked with Laird first as an outside contractor with a focus on the economic effects of Vietnamization.[23] Though only thirty-three, Shields would prove he had the training, the organizational skills, and the compassion necessary to pull off the multilayered return and reunion smoothly.

Many issues had to be dealt with, in addition to the physical pickup and transport of the men. Operation Homecoming was a moving target. "First, we didn't know how many men were going to be released, nor were we sure of their identity, or their medical condition." At this stage, the government did not even know for sure where the men would be released. As a result, Shields and the hundreds of staff under him set up reception centers and medical treatment facilities in several different locations—there was even a welcome home center set up in Germany. They had to plan for every contingency.

Just as important in Shields's plans was the emotional and mental health component of the homecoming operation. "We also had to ensure that their reunions with their families, for many involving a separation of more than five years, was accomplished with care and understanding."[24] Shields's commonsense approach was to shield the returnees from the onslaught of press coverage and interviews as much as possible. After years of confinement, sometimes in solitary, the noise, bustle, and clamor of the press corps was sure to be disorienting, if not frightening, to some of the men.

President Nixon supported Shields's plan and stayed out of the limelight when the POWs returned. When speculation arose that the president would appear at Travis Air Force Base, in Northern California, to greet the first batch of prisoners, he quickly put the rumor to rest. "These are men who have been away sometimes for years. They have a right to privacy and a right to be with their families just as quickly as they possibly can. And I am going to respect that right."[25]

A total of six hundred prisoners of war (591 Americans and nine foreign nationals) would return home in groups of forty. Those who had been captured first would also come home first. All American prisoners would first pass through Clark Air Base, in the Philippines, then be flown to the United States to their home bases. Of the 591 Americans, more than half (325) were Air Force, followed by Navy (138), Army (77), Marines (26), and civilians (25). Their time of captivity ranged from a few days to almost nine years. The prisoner releases would take place from February 12 through March 29, 1973.[26]

The National League weighed in on the Operation Homecoming

plans, though its input was not solicited by the government. As board chair, Phyllis sent Shields recommendations from the League's own Committee on Repatriation, Rehabilitation, and Readjustment in late December of 1972. The most important recommendations included: helping to pay for education for the POW/MIA children; recommendations that the DoD work with the VA hospitals to sensitize them to issues they would face in treating the returning POWs; and a directive that draft boards exempt sons of returning POWs for at least one year after their father's return.[27]

Operation Homecoming was a tall order to fill and a Herculean organizational task. In addition, the operation would take place under a harsh media spotlight, with grieving MIA families in the background. "Intense pressures could be anticipated from families, members of Congress, news commentators, and editorial writers for fulfillment of the government's assurances that the fullest possible accounting would be obtained."[28] Still, Shields and his team were determined to pull Operation Homecoming off to the best of their ability. They felt the country owed it to both the men and their families to get it right.

On February 12, 1973, 116 men who years earlier had been high-flying Navy, Air Force, Marine, and Army pilots shuffled, limped, or were carried off three government C-141 military transport planes at Clark Air Base. The first two planes held 40 POWs with the third holding the last 36 prisoners. The first group to return, the men had suffered years of brutal torture, spent months and sometimes years shackled in solitary confinement, and starved in rat-infested, mosquito-laden prisons. They had finally left their cells in the infamous Hanoi Hilton and its associated jails—for home and the families they had not seen in years.

These first POWs to set foot on the base in the Philippines—the planes would come to be known as *Hanoi Taxis*—had spent the longest time in captivity: between six and eight years. Captain Jeremiah Denton, one of the most senior naval officers to be held prisoner, was the first man off the plane. He would be the spokesman for the first group of returnees.

With tears in his eyes, Denton gave an address to the nation on behalf of all the returning POWs: "We are honored to have had the opportunity to serve our country under difficult circumstances. We are profoundly grateful to our commander in chief and to our nation for this day." In his memoir, Denton recalled that he felt like something was still missing from his remarks. "I hadn't said all that was in my heart. Final, unrehearsed words slipped from me." He paused before the right words tumbled forth: "God bless America!"[29]

Though some cynics later accused the government of coaching Denton and other POWs on their speeches, nothing could have been further from the truth. It may have seemed old-fashioned and "square" to antiwar activists such as Philip Berrigan, who stood among these accusers, but as Navy POW Captain Howard Rutledge later stated, "This thing all came from the heart."[30]

Several days later, on February 15, at 2:35 a.m., Jerry Denton, Jim Mulligan, and Paul Galanti emerged from a C-9 military transport plane at Naval Station Norfolk. Jim was quickly mobbed by Louise and their six sons. Louise put aside the years of battle she had done, with two presidential administrations and innumerable government staff, and thanked God that her husband was finally home. (She would keep her BULLSHIT stamp forever, though, just in case.)

Jane stood on the tarmac, glowing with pride. With her were the couple's five sons, two daughters, and two new daughters-in-law. The look of pure joy on Jane and Jerry's faces as they held each other close lit up the runway. The Denton family would stay up all night that evening as Jerry debriefed them on all that had happened to him while in prison.[31] Jerry later wrote, "Of all the emotions I have experienced, nothing yet compares with my feeling of pride at the strength of character shown by my family while I was away and during my recovery period. Jane especially cannot get enough credit."[32]

Phyllis was nervous about her husband's homecoming. She had matured while he was away, from a shy young housewife into an international diplomat. In a newspaper article published a few days before Paul's release, she had confessed to having some worries related to Paul's years in captivity. "We'll never catch up with our contemporaries.

We'll be behind in education, finances, social life and having a family." Navy psychiatrists had warned Phyllis that she and Paul would probably face arguments during the first thirty minutes they were back together.[33]

Phyllis and the Navy psychiatrists were all wrong.

Almost the minute that fun-loving, laid-back Paul saw his wife, Phyllis's worries seemed to melt away. He quoted poetry to her the minute he got off the plane and swept her into his arms for a very public kiss. (Ever mischievous, Paul later admitted that he swiped the poem from a newspaper on the way home.[34])

The next day, Jane, Louise, and Phyllis held a press conference at Portsmouth Naval Hospital, where their husbands were all being held for medical testing and intelligence debriefing. Jane was bubbly and upbeat about her husband's return: "We have had no difficulties with the adjustment. This is the happiest week of our lives." Louise said the same thing of her experience. There were no adjustment issues, and the family was enjoying reconnecting with one another. "As far as I can determine, Jim Mulligan is the same man now as when he went over," she noted fondly. The anger that had kept Phyllis going for so long seemed to have evaporated: "I'm not even going to regret the time we missed," she declared, incredulous that Paul was finally home.[35] "The reunion surpassed my expectations," Phyllis admitted. "A lot of the problems I was concerned about just weren't there."[36]

The men had another visitor besides their wives and families during this time—a benevolent but shadowy figure who had thrown a lifeline to the prisoners during their captivity by working in tandem with their wives. A man they did not know yet, but who knew each of them well: Bob Boroughs, soon to be known as "Mr. POW" among the naval prisoner-of-war community.[37]

Boroughs had also brought his twelve-year-old daughter, Merriann, with him to the debriefing. (It's hard to believe, in today's top-secret world, that you could once bring your kid with you for intelligence work.) Merriann kept a scrapbook and a diary of the POWs return. In her very neat print handwriting, she wrote about their day at Portsmouth Naval Hospital: "Dad went into the suites to set up for the prisoners and their wives, to talk to Captain Mulligan and Captain Denton. After a few minutes, we got to see Mrs. Mulligan and her husband Captain Mulligan. I was so happy to meet him, I didn't know what to say. We also got to see Captain Denton and his wife Jane, Mrs. Galanti and Lieutenant Cmdr. Galanti's parents."

Jim Mulligan wrote Merriann a note, which she kept pasted neatly in her scrapbook on the next page. It read:

> Merriann,
> Thanks for keeping faith in the Hanoi P.O.W.s—
> > Good luck and God bless you.
> > > Jim Mulligan
> > > Captain U.S. Navy
> > > 2-17-73[38]

Merriann would later paste another thank-you note in her scrapbook from Jim Stockdale, who would also be debriefed by her dad. "There has been no other man who has helped either myself or my family so much as your wonderful Dad! . . . You are a lucky daughter."[39]

While reunions among the Navy families were taking place in Norfolk, Andrea and Donald Rander were reunited at the Army's Valley Forge hospital, in Pennsylvania. The Army psychologists had tried to prepare her for the reunion, advising her, "You have to decide how to greet him. What to leave in, and what to leave out."

Andrea had been very optimistic and upbeat, as was her nature. "I would just be my wifely self!" But still, it was a shock for her to see him looking so thin. Donald swept his wife up in a dramatic embrace, and her worries disappeared. That fall, the reunited couple would finally take that honeymoon they had never had, in Montego Bay, Jamaica. They needed to make up for lost time.[40]

The day before Jim Stockdale returned home to the West Coast was Valentine's Day. A true romantic, Jim sent Sybil a dozen red American Beauty roses and a note that read "God Bless You, Syb. All my love,

Jim." Jim Jr., Stan, and Taylor spent hours preparing a gigantic banner reading WELCOME HOME, which they draped across the porch roof at 547 A Avenue on the morning of February 15.

When Jim finally arrived on the tarmac at Naval Air Station Miramar, in north San Diego, Sybil, Jim Jr., Stanford, and Taylor were waiting. (Sid would be home in time for dinner; his family did not want him to miss the championship hockey game he was playing in that day at South Kent Prep.) The Stockdale boys' now famous dad gave a short but poignant speech, quoting the Greek Stoics, whose philosophies had sustained him in prison. He then smiled at his family and declared, "We're home. America, America, God shed His grace on thee."[41] Then Sybil and the boys tackled him in a mad rush. Sybil would never forget seeing her beloved husband, now gaunt and silver-haired, approach her. "We come together with so much force and emotion that for a split second I think we might topple over."[42]

The Stockdales drove to nearby Balboa Hospital, where Jim would be staying for his medical checkups. That evening, the whole family came together for their first meal in more than seven years. They devoured juicy steaks and talked about Sid's victorious hockey game. Jim Jr. drove the younger boys home to Coronado, but Sybil stayed with Jim, despite the lack of a double bed. The couple decided to sleep on the carpeted floor together, amid a nest of pillows and blankets. Sybil and Jim cracked open a bottle of champagne to celebrate their reunion. As they drifted blissfully off to sleep, Sybil noted with satisfaction "how completely wrong our briefers had been about the sexual impotence."[43]

Another expectation the military psychologists had, which they would later be stunned to find themselves completely wrong about, was the strikingly low occurrence of PTSD among Hanoi Hilton prisoners of war. During a fourteen-year postwar study period, researchers at the Robert E. Mitchell Center for Prisoner of War Studies, run by the Navy in Pensacola, noted that "only 4 percent of the aviator POWs, all of them officers, experienced PTSD."[44] What contributed to this extraordinary resilience among the men?

With few exceptions, the prisoners were highly educated, most were college graduates, and many had attended elite American military academies. They tended to be older and more mature than the average draftee. All aviators flying in combat zones were required to attend SERE school. As a result, these pilots became "the products of one of the most rigorous military training systems in existence at the time."[45]

The bonding and mentoring that occurred while the men were imprisoned and the unity that resulted among these servicemen were unprecedented in the history of warfare. Jim Stockdale would later describe his role in prison as "'presiding over a unique society.' This society was built upon mutual care, unity, and optimism in the face of adversity. Newly captured prisoners would later speak of being 'mentored' by the more experienced prisoners."[46] Unlike enlisted Vietnam vets, who often returned home to hostile antiwar sentiment, Vietnam POWs were treated to ticker-tape parades, a White House gala hosted by President Nixon, and ongoing admiration in their communities. "Their suffering was acknowledged, processed, meditated upon, and even celebrated by their culture."[47]

Though Jim didn't realize it at the time, his capable and accomplished wife had established a mirror society on the home front among the POW/MIA wives. Sybil's New Girl Villages were built upon remarkably similar principles. While the women were not threatened with death if they spoke to one another via the tap code their husbands had used to communicate within their prison walls, they were told to "keep quiet" and warned about the supposed harm they would cause their husbands if they spoke out. Both the POWs and their female partners ultimately defied their captors—or, in the case of the wives, their government handlers—to beat their respective systems.

Though there would be exceptions among the men in terms of PTSD, Donald Rander being one of them,[48] "the Hanoi Hilton experience is a unicorn in the literature of trauma, a case in which the perfect storm of circumstances converged to produce a group of people who defied the odds."[49]

The MIA wives, like Helene and Kathleen, looked on from the wings, many feeling left out and concerned that the MIA situation was

being forgotten by some in the midst of the POWs' triumphant return home. Helene recalled seeing the famous cover of *Newsweek* featuring her friend and League colleague Phyllis and her returned POW
husband, Paul, and being "simultaneously thrilled and saddened."[50]
The MIA wives and families knew that the window of opportunity
to find their husbands was running out: with the return of the POWs,
the country had the Hollywood ending it wanted, and after it was
over everyone would forget about the missing men forever.

Helene and her children, Cindy and Robbie, had watched the POW
homecoming ceremonies on TV, still hoping against hope that Herman would be among the men. Like many of the MIA wives, Helene
felt disheartened. She felt deserted, too, after so many of her POW
wife friends had left the League. Helene would remain in her post as
the national coordinator of the League until her term was finished, in
the fall of 1973.[51]

In late May of 1973, Helene would testify before the House Committee on Foreign Affairs about the missing men. She spoke both from
her viewpoint as the coordinator of the National League and from a
personal standpoint, as the wife of one still missing in action. "In the
recent joyous reunion of 590 of our POW families—a joy in which
we and all Americans shared—it appears many of our countrymen
may have lost sight of the fact that almost two-thirds of our men who
were missing and imprisoned in Southeast Asia did not come home."[52]
Helene and all the MIA wives and families wanted an accounting of
the men immediately. "We want this accounting now; we want our
dead returned; we want our search teams allowed to go into all areas
of Southeast Asia."[53]

For Kathleen Johnson, the time from her husband's disappearance
until the return of the POWs, in the spring of 1973, was like one long
day. Dates and times were hard to recall. Perhaps, she admitted later,
this was her way of coping with the unthinkable. She had been absolutely convinced the entire time that he was alive and fought hard to
do everything possible to get news of his fate and to bring him home.
Bruce used to say to her before he left for Vietnam, "There's no doubt
in my military mind that I'll be home." His faith in God, country,

and family were strong. She could not imagine any other outcome for him than what he promised her.[54]

It was simply not to be. Neither Herm nor Bruce would return home in 1973. Helene and Kathleen would continue their vigils. Though MIA wives often felt adrift and alone, their POW wife sisters would continue to support them by always keeping the MIAs in mind. Andrea and her family have a tradition that began during the war and continues to this day: "Before we eat, we still stay 'God Bless the POWs and MIAs.' I don't know if that will ever end. We still have to keep hope alive."[55]

After the POWs' successful return, Nixon's next priority was to follow through on the promised accounting of those missing in action. In a private, now declassified memo from early April of 1973, Nixon told Shields to let the MIA families know: "On the MIAs, you say the President personally will follow through on scrupulous adherence by North Vietnam on this. We will leave no stone unturned. All those families, waiting, hoping. They must know the certainty of their men's fate."[56]

Nixon seemed to have had the intent to follow through with this accounting, but the Watergate break-in had widened into a political tsunami that would sweep the president and much of his staff from office. The president's inherent mistrust of the press and his political rivals, which had first manifested itself in his reaction to the Pentagon Papers leak, had spun out of control. In her memoir, *Washington Post* owner and publisher Katharine Graham would recount that Watergate's "sheer magnitude and reach put it on a scale altogether different from past political scandals."[57] Nixon biographer Evan Thomas wrote, "By the summer of 1974, the U.S. government was essentially running without an effective president. Indeed, it had been running on autopilot for at least a year."[58] On August 8, 1974, Richard Milhous Nixon would become the first president in American history to resign.

Despite this disgrace, Watergate would not dim the loyalty felt by most POWs—and their wives—for the former president. Most of this population would remain loyal to Nixon: in the men's view, he was the president who finally brought them home from Hanoi. (The returned prisoners would present Nixon with a plaque inscribed TO OUR LEADER, OUR COMRADE, RICHARD THE LIONHEARTED.[59]) Though some of the women had switched political sides during the war, out of sheer frustration with its length, most would admit that Nixon had been a massive improvement over LBJ. His administration, unlike Johnson's, had treated the women with respect and supported their concerns. This laudatory view of Nixon within the POW/MIA community has remained consistent over the years.[60]

After Nixon's resignation, his vice president, Gerald Ford, would become the nation's thirty-eighth president. Though American troops had been withdrawn and the POWs returned, Vietnam remained a war zone. In April of 1975, President Ford and Secretary of State Kissinger would make one last attempt to save U.S. ally South Vietnam by requesting $722 million in emergency military aid for the beleaguered nation. But Americans and the U.S. Congress were unwilling to support further monetary aid. On April 23, Ford announced that American involvement in Vietnam was over and the war there was a lost cause.[61]

On April 30, Saigon fell to the North Vietnamese Army. An eleventh-hour American airlift by seventy Marine helicopters had evacuated a thousand American civilians and seven thousand South Vietnamese the day before. But "tens of thousands of South Vietnamese who had been followers of the American-backed regime were left to face the wrath of the impending Communist takeover. Many would be killed or 're-educated.' Still others would eventually make their way out as refugees."[62] Saigon was immediately renamed Ho Chi Minh City, in honor of the deceased Communist leader.[63]

Although Article 8 of the Paris Peace Accords "called for mutual assistance among the parties in accounting for the missing Americans, immediate postwar hostilities limited access to many sites." When Saigon fell to the Communists, so did the hopes of MIA families. Searches were completely shut down from this date until the early 1980s.[64]

Save for one MIA who remains listed as a POW for symbolic purposes, all American servicemen still missing in action were "presumed dead" in 1978. This declaration included Herman Knapp and Bruce Johnson.[65]

Though there have been numerous attempts to find them, the remains of Herman and Bruce have never been recovered.[66] The Defense POW/MIA Accounting Agency (DPAA)—known until 2015 as the Joint POW/MIA Accounting Command (JPAC)—is the U.S. government agency whose grim duty it is to attempt to recover remains from MIAs of all American wars. The most recent DPAA report on the Vietnam War missing lists a total of 1,598 still unaccounted for in Southeast Asia. This includes servicemen lost in Vietnam, China, Laos, and Cambodia, and MIAs from every military branch, as well as thirty-one civilians.[67]

Helene and Kathleen both have strong religious faiths that have sustained them throughout their ordeals. Both women desperately wanted their husbands' remains home for years. However, six forensic digs have turned up only remnants of Herm's plane and clothing and no human remains. Helene questions the point of continuing to search. Each dig brings a fresh sense of trauma. "I don't need human remains. I know he is in heaven," she says.[68]

Kathleen still wishes Bruce could be buried with his family in Salina, Kansas. She has no body to claim for them. But she and her children do have something from him that they all share and treasure: Bruce's red Bible, which was sent back with his things from Vietnam all those years ago. It had a moist, dank jungle smell when Kathleen first received it. "It smelled like Vietnam for decades."[69]

Eighteen

TO THE FIRST LADIES
OF AMERICA!

FOR THE RETURNED POWS, life had gone from grim to glam in a matter of weeks.

The men and their wives were celebrated like royalty at parties all over the country.

In April, Ross Perot teamed up with California governor Ronald Reagan for a fabulous fête. "I was determined to welcome these people home as true heroes."[1] He and the Reagans hosted a big parade for them in San Francisco on April 27, 1973. The parade remains one of the biggest in the history of San Francisco. Only one lone protester showed up.

The POWs and their wives were carried down the parade route in trolleys and convertibles as the television cameras rolled. Governor Reagan hosted the evening gala at the Governor's Mansion. Senator McCain was present and recalled it fondly: "The welcome-home party arranged by the Reagans was unbelievable."[2] The future president and First Lady knew how to throw a party. Sybil, of course, was involved in the planning and, as Perot recalled, "Sybil made it all go just right."[3]

On June 3, Perot would host another incredible event. The Texan flew all the POWs and their wives and girlfriends out to Dallas for a VIP party at the Cotton Bowl. Sybil, Jane, and Phyllis attended many of these parties and were thrilled to have their men back home.[4]

Carole Hanson, former chair of the National League, was also invited. Although she was an MIA wife, she was honored at the party for her activism on behalf of the POWs and the MIAs. That date happened to be the anniversary of her MIA Marine husband's shoot-down. The gunner on Steve's helicopter had been able to confirm Steve's death when he returned home. Carole finally knew for sure that he was deceased. Despite being crushed by the news, Carole looked back on those dark years with appreciation for what the Nixon government had done to help the POW/MIA wives and their cause. "If another kind of President, with less resolve to bring our men home, had been in the White House, I think the North Vietnamese would have kept them to bargain with later which would have continued the anguish for the POW/MIA families."[5]

Carole did not want to go to the Perot party, fabulous as it sounded, but her mother encouraged her to attend. At the Cotton Bowl party, she met a returned POW named Jim Hickerson.[6] She remembered that Tony Orlando was there that night, singing his 1973 hit "Tie a Yellow Ribbon Round the Ole Oak Tree." Carole started crying, and Jim kissed her on the cheek. Later he would call it "the most expensive kiss I ever gave!"[7] The former National League chair would marry returned POW Jim Hickerson on December 14, 1974.[8]

But the gala to end all galas occurred on May 24, 1973, at the White House.

On that night, the POWs found themselves in a setting that just months earlier would have seemed unimaginable—as guests of President Richard Nixon and First Lady Pat Nixon at the most lavish dinner in White House history. Under awnings of gold-and-red-striped tents set up on the South Lawn, the POWs were honored at a party that included their wives, girlfriends, and family members. The women wore long gowns of chiffon and embroidered damask, with elaborate hairstyles and long-lashed, doe-eyed makeup.[9]

Kissinger had just gotten back from Paris, where he had been working to negotiate another cease-fire. Though exhausted, he was in a jovial and festive mood. In his thick German accent, Kissinger told Paul Galanti, with a wink, "Your vife, she was *so* much trouble!"[10] Jim and Sybil Stockdale hung out with Bob Hope—in fact, Jim introduced the gala's telecast of the event with Hope while the Dentons danced the night away under the striped awning.

Nixon speechwriter Ken Khachigian, who attended the gala and reported on the event, remembered, "The wives were mobbing Henry and Mel Laird like they were Hollywood celebrities . . . The ladies were all kissing Henry like he was a movie star. Everyone had cigars, champagne was flowing."[11]

The MIA wives had not been invited to the gala that evening. Helene and Kathleen stayed home. As Roger Shields explained, "There were thousands of MIA family members—no way to include them in the gala, which was specifically for the men who had returned."[12]

Though nattily turned out that evening in their dress uniforms, many of the POWs were a shocking sight. Some wore eye patches, others arrived wearing casts for their broken arms and legs. Naval commander and future U.S. senator and Republican presidential nominee John McCain hobbled into the reception on crutches. He would never again be able to comb his own hair or raise his arms above his head, due to the vicious rope torture and beatings he received while imprisoned in the infamous Hanoi Hilton.[13]

Despite these injuries, he was grateful to be home with his integrity intact. Kissinger remembered how McCain had tracked him down that evening for one purpose: "He wanted to thank me for saving his honor" during the war negotiations. McCain would repeat his thanks many years later at Kissinger's ninetieth birthday party.[14]

After the arrival and seating of all the guests, President Nixon gave the welcoming remarks, followed by the POW choir (formed in prison), which sang the "POW Hymn" and recited the Lord's Prayer. Navy captain Charles R. Gillespie gave the Invocation, and the United States Marine drum and bugle corps paraded the colors.[15]

At 8:20 p.m., dinner was served. The White House menu that evening was a POW food fantasy come true. Men who had subsisted on watery soup laced with feces in Hanoi now sipped champagne. The men finally had the all-American meal many had dreamed of while in prison: roast sirloin of beef au jus, tiny new potatoes, and straw-berry mousse for dessert.[16]

Popular performers and movie stars Bob Hope, John Wayne, Sammy Davis Jr., and Phyllis Diller entertained the men and their dates after dinner. Irving Berlin sang "God Bless America" with Pat and Richard Nixon.

When the president lifted his glass for an official toast, he did not salute the prisoners of war; the official White House protocol, as Nixon pointed out, was that toasts should be made to ladies. In an elegant and emotional tribute to the POW wives, mothers, and significant others, the president said, "They were and are the bravest and most magnificent women I have ever met in my life."

Nixon then asked all the men in the room to stand up. He continued:

"As president of the United States, I designate every one of the women here, the wives, the mothers, and others who are guests of our POWs, as First Ladies.

"Gentlemen, to the First Ladies of America—the First Ladies!"[17]

Khachigian, Nixon's speechwriter for the event, had given him twenty pages of notes with different options for toasts and remarks. Instead Nixon decided to prepare the speech on his own. "It virtually all came from his own pen," Khachigian said. "The words came from him."[18]

For wives who were reunited with their husbands, there was the giv-ing up of hard-earned power and influence and adapting to having a husband who had been absent for years back home again. It was a huge adjustment for both halves of each couple.

Jane and Jerry returned to Mobile, their joint hometown, for a ticker tape parade that would be a prelude to Jerry's later Senate career. While Jane felt he had done enough for his country, he wanted to reform an America he felt was in moral peril. He would become a Republican senator for Alabama in 1980, the first Catholic ever elected to state-wide office in that state. Jane would step back comfortably into her domestic role as a wife and mother but would find that her time as a Senate wife intruded upon her family life. When Jerry became an Alabama senator, she once again had to share with the American public the husband she so wanted to protect. Despite this, she jumped into life as a senator's wife with enthusiasm and grace, and became known for her efforts to improve mental health facilities.

Jane died on November 22, 2007, Jerry on March 28, 2014. The Dentons are buried next to each other at Arlington National Cemetery.[19]

Phyllis's anticipatory fears of not being able to adjust psychologically to her husband's return proved to be groundless. An iconic photo of a glowing Phyllis in a powder-blue suit, reunited with her handsome, just-returned POW husband, Paul, made the February 26, 1973, cover of *Newsweek*. She became pregnant with their first child within a year of his homecoming.

The former star negotiator quickly relinquished her position as chair of the National League for this long-awaited role as wife and mother. Phyllis would put her formidable leadership skills on ice while her two sons, Jamie and Jeff, were young. She found being a mother to be one of the most important but hardest jobs ever. When the boys were little, she wrote, "My idea of heaven—morning quiet, coffee, paper."[20] That clearly would not be happening for her for a long time, with little boys running around. But soon enough, she was back at it. She and Paul would become renowned for their activism on behalf of POWs, and both would lend their star power to charitable causes both locally and nationally.[21]

Phyllis would die unexpectedly of leukemia on April 23, 2014. At her memorial service in Richmond on April 29, her good friend Ross Mackenzie, the former editorial page editor of *The Richmond News Leader* and *The Richmond Times-Dispatch*, eulogized her, noting that her principal detestation was "complaining. Phyllis rarely manned her Complaint Department window—usually had it slammed shut. Her email address, for heaven's sake, was 'no whining.'" (I can confirm that: Phyllis's email was nowhining@comcast.net—she was in my mother's book club.)

Everyone at Phyllis's memorial service that day at First Presbyterian Church went out the door repeating what Mackenzie always said about Phyllis: "What a gal!"[22]

Like Jerry and Jane, Phyllis is buried at Arlington Cemetery.

Andrea and Donald would stay in good touch with Phyllis and Paul, going boating with them in Virginia and exchanging Christmas cards for years. Sadly, Donald, known to his family as "the Don," would suffer from PTSD. Andrea desperately wanted to save their marriage but was powerless to do so in the face of his severe symptoms. She recalled years later, "Donald was definitely the victim of PTSD. We kept hearing 'shell-shocked.' That meant nothing to me . . . I NOW know more about the diagnosis and how veterans suffer from the syndrome. In my mind and heart, it was the reason our marriage failed." The woman who had fought so hard on every level to get her husband back from prison now found that her husband was trapped by his own trauma. "The symptoms I saw in him were shocking. He tried so very hard to control what he was going through. Sometimes it only made it worse. He became so apologetic for his actions. He did so much to make up for his actions, but it's as if they would again overtake him. I reflect, and it makes me sad. He was such a decent man, with lots of love in his heart."[23] Donald and Andrea ultimately divorced in 1993, but their children thrived, and Andrea enjoyed a long career in the health care field.[24]

Andrea would fly to Coronado to visit Sybil for a milestone birthday and kept in touch with her West Coast POW/MIA wife friends. Donald died on April 21, 2005, and is buried at Arlington Cemetery.[25] Andrea's motto, gleaned from her years as both a mental health hotline operator and as a POW/MIA wife? "Never a problem, only a situation." If anyone learned to roll with the punches, it was this petite, stylish, determined woman, New York born and bred.[26]

Louise and Jim have remained in Norfolk for all these years. When Jim returned to his six long-haired sons, it was a big adjustment for all. Louise and Jim's close friends got the returned POW through a tough transition period. "My close friends and my wife sheltered me. Louise is the mother blanket . . . In the long run, my personal life has been very successful thanks to Louise." After being in charge of everyone and everything for so long, Louise admitted, "I had been independent and he was so protective. He didn't even want me to drive . . . I was his security." Over time, everyone adjusted to their new roles and relaxed, but it took time, love, and patience on both sides.[27]

Louise and Jim's proudest achievement is clearly their tight-knit family. The couple has seventeen grandchildren—in Louise's words, "scattered to the winds, with professions from Composer to Genetic counseling at MD Anderson [Cancer Center in Houston]! We also have 13 Great Grandchildren."[28]

Bob Boroughs, his wife, Ruth, and his four children (Merriann, Lynn, Bob Jr., and Tom) would remain friends for life with the Navy POW wives and families. They would remain especially close to the Stockdales, visiting them both in California and in Connecticut at Sybil's family summer beach retreat.[29] Bob and Ruth are buried together at Arlington Cemetery, resting not far from Phyllis's grave.

Sybil had perhaps the hardest time of all the wives stepping back into her domestic role. After running a powerful humanitarian organization and then political lobby for many years, it was difficult to go back to normal life. Jim and Sybil both agreed in their memoir, *In Love and War,* "It was going to be hard if not impossible to ever again find the outside challenge, excitement, and fulfillment each of us, in our own spheres, knew in the dark days of war."[30]

Sybil and Jim's strong and enduring marriage never faltered, however. Their book became a classic war memoir and, later, a major television movie, despite opposition from the Department of Defense, which, Sybil recalled, "refused to lend any support for the movie [because] our Chapter 1 does not agree with government policy about our history." That was not about to deter Sybil or Jim from telling their story and the story of the Vietnam War as it really happened.

"History is not a matter of policy, as we all know," Sybil emphasized. "It is a matter of truth."[31] Sybil and her League of Wives remain role models for courageous women who speak truth to power today.

EPILOGUE

"That Other Stockdale Naval Hero(ine)"

United States Naval Academy Chapel, Annapolis, Maryland
November 6, 2015, 10:30 a.m.
A Service Celebrating the Life of Mrs. Sybil Bailey Stockdale

FRIENDS AND FAMILY POURED into the Naval Academy Chapel, in Annapolis, on this warm but gray fall day to remember Sybil. She and Jim had met at the academy fifty years earlier, on a blind date. They could never have imagined when they met how momentous their lives together would be and how many men's and women's lives they would impact. Many of Sybil's POW wife friends attended her service, Dot McDaniel, Patsy Crayton, Marty Halyburton, Louise Mulligan, and Lorraine Shumaker among them. Many of their husbands, former POWs, also attended. Six female midshipwomen, trim and confident in their immaculate white dress suits, carried Sybil's heavy mahogany coffin, festooned with roses, up the church aisle. Sybil would likely have appreciated that touch.

Vice Admiral Walter E. "Ted" Carter and his wife, Lynda, spoke together from the chapel pulpit about the dual experiences the Stockdales had during Vietnam, and about how they were full and equal partners in coding secret messages that allowed them to communicate about the prisoner abuse Jim and his fellow soldiers experienced.

The implicit trust that each of the Stockdales had in each other allowed this risky and dangerous endeavor to succeed.

It should come as no surprise that James Stockdale was awarded the Medal of Honor, the nation's highest award for valor, in 1976.[1] What fewer people learned about was that in 1979 Sybil became the only wife of an active-duty naval officer to receive the Navy Distinguished Public Service Award. Part of the citation reads:

> By her courageous and determined actions, Mrs. Stockdale performed an outstanding public and humanitarian service for captured and missing military members of all services, their families and the American people. Her actions and her indomitable spirit in the face of many adversities contributed immeasurably to the successful safe return of American prisoners, gave hope, support and solace to their families in a time of need and reflected the finest traditions of the Naval service and of the United States of America.[2]

Each of the Stockdales' three living sons, Taylor, Sid, and Jim Jr., spoke movingly about their mother. Each remembered the unique bond they had formed with her. Taylor noted that his mother often talked about wanting to be a princess, about wanting to find her Prince Charming and to live happily ever after. He observed that his mother was indeed reunited with her Prince Charming after many years and many hardships.[3]

Sybil and her POW and MIA wife friends did not have the luxury of being damsels in distress, though. Fate and history made them all into something else, something far more substantial. These by-the-book military wives were transformed by circumstance into international diplomats, hostage negotiators, coders of secret letters, and POW/MIA activists for their husbands and for their country. Sybil, Jane, Phyllis, Louise, Andrea, Helene, and Kathleen did not need knights to save and defend them. In fact, when politicians called them "girls" and patted them on the head, telling them not to "worry," they got angry. Angry and frustrated enough to take their fate and their husbands' fates into their own capable hands. They became dragon slayers, facing the monsters of government indifference, poor diplomacy, and wartime violence—relying primarily on one another and their own inner resolve. "You have got to understand," Sybil would tell Jim after the war, "the POW wives who worked with me were not victims. They were fighters and we were at war with our own government as well as that of the enemy."[4]

These female freedom fighters never got to be princesses. Instead they got to be warrior queens who fought for their husbands' freedom and an accounting of the missing men—and won. As a group, these ladies became a powerful force that saved their families and ultimately changed the role of military wives and the fate of American POWs. These women were a self-created lobby that not only forced their government to listen to them but also convinced the government that their opinion mattered.

If these military wives hadn't rejected the "keep quiet" policy and spoken out, the POWs might have been left to languish in prison long after the last helicopter lifted off the roof of the U.S. embassy in April 1975. More surely would have died in prison from maltreatment and lack of medical care. They demanded the accounting of the MIAs that was built into the Paris Peace Accords. They wanted answers, not platitudes, hard facts even if they were distressing, and accountability for both the prisoners and the missing. Only months after their return home would Jerry, Jim, Paul, and their fellow captives, like John McCain, realize how much credit the POW/MIA wives deserved for the end of the Vietnamese torture campaign and for their safe return to the States. Without the National League and the wives' relentless lobbying of the president, his national security adviser, the Defense Department, the State Department, and Congress, the women's covert work, their savvy media campaign all across the globe, and their own personal sacrifices, the entire prisoner and missing scenario might have been ignored by a largely oblivious American nation and the world.

Jeremiah Denton would credit his wife and her League friends with the noticeable change in POW treatment that came about in 1969. He claimed that without the women's help, certain POWs who were on the brink of death would have most certainly died in captivity. "In my analysis, the wives' campaign was at least partly responsible for the huge change that took place—the change from night to day—in our treatment" in the fall of 1969.[5]

Interviewed in 1986, thirteen years after his return home, Jim Mulligan also felt strongly that his outspoken wife had been instrumental in his rescue. "Louise is even better with politics than I am because she can cut them off at the legs if she has to . . . it's a good thing Louise came along when she did." Mulligan went on to say that the women's efforts "helped get the POWs released sooner than they otherwise would have been."[6]

In 2016, Senator John McCain said much the same thing that Denton had said years before. He claimed that the POW/MIA wives' intervention had made all the difference. "Our treatment changed dramatically. It went from bad—in my case, solitary confinement— to being with twenty-five others . . . It was a decision made by the Politburo. It was not gradual." McCain firmly believes that "some of us may not have been alive had it not been for that change in treatment." He confirmed that "keep quiet" was the wrong call. The wives' instincts had been right all along.[7]

Even the government finally admitted as much. Dick Capen, Melvin Laird's assistant secretary of defense, remembered, "Until 1969, little had been done to defend the rights of these men under the provisions of the Geneva Conventions. The international outrage generated in 1969 saved lives."[8] Sybil had gone public in 1968 on the West Coast, followed soon after by Louise Mulligan on the East Coast. The government backed the women up in 1969 and amplified their voices. But the POW/MIA wives and families and later their National League of Families began the process, putting the word out there, first in the media. They knew better than anyone what to do. Had it not been for the National League and the POW/MIA wives' efforts, the world might never have known about the POW/MIA issue. For the men who could not have survived additional torture, the women were their personal SEAL Team Six.

Some historians claim that the Nixon government used the women for its own ends. However, these women also used the Nixon administration to amplify their views, recruit members for the National League, and support worldwide publicity highlighting the POW and MIA situations. They were not puppets but partners, frequently directing the president and his staff on this issue. The women became POW/MIA experts because of their devoted and fierce connection to their husbands. They had a lot more to lose than any government administrator.

As Sybil explained years later, "Of course we [the League] had authority. It was our business. Otherwise you see when Harriman was saying they had the keep quiet policy going—they took our authority or any authority away from us. And that was not ok. For the government to have the authority, the sole authority—heaven help us—no way."[9] When the League was accused of being controlled by the Nixon administration, 1970–71 League chair Carol North vehemently disagreed: "Sure there's been a calculated campaign . . . but it's *our* calculated campaign."[10]

It was a campaign that Sybil, Jane, Louise, Phyllis, Andrea, Helene, Kathleen, and their League of Wives dared to imagine and implement.

ACKNOWLEDGMENTS

I couldn't believe it when my mother, Anne Hardage, sent me the obituary of her good friend and fellow book club member Phyllis Galanti. Phyllis died unexpectedly on April 23, 2014. This vibrant former POW/MIA advocate and pillar of her Richmond, Virginia, community was suddenly gone. After her death, my friends on staff at the Virginia Historical Society, now the Virginia Museum of History and Culture in Richmond, informed me that they had something they thought I might want to see: Phyllis's papers.

Phyllis's archive led me across the country to the women who ultimately united to form the National League of Families of American Prisoners and Missing in Southeast Asia under the leadership of Sybil Bailey Stockdale, the League's one and only founder. While Phyllis opened the door to the story, Sybil was the shining center of it. I met Sybil only one time before she passed away, but even confined to a wheelchair and ill with Parkinson's, she had tremendous presence. I am eternally grateful to Sybil and Jim Stockdale's sons, Sid, Jim, and Taylor, for allowing me to see and work with their mother's diary before it was open to other scholars at the Hoover Institution, where her papers now reside. Their interviews, trust, and support made a huge difference in the story I was ultimately able to tell. I am especially grateful to Sid and Nan Stockdale for going out of their way to help me with sources, contacts, and photographs.

Sybil's friends and fellow POW/MIA wives shared their memories freely with me while I worked for four years on the project. Many thanks are owed to Patsy Crayton, Jenny Connell Robertson, Debby Burns Henry, Karen Butler, Sandy Dennison, Marie Estocin, Chloe Moore, Sherry Martin, Shirley Stark, and Regina Bidstrup. Thanks also to Carole Hanson Hickerson, Bebe Woolfolk, and Gail Orell.

Phyllis's husband, Paul, and her sons, Jamie and Jeff, could not have been more helpful or supportive of this book. Her best friend Judi Clifford was a treasure trove of information, as were Phyllis and Paul's dear friends Ross and Ginni Mackenzie. I thank them all for working with me.

I wish I could have met Jane Denton, who passed away in 2007. Thanks to my old friend J. E. B. Stuart III for his introduction to Mike Denton, one of Jane's children. Mike introduced me to the entire Denton clan, who graciously allowed me access to Jane's private diaries from the Vietnam era. Madeleine Denton Doak made sure I had copies of all the relevant diaries and documents; Jerry III allowed us to film interviews in his home; thanks also to Mary Denton Lewis, Don Denton, Billy Denton, and finally to Jim Denton, who was such a help to me with sources and contacts before he passed away June 18, 2018. Grateful thanks also to Louise Mulligan, who graciously allowed me to interview her on the phone, in person, and on film; to Dorothy (Dot) McDaniel, her husband, Red, and their son Mike; to Janie Tschudy and her husband, Bill; to Marty and Porter Halyburton; and to Ted and Fifi Sienicki for their interviews.

I was thrilled to connect with the lovely Andrea Rander, whose eloquent perspective enriched the entire story. Her daughter, Page Rander, loaned me amazing family photos for the book. I was also fortunate to locate the children of Bob Boroughs. Thanks to his daughter Lynn Boroughs Amwake, Merriann Boroughs Lynch, Bob Boroughs Jr., and Tom Boroughs for their interviews and for helping me obtain their father's military records. Many thanks also to their dad's former colleague at Naval Intelligence Pat Twinem for speaking with me.

Through my friend and colleague Colorado Springs Pioneers Museum Curator Leah Witherow and CSPM board members Pam Marsh, Darryl Thatcher, and Terry Thatcher, I was introduced to the vivacious Helene Knapp, who became one of the MIA wives I focused on most in the book. Many thanks to Helene for sharing her amazing story. Thanks also to former Springs resident Joan Pollard for her insights, and to Harlan and Alice Ann Ochs of Colorado Springs for their much-appreciated support.

My thanks go out to two Texas MIA wives, Sallie Stratton and Sandy McElhanon, for their poignant interviews; to Ross Perot, who allowed me to interview him about his work on behalf of American POWs and MIAs; and to Perot staffers Libby Craft and Sandra Dotson for their diligent assistance with my research.

Senator Bob Dole was one of the few politicians in Washington who supported the POW/MIA wives in the early days of their fight. It was an honor and a privilege to work with him. Thanks to Marion Watkins for coordinating my interviews with the senator.

I was thrilled to meet and interview Senator John McCain in 2016. Having been such a maverick himself, I feel sure he appreciated the grit and determination of the League of Wives. Thanks to Julie Tarallo in the senator's D.C. office for helping schedule his interview and for helping me with follow-up materials. I was also grateful to have been able to interview Dr. Henry Kissinger for this book. Thanks to Jessee Leporin for facilitating our meeting in New York. Many thanks are also due to Ambassador Richard Capen and Dr. Roger Shields, both members of the Nixon administration who were deeply involved in POW/MIA issues and were so patient and available to me.

Thank you to the fabulous Audrey Coleman-McKanna, and Sarah Gard D'Antonio, and Chloe Moore at the Robert and Elizabeth Dole Archive and Special Collections and the Dole Institute of Politics at the University of Kansas in Lawrence, for all their guidance and help in the archive and for introducing me to MIA wife Kathleen Johnson Frisbie. Similar thanks go to my wonderful friends and former museum colleagues Paige Newman, Graham Dozier, Andy Talkov, and Jamison Davis at the Virginia Museum of History and Culture, and to Paul Levengood at the Virginia War Memorial. Thanks to Danielle Scott-Taylor, Sarah Patton, Linda Bernard, and Diana Sykes at the Hoover Institution Archives at Stanford; Candice Hooper at the Coronado Public Library; Jonathan Movroydis, Jim Byron, Greg Cumming, and Jason Schwartz at the Richard Nixon Foundation and Library, as well as Ken Khachigian; and to Dr. Wendy E. Chmielewski, curator of the Swarthmore College Peace Collection.

I was so lucky to already know historian Marc Leepson, arts editor of the *VVA Veteran* magazine and author of the *Dictionary of Vietnam* and many other books. Marc was my go-to guru whenever I had any questions regarding the Vietnam War. Thanks also to four other outstanding scholars who helped me understand the wives' story within the larger historical and psychological context: Dr. Luke Nichter, Dr. Irwin Gellman, Dr. Frank Ochberg, and Dr. Virgil Dean.

A big shout-out to the talented Luis Blandon, my primary researcher, who always went the extra mile to help me track down hard-to-find sources and people. Many thanks also to researchers Jenny Fichmann, Max Friedman, Ann Trevor, and Chloe Lucchesi-Malone for their excellent work. And thanks also to filmmaker Mark Fastoso for his fine film work and to Tyler Lemon for his helpful audio notes.

I cannot say enough wonderful things about my editor, Michael Flamini, and his editorial assistant, Gwen Hawkes. Michael is warm, witty, and wise, with a great eye for women's stories. Gwen has a young, fresh perspective on American history and was a joy to work with. I was also very fortunate to connect with Will Palmer, Copy Editor Extraordinaire. Thanks to Young Lim for his superb cover design, Donna Noetzel for the interior photo design, and Laura Hanifin for her expert help with obtaining hard-to-find photos and copyrights.

Many thanks go my literary agent, Katherine Flynn, at The Kneerim & Williams Agency, for her superb help and guidance with the book, and to my top-notch film agent, Jason Richman, at United Talent Agency. Thanks also to my writer friends and colleagues Diane Kiesel, Kitty Kelley, Beth Macy, Dean King, Will Swift, and Alvin Townley, as well as supportive friends Judith Williams, Teri Blandon, and Kemper Sublette.

Finally, thanks to my mother, Anne Hardage, who has read every chapter of this book multiple times and who has always encouraged me to write, and to my sister Morgan for always making me laugh and giving sound advice. Kudos to my husband, Chris, for his tech support and for wrangling our two teenagers, Anne Alston and James, and to my mother-in-law, Linda Lee, for helping with the kids when I was out of town working on the book. Anne Alston and James, I hope one day you will discover that you *like* history.

Maybe you will even read this book.

NOTES

Prologue

1 Leslie Hubbard Crawford, *Images of America: Coronado* (Charleston, SC: Arcadia, 2010), 59–70.

2 "A Brief History of the Hotel del Coronado," Hotel del Coronado website, accessed January 15, 2016, https://hoteldel.com/press_type_taxonomy/history.

3 Ibid.

4 Ibid.

5 Sid Stockdale, in conversation with the author, June 17, 2015.

6 Crawford, *Coronado*, 113.

7 Sid Stockdale, in conversation with the author, June 17, 2015.

Chapter One: The Right Wife

1 Tom Wolfe, *The Right Stuff* (New York: Picador, 1979), 13.

2 Dr. Ganesh A and Dr. Catherine Joseph, "Personality Studies in Aircrew: An Overview," *Indian Journal of Aerospace Medicine* 49, no. 1 (2005): 54–62.

3 Anne Briscoe Pye and Nancy Shea, *The Navy Wife* (New York: Harper & Row, 1965), 101.

4 Marian Novak to the author, April 10, 2017.

5 Pye and Shea, *Navy Wife*, 94–95.

6 Ibid., 4.

7 Donna Moreau, *Waiting Wives: The Story of Schilling Manor, Home Front to the Vietnam War* (New York: Atria, 2005), 151.

8 Nancy Shea, *The Air Force Wife* (New York: Harper & Brothers, 1951), 1.

9 Ibid., 6.

10 Jim Stockdale and Sybil Stockdale, *In Love and War: The Story of a Family's Ordeal and Sacrifice During the Vietnam Year* (Annapolis, MD: Naval Institute Press, 1990), 65.

11 Ibid., 65–69; Alvin Townley, *Defiant: The POWs Who Endured Vietnam's Most Infamous Prison, the Women Who Fought for Them, and the One Who Never Returned* (New York: Thomas Dunne, 2014), 8–9; "Admiral James B. Stockdale, USN," American Academy of Achievement, accessed October 26, 2016, www.achievement.org/achiever/admiral -james-b-stockdale.

12 Craig Howes, *Voices of the Vietnam POWs: Witnesses to Their Flight* (New York: Oxford University Press, 1993), 242.

13 Stockdale and Stockdale, *In Love and War,* 37.

14 Sybil Stockdale résumé, collection of Sid Stockdale.

15 Bebe Woolfolk, in conversation with the author, November 27, 2015.

16 Stockdale and Stockdale, *In Love and War,* 41.

17 Bebe Woolfolk, in conversation with the author, November 27, 2015.

18 Stockdale and Stockdale, *In Love and War,* 45.

19 Ibid., 45–46.

20 Ibid., 49–52.

21 Marian Novak to the author, April 10, 2017.

22 Michael J. Allen, *Until the Last Man Comes Home: POWs, MIAs and the Unending Vietnam War* (Chapel Hill: University of North Carolina Press, 2009), 25.

23 Stockdale and Stockdale, *In Love and War,* 53.

24 Jeremy Allen, "SERE School Celebrates 50 Years of Training," United States Navy website, accessed August 5, 2018, www.navy.mil/submit /display.asp?story_id=68336.

25 Rod Powers, "United States Military Code of Conduct: Military Rules for Prisoners of War," The Balance Careers, accessed August 5, 2018, www.thebalancecareers.com/united-states-military-code-of-conduct -3354185.

26 Rachel Starnes, *The War at Home: A Wife's Search for Peace (and Other Missions Impossible)—A Memoir* (New York: Penguin, 2016), 40–41.

27 Stockdale and Stockdale, *In Love and War,* 72–73; Jim Stockdale Jr., email message to author, February 24, 2016.

28 Jim Stockdale Jr., email message to author, December 17, 2016.

29 Ibid.

30 Sid Stockdale, in conversation with the author, June 17, 2015.

31 Jim Stockdale Jr., email message to author, December 17, 2016.

Chapter Two: It Can't Happen to Us . . .

1 "Virginia Beach Drive-In," Drive-Ins.com, accessed March 31, 2017, http://drive-ins.com/theater/vatvirg/virginia-beach-drive-in-virginia-beach-va.

2 Jane Maury Denton diary, July 17–18, 1965, JJDPC.

3 Jeremiah A. Denton Jr. with Ed Brandt, *When Hell Was in Session* (Clover, SC: Commission Press, 1976), 20–21.

4 Jane Maury Denton diary, July 18, 1965, JJDPC.

5 Denton, *When Hell Was in Session,* 10.

6 Bill Tschudy, in conversation with the author, April 11, 2017.

7 Vice Admiral B. J. Semmes Jr., Chief of Naval Personnel, to Jane Denton, telegram, July 23, 1965, Jeremiah Denton CACO (Casualty Assistance Calls Officer) file, collection of Mike Denton.

8 Jane Maury Denton diary, July 23, 1965, JJDPC.

9 Janie Tschudy, in conversation with the author, March 21, 2017.

10 Denton, *When Hell Was in Session,* 21.

11 Jane Maury Denton diary, August 27, 1965, JJDPC.

12 Stockdale and Stockdale, *In Love and War,* 79–84.

13 Ibid., 83.

14 Ibid., 83–87.

15 Katherine Kennedy Clark obituary, September 16, 2005, collection of Doris Beatty.

16 Stuart I. Rochester and Frederick Kiley, *Honor Bound: The History of American Prisoners of War in Southeast Asia* (Washington, DC: Historical Office of the Office of the Secretary of Defense, 1998), 99.

17 "Under Difficult Circumstances: Jeremiah Denton and Military Service During the Cold War. Particularly in Vietnam and During the Era of President Lyndon Johnson," 19, Jeremiah Denton CACO file, collection of Mike Denton.

18 Robert G. Angevine, "Hiding in Plain Sight: The US Navy and Dispersed Operations Under EMCON, 1956–1972," *Naval War College Review* 64, no. 2 (Spring 2011): 80–81.

19 Jane Maury Denton diary, July 29, 1965, JJDPC.

20 Merle Pribbenow, "Treatment of American POWs in North Vietnam," Woodrow Wilson International Center for Scholars, February 14, 2012, www.wilsoncenter.org/publication/treatment-american-pows-north-vietnam.

21 Bill Tschudy, in conversation with the author, April 11, 2017.

22 Jane Denton, written notes, n.d., Jeremiah Denton CACO file, collection of Mike Denton.

23 Rochester and Kiley, *Honor Bound,* appendix 3, 598–618.

24 Ibid., 5.

25 Marc Leepson, in conversation with the author, 2016–2018.

26 "Ngo Dinh Diem," *Encyclopedia of World Biography*, accessed August 2, 2018, www.encyclopedia.com/history/encyclopedias-almanacs-tran scripts-and-maps/ngo-dinh-diem; Geoffrey C. Ward and Ken Burns, *The Vietnam War: An Intimate History* (New York: Knopf, 2017), 79–80.

27 Dr. Luke Nichter, email message to author, October 30, 2017.

28 Larry J. Sabato, *The Kennedy Half-Century* (New York: Bloomsbury, 2013).

29 H. R. McMaster, *Dereliction of Duty: Lyndon Johnson, Robert McNamara, the Joint Chiefs of Staff, and the Lies That Led to Vietnam* (New York: Harper Perennial, 1997), 5.

30 Mark K. Updegrove, *Indomitable Will: LBJ in the Presidency* (New York: Skyhorse, 2012), 190.

31 McMaster, *Dereliction of Duty*, 63; Denton, *When Hell Was in Session*, 23.

32 McMaster, *Dereliction of Duty*, 108.

33 David Halberstam, *The Best and the Brightest* (New York: Random House, 1992), 229.

34 Robert S. McNamara with Brian VanDeMark, *In Retrospect: The Tragedy and Lessons of Vietnam* (New York: Vintage, 1996), 357.

35 Halberstam, *Best and the Brightest*, 247.

36 Janie Tschudy, in conversation with the author, March 21, 2017.

37 Richard Capen, in conversation with the author, March 30, 2017.

38 Ibid.

39 Halberstam, *Best and the Brightest*, 247.

40 Janie Tschudy, in conversation with the author, March 21, 2017.

41 Debby Burns Henry, in conversation with the author, May 2, 2016.

42 David J. Morris, *The Evil Hours: A Biography of Post-Traumatic Stress Disorder* (New York: Houghton Mifflin Harcourt, 2015), 48–49.

43 Stanley Karnow, *Vietnam: A History—The First Complete Account of Vietnam at War* (New York: Penguin, 1984), 366–76; Stockdale and Stockdale, *In Love and War*, 3–36.

44 McMaster, *Dereliction of Duty*, 125.

45 Ibid., 133.

46 Stockdale and Stockdale, *In Love and War*, 36, 499–505.

47 Howes, *Voices of the Vietnam POWs*, 238.

48 Ibid., 101–14; Townley, *Defiant*, 2–3.

49 Townley, *Defiant*, 18–19.

50 Eagles, "Hotel California," composed by Don Felder, Glenn Frey, and Don Henley, on *Hotel California* (Asylum Records, 1976).

Chapter Three: A Great Society for Some, Not for All . . .

1 Associated Press, *The World in 1965: History as We Lived It* (New York: Associated Press, 1965), 9.

2 Lyndon B. Johnson, "The President's Inaugural Address," January 20, 1965, American Presidency Project, accessed August 2, 2018, www.presidency.ucsb.edu/ws/?pid=26985.

3 Betty Friedan, *The Feminine Mystique,* 50th anniv. ed. (New York: W. W. Norton, 2013), 461–62; Gail Collins, *America's Women: 400 Years of Dolls, Drudges, Helpmates, and Heroines* (New York: William Morrow, 1997), 433–34.

4 "Republican Motherhood," in *Women's Studies Encyclopedia,* ed. Helen Tierney (Santa Barbara, CA: Greenwood Press, 2002).

5 Gail Collins, *When Everything Changed: The Amazing Journey of American Women from 1960 to the Present* (New York: Little, Brown, 2009), 5.

6 Karen Taylor, "Cult of True Womanhood," in *Women's Studies Encyclopedia,* ed. Helen Tierney (Santa Barbara, CA: Greenwood Press, 2002).

7 Sybil Stockdale diary, n.d., 18–19, box 11, folder 22, SBSP; Stockdale and Stockdale, *In Love and War,* 118–19.

8 Stockdale and Stockdale, *In Love and War,* 118–20; Sybil Stockdale diary, September 1965, 1–3, box 11, folder 22, SBSP.

9 Stockdale and Stockdale, *In Love and War,* 121.

10 Sid Stockdale, in conversation with the author, June 8, 2015.

11 Evelyn Grubb and Carol Jose, *You Are Not Forgotten* (St. Petersburg, FL: Vandamere Press, 2008), 50–51.

12 "Families of Men Missing in Vietnam Fight Legal Battles," *Washington Post,* August 26, 1966, box 2, SBSP.

13 Photo of Lyndon B. Johnson with Sybil Stockdale, box 5, SBSP.

14 Howes, *Voices of the Vietnam POWs,* 244–45.

15 Dorothy McDaniel, *After the Hero's Welcome: A POW Wife's Story of the Battle Against a New Enemy* (Chicago: Bonus Books, 1991), 41.

16 Sybil Stockdale to Captain James Andrews, September 29, 1966, box 2, SBSP.

17 Grubb and Jose, *You Are Not Forgotten,* 51–52.

18 Janie Tschudy, email message to author, May 2, 2017.

19 Sybil Stockdale diary, n.d., 24–25, box 11, folder 22, SBSP; Sybil Stockdale, "Reflections of a POW Wife" speech, JSSP, 5.

20 Stockdale and Stockdale, *In Love and War,* 125–27; Sybil Stockdale diary, n.d., 1, box 11, folder 22, SBSP.

21 Stockdale and Stockdale, *In Love and War,* 130.

22 Ibid., 132–34; Sybil Stockdale diary, n.d., 2, box 11, folder 22, SBSP.

23 Sybil Stockdale diary, n.d., 2, box 11, folder 22, SBSP.

24 Stockdale and Stockdale, *In Love and War,* 135.

Chapter Four: Wives or Widows?

1 Denton, *When Hell Was in Session,* 96–97.

2 Jeremiah Denton III, in conversation with the author, May 7, 2016; *Jeremiah,* directed by Mark Fastoso (Birmingham: Alabama Public Television, 2015); Townley, *Defiant,* 76–78.

3 James S. Denton, "Editor's Introduction: In Hanoi, Going Forward and Backward," World Affairs Institute, January/February 2014, accessed May 24, 2016, http://worldaffairsjournal.org/article/editor's-intro duction-hanoi-going-forward-and-backward; Townley, *Defiant,* 78.

4 Jeremiah Denton III, in conversation with the author, May 7, 2016.

5 Denton, *When Hell Was in Session,* 89–90.

6 Andre Wiest and Chris McNab, *The Illustrated History of the Vietnam War* (New York: Metro Books, 2015), 33–34.

7 Stockdale and Stockdale, *In Love and War,* 120.

8 Ibid.

9 Steven L. Smith, "The Reluctant Sorority: Stories of American Wives of Prisoners of War and Missing in Action, 1965–1973; Lessons in Exercising Leadership in the Absence of Power" (PhD diss., University of San Diego, April 2006), 82–83; Debby Burns Henry, personal scrapbook.

10 Pye and Shea, *Navy Wife,* 152.

11 Smith, "Reluctant Sorority," 66.

12 Rochester and Kiley, *Honor Bound,* 189.

13 Geneva Conventions description, "Return with Honor," *American Experience,* PBS, aired November 2000, accessed December 7, 2015, www.pbs.org/wgbh/amex/honor/filmmore/ps-geneva.html (webpage discontinued).

14 Dorothy and Red McDaniel, in conversation with the author, January 18, 2018.

15 Stockdale and Stockdale, *In Love and War,* 149–202; Townley, *Defiant;* Howard and Phyllis Rutledge, *In The Presence of Mine Enemies: 1965–1973—A Prisoner of War* (Old Tappan, NJ: Fleming H. Revel, 1973), 24–27, 45–47; Denton, *When Hell Was in Session.*

16 Denton, "Editor's Introduction: In Hanoi."

17 Pat Twinem, in conversation with the author, June 6, 2017.

18 Stockdale and Stockdale, *In Love and War,* 135–37; Sybil Stockdale diary, n.d., 53–56, box 11, folder 22, SBSP.

19 Robert Sams Boroughs Jr., military records, Department of the Navy, Bureau of Naval Personnel, various pages, Boroughs family private collection.

20 Merriann and Bernard Lynch, in conversation with the author, July 20, 2017; Bob Boroughs's military superior's comments, Boroughs military records.

21 Sybil Stockdale diary, n.d., 55, box 11, folder 22, SBSP.

22 Merriann Boroughs Lynch, in conversation with the author, February 8, 2017; Stockdale and Stockdale, *In Love and War,* 137.

23 Pat Twinem, in conversation with the author, June 7, 2017.

24 Ibid.

25 Stockdale and Stockdale, *In Love and War,* 135–37; Sybil Stockdale diary, n.d., 64, box 11, folder 22, SBSP.

26 Stockdale and Stockdale, *In Love and War,* 140–41.

27 Rochester and Kiley, *Honor Bound,* 195.

28 Ibid., 194–200.

29 "Return with Honor," *American Experience.*

30 Interview with Bob Shumaker in *Jeremiah,* directed by Mark Fastoso (Birmingham: Alabama Public Television, 2015).

31 Rochester and Kiley, *Honor Bound,* 198.

32 "Return with Honor," *American Experience.*

33 Rochester and Kiley, *Honor Bound,* 196–97.

34 Ibid., 206.

35 "Return with Honor," *American Experience;* Rochester and Kiley, *Honor Bound,* 206.

36 Rochester and Kiley, *Honor Bound,* 199.

37 Stockdale and Stockdale, *In Love and War,* 72–73; Denton, *When Hell Was in Session,* 28–29.

38 Stockdale and Stockdale, *In Love and War,* 49; Vernon E. Davis, *The Long Road Home: U.S. Prisoner of War Policy and Planning in Southeast Asia* (Washington, DC: Historical Office of the Office of the Secretary of Defense, 2000), 7–11; Senate Committee on Government Operations, *Communist Interrogation, Indoctrination and Exploitation of American Military and Civilian Prisoners* (Washington, DC: United States Government Printing Office, 1957), Senate Report no. 2832, 84th Cong., 1–2, 6–23.

Chapter Five: A Reluctant Sorority

1 Davis, *Long Road Home,* 42–43.

2 "The National League of Families of American Prisoners of War and Missing in Action in Southeast Asia," paper by unidentified author, n.d., 14–15, JSSP.

3 Michael J. Allen, *Until the Last Man Comes Home: POWs, MIAs and the Unending Vietnam War* (Chapel Hill: University of North Carolina Press, 2009), 20.

4 Ibid., 18–19.

5 Sallie Stratton, in conversation with the author, September 7, 2017.

6 Sybil Stockdale, oral history interview with Steven L. Smith, June 16, 2000, 4, in Smith, "Reluctant Sorority."

7 Rochester and Kiley, *Honor Bound*, 202, 206; Davis, *Long Road Home*, 77, 80–84.

8 Davis, *Long Road Home*, 84.

9 Stockdale and Stockdale, *In Love and War*, 140.

10 Sybil Stockdale, "Reflections of a POW Wife" speech, 5–6, JSSP; Stockdale and Stockdale, *In Love and War*, 141.

11 Sybil Stockdale diary, n.d., 60, box 11, folder 22, SBSP.

12 Rudy Abramson, *Spanning the Century: The Life of W. Averell Harriman, 1891–1986* (New York: William Morrow, 1992), 51–52.

13 Lynne Olson, *Citizens of London: The Americans Who Stood with Britain in Its Darkest, Finest Hour* (New York: Random House, 2010), 239–43, 389–90.

14 Abramson, *Spanning the Century*, 603.

15 Olson, *Citizens of London*, 58.

16 Ibid., 54.

17 Stockdale and Stockdale, *In Love and War*, 141.

18 Sybil Stockdale diary, n.d., 61, box 11, folder 22, SBSP.

19 Ibid.; Stockdale and Stockdale, *In Love and War*, 141–43.

20 Sybil Stockdale diary, n.d., 60, box 11, folder 22, SBSP.

21 Sybil Stockdale to POW/MIA wives, August 10, 1966, box 2, SBSP.

22 Ibid.

23 Stockdale and Stockdale, *In Love and War*, 143.

24 Sybil Stockdale to POW/MIA wives, August 10, 1966, box 2, SBSP.

25 Sybil Stockdale, "1968: What Was Changing," 5, box 3, SBSP.

26 James G. Andrews, USN Assistant Chief for Morale Services, to Mrs. Jeremiah Denton, November 7, 1966, Jeremiah Denton CACO file, collection of Mike Denton.

27 Jane Denton to Governor Harriman, n.d., Jeremiah Denton CACO file, collection of Mike Denton.

28 Bruce Henderson, "Dieter Dengler's Great Escape from Laotian POW Camp," HistoryNet, July 12, 2010, www.historynet.com/dieter-denglers -great-escape-from-laotian-pow-camp.htm.

29 Jane Denton to Averell Harriman, n.d., Jeremiah Denton CACO file, collection of Mike Denton.

30 *Stockdale Family Cookbook*, JSSP.

31 Sherry Martin, in conversation with the author, January 30, 2016.

32 Stockdale and Stockdale, *In Love and War*, 51.

33 Sandy Dennison, in conversation with the author, March 9, 2016.

34 Karen Butler, remarks at Sybil Stockdale memorial service, Coronado, CA, November 14, 2015.

35 Sybil Stockdale, oral history interview with Steven L. Smith, June 8, 2000, 4, in Smith, "Reluctant Sorority."

36 Sybil Stockdale, speech notes on "Six Stages of Being a POW Wife," n.d., 1, JSSP.

37 Ibid.

38 "Operation Rolling Thunder," History.com, accessed June 20, 2016, www.history.com/topics/vietnam-war/operation-rolling-thunder; Karnow, *Vietnam: A History,* 415, 454.

39 Stockdale, speech notes on "Six Stages of Being a POW Wife."

40 Sherry Martin, in conversation with the author, January 30, 2016.

41 Jenny Connell Robertson, email message to author, September 26, 2017.

42 Debby Burns Henry, email messages to author, September 22 and 26, 2017.

43 Karen Butler, Debby Burns Henry, Patsy Crayton, Shirley Stark, and Jenny Connell Robertson, oral history interview with Heath Hardage Lee, January 16, 2016, REDASC.

44 Karen Butler, email message to author, September 24, 2017.

45 Stockdale and Stockdale, *In Love and War,* 225–26.

46 Friedan, *Feminine Mystique,* 1.

47 Captain Gordon I. Peterson, USN (Ret.), and David C. Taylor, "A Shield and a Sword: Intelligence Support to Communications with US POWs in Vietnam," *Studies in Intelligence* 60, no. 1 (March 2016). 5, Stockdale and Stockdale, *In Love and War,* 141.

48 Sybil Stockdale diary, n.d., 64, box 11, folder 22, SBSP; Stockdale and Stockdale, *In Love and War,* 141.

49 Sybil Stockdale diary, n.d., 64, box 11, folder 22, SBSP; Jenny Connell Robertson, in conversation with the author, January 16, 2016; Debby Burns Henry, in conversation with the author, January 16, 2016.

50 Janie Tschudy, in conversation with the author, March 21, 2017.

51 Admiral B. J. Semmes to Jane Denton, March 27, 1967, Jeremiah Denton CACO file, collection of Mike Denton.

52 Grubb and Jose, *You Are Not Forgotten,* 71.

Chapter Six: New Girl Village

1 Sheila Weller, "It Happened in 1967," *Vanity Fair,* March 2017, 199.

2 Bhuma Shrivastava and Gerry Smith, "Rolling Stone, Music Chronicle Spanning Rock to Rap, Up for Sale," Bloomberg, September 19, 2017.

3 Joe Hagan, *Sticky Fingers: The Life and Times of Jann Wenner and Rolling Stone Magazine* (New York: Knopf, 2017), 75–76.

4 Weller, "It Happened in 1967," 199–200.

5   Collins, *When Everything Changed,* 170.

6   Ray A. Smith, "The Power Suit Gets an Update," *Wall Street Journal,* September 13, 2017, A13.

7   Everett Alvarez Jr. and Anthony S. Pitch, *Chained Eagle: The Heroic Story of the First American Shot Down over North Vietnam* (Washington, DC: Potomac Books, 2005), 94, 101, 108.

8   McDaniel, *After the Hero's Welcome,* 41.

9   Jane Maury Denton diary, January 8, 1967, JJDPC.

10 Amy Swerdlow, *Women Strike for Peace: Traditional Motherhood and Radical Politics in the 1960s* (Chicago: University of Chicago Press, 1993), 1.

11 Ibid., 2.

12 Ibid., 3, 134.

13 Swerdlow, *Women Strike for Peace,* 134–35; James W. Clinton, *The Loyal Opposition* (Niwot: University Press of Colorado, 1995), 180–81.

14 Swerdlow, *Women Strike for Peace,* 217.

15 Stockdale and Stockdale, *In Love and War,* 204.

16 S. Steven Powell, *Covert Cadre: Inside the Institute for Policy Studies* (Ottawa, IL: Green Hill, 1988), 15–16; Robert Chandler, *Shadow World: Resurgent Russia, the Global New Left, ad Radical Islam* (Washington, D.C. Regnery Publishing, 2008), 190.

17 Jenny Connell Robertson, email message to author, September 19, 2017.

18 Jane Maury Denton diary, February 4–6, 1967, JJDPC.

19 Jeremiah Denton III, unpublished memoir (2017), 135, collection of Jeremiah Denton III; Jeremiah Denton III, in conversation with the author, May 8, 2016.

20 Jeremiah Denton III, unpublished memoir (2017), 119, collection of Jeremiah Denton III.

21 Jane Maury Denton diary, February 4–6, 1967, JJDPC.

22 Sybil Stockdale diary, n.d., 70, box 11, folder 22, SBSP.

23 Ibid., 71; Stockdale and Stockdale, *In Love and War,* 207.

24 Sybil Stockdale diary, n.d., 70–71, box 11, folder 22, SBSP.

25 Stockdale and Stockdale, *In Love and War,* 208; Sybil Stockdale diary, n.d., 71–72, box 11, folder 22, SBSP.

26 Allen, *Until the Last Man,* 25.

27 Ibid.

28 Sybil Stockdale, oral history interview with Steven L. Smith, 2, June 16, 2000, in Smith, "Reluctant Sorority."

29 Jane Maury Denton diary, March 1, 1967, JJDPC.

30 Jenny Connell Robertson, Karen Butler, and Debby Burns Henry, in conversation with the author, January 16, 2016.

31 Patsy Crayton, "Ladies of the National League," interview by Heath

Hardage Lee, *The League of Wives: Vietnam's POW MIA Allies & Advocates* exhibit, January 16, 2016, REDASC; Patsy Crayton, in conversation with the author, February 16, 2018.

32 Allen, *Until the Last Man,* 26–27.

33 Townley, *Defiant,* 31.

34 Ibid., x.

Chapter Seven: The League of Wives

1 Judi Clifford and Paul Galanti, in conversation with the author, May 2016–December 2017.

2 Jane Maury Denton diary, March 4, 1967, JJDPC.

3 Ibid.

4 Ibid.

5 Mrs. James A. Mulligan Jr. to Governor Averell Harriman, Ambassador at Large, Washington, DC, April 8, 1967, record group 59, National Archives at College Park, College Park, MD.

6 Phyllis Eason Galanti to Averell Harriman, April 10, 1967, folder 5, PEGP.

7 Jane Maury Denton diary, April 4, 1967, JJDPC.

8 Ibid.

9 Helene Knapp, "Helene's Memoire from the Years 1946–1978" (unpublished memoir, 1978), 8; Helene Knapp, in conversation with the author, March 15 18, 2015.

10 McDaniel, *After the Hero's Welcome,* 30.

11 Ibid., 39.

12 Ibid., 41–42.

13 Jane Maury Denton diary, July 18, 1967, JJDPC.

14 Dorothy McDaniel, in conversation with the author, January 16, 2018.

15 Ibid.

16 Ibid.

17 Jane Maury Denton diary, July 31, 1967, JJDPC.

18 Stockdale and Stockdale, *In Love and War,* 218; Douglas Martin, "Jack Anderson, Investigative Journalist Who Angered the Powerful, Dies at 83," obituary, *New York Times,* December 18, 2005.

19 Stockdale and Stockdale, *In Love and War,* 218–19; Sybil Stockdale diary, n.d., 80–81, box 11, folder 22, SBSP.

20 Sybil Stockdale diary, n.d., 80–85, box 11, folder 22, SBSP; Stockdale and Stockdale, *In Love and War,* 219–22.

21 Sybil Stockdale to Phyllis Galanti, December 1, 1966, folder 4, PEGP.

22 Phyllis Galanti to other POW wives, August 16, 1967, folder 5, PEGP.

23 Grubb and Jose, *You Are Not Forgotten,* 74.

24 Sybil Stockdale, "Thank you, Mr. Watterson" speech, n.d., JSSP.

25 Stockdale and Stockdale, *In Love and War,* 216.

26 Pat Twinem, in conversation with the author, June 6, 2017.

27 Stockdale and Stockdale, *In Love and War,* 225.

28 Sybil Stockdale diary, n.d., 89, box 11, folder 22, SBSP.

29 Stockdale and Stockdale, *In Love and War,* 225; Sybil Stockdale diary, n.d., 88–89, box 11, folder 22, SBSP.

30 Shirley Stark, email message to author, September 26, 2017.

31 Stockdale, "Thank you, Mr. Watterson" speech.

32 Sybil Stockdale, oral history interview with Steven L. Smith, June 16, 2000, in Smith, "Reluctant Sorority."

Chapter Eight: Incredibly Screwed Up

1 OldTimeCandy.com, accessed November 6, 2017.

2 Sid Stockdale, email message to author, November 4, 2017.

3 Sybil Stockdale diary, n.d., 87, box 11, folder 22, SBSP.

4 Stockdale and Stockdale, *In Love and War,* 226–27; Sybil Stockdale diary, n.d., 86–88, box 11, folder 22, SBSP.

5 *Jeremiah,* directed by Mark Fastoso (Birmingham: Alabama Public Television, 2015).

6 Sybil Stockdale diary, n.d., 90, box 11, folder 22, SBSP.

7 Stockdale and Stockdale, *In Love and War,* 227.

8 Karnow, *Vietnam: A History,* 547.

9 Walter Cronkite, "We Are Mired in a Stalemate," editorial, CBS News, broadcast February 27, 1968, accessed August 3, 2018, www.ushisto ryatlas.com/era9/USHAcom_PS_U09_tet_R2.pdf; Walter Cronkite, *A Reporter's Life* (New York: Knopf, 1996), 258.

10 Cronkite, *Reporter's Life,* 258.

11 William J. Luti, "Did Fake News Lose the Vietnam War?" *Wall Street Journal,* January 20, 2018, A15.

12 John McCain with Mark Salter, *Faith of My Fathers* (New York: Random House, 1999), 192.

13 McCain, *Faith of My Fathers,* 192–94.

14 John S. McCain, "John McCain, Prisoner of War: A First-Person Account," *U.S. News & World Report,* January 28, 2008; McCain, *Faith of My Fathers,* 189–97.

15 McCain, *Faith of My Fathers,* 192.

16 Jane Maury Denton diary, January 31, 1968, JJDPC.

17 Clinton, *Loyal Opposition,* 25.

18 *Hearings on New Mobilization Committee to End the War in Vietnam, part I, before the House Committee on Internal Security,* 91st Cong.

(1970), Committee Exhibit No. 14, 4021, in collection of Max Freid-man.

19 Jane Maury Denton diary, January 31, 1968, JJDPC; Janie Tschudy, in conversation with the author, December 17, 2015.

20 Daniel Berrigan, *Night Flight to Hanoi: War Diary with 11 Poems* (New York: Harper & Row, 1968), x.

21 Ibid., xv.

22 Ibid., x.

23 Stockdale and Stockdale, *In Love and War,* 295.

24 Clinton, *Loyal Opposition*, 59–60.

25 Bob Boroughs to Sybil Stockdale, February 12, 1968, box 3, SBSP.

26 McDaniel, *After the Hero's Welcome*, 48.

27 Janie Tschudy, in conversation with the author, December 17, 2015; Judi Clifford, email message to author, November 18, 2017.

28 Sybil Stockdale diary, n.d., 73, box 11, folder 22, SBSP.

29 Jim Stockdale II, "My Father, the Spy in the Hanoi Hilton," *Daily Beast,* April 27, 2015, accessed November 15, 2017, www.thedailybeast.com/my-father-the-spy-in-the-hanoi-hilton.

30 Sybil Stockdale diary, n.d., 64, box 11, folder 22, SBSP.

31 "The National League of Families of American Prisoners of War and Missing in Southeast Asia," paper by unidentified author, n.d., 22, JSSP.

32 Stockdale, "My Father, the Spy."

33 Sybil Stockdale, oral history interview with Steven L. Smith, June 16, 2000, in Smith, "Reluctant Sorority."

34 Louise Mulligan, oral history interview with Heath Hardage Lee, December 10, 2016, REDASC; McDaniel, *After the Hero's Welcome,* 48.

Chapter Nine: You Say You Want a Revolution?

1 Danny Miller, "Eartha Kitt, CIA Target," *HuffPost,* December 27, 2008 (quoting *New York Times*), accessed January 27, 2018, www.huffingtonpost.com/danny-miller/eartha-kitt-cia-target_b_153684.html; Editors of Life, *Life 1968: The Year That Changed the World* (New York: Life Books, 2018), 54.

2 Davis, *Long Road Home,* 161.

3 Amanda Foreman, "Remembering the Pueblo: Hostages as Propaganda Tools," *Wall Street Journal,* January 23, 2018.

4 Davis, *Long Road Home,* 160.

5 Edwin H. Brandt, "The Moving Finger Rites," *Esquire,* December 1969, 253.

6 Sybil Stockdale diary, n.d., 98, box 11, folder 22, SBSP.

7 Patrick J. Buchanan, "With Nixon in '68: The Year America Came Apart," *Wall Street Journal,* April 7–8, 2018.

8 Karnow, *Vietnam: A History,* 510.

9 Mark K. Updegrove, *Indomitable Will: LBJ in the Presidency* (New York: Skyhorse, 2012), 248.

10 Stockdale and Stockdale, *In Love and War,* 299.

11 Andrea Rander, in conversation with the author, June 29, 2018.

12 Andrea Rander, in conversation with the author, May 7 and June 29, 2018; Sybil Stockdale to Louise Mulligan ("Dear Wives and Families of the MIA and POW, En Route to California"), October 11, 1969, collection of Louise Mulligan.

13 Sybil Stockdale, "1968: What Was Changing," 5, box 3, SBSP.

14 Bob Boroughs to Sybil Stockdale, April 12, 1968, box 3, SBSP.

15 Niall Ferguson, *Kissinger, 1923–1968: The Idealist* (New York: Penguin Press, 2015), 813–815.

16 Sylvia Poggioli, "Marking the French Social Revolution of '68," *Morning Edition,* NPR, May 13, 2008.

17 Ferguson, *Kissinger,* 814.

18 Ibid.; Abramson, *Spanning the Century,* 644, 661.

19 Abramson, *Spanning the Century,* 660.

20 Ibid., 660–61.

21 Jonathan Coleman, "Harold Wilson, Lyndon Johnson and the Vietnam War, 1964–68," American Studies Today Online, December 7, 2004, accessed December 11, 2017, www.americansc.org.uk/Online/Wilsonjohnson.htm.

22 Stockdale and Stockdale, *In Love and War,* 295.

23 Sybil Stockdale diary, n.d., 5, box 11, folder 22, SBSP.

24 Allen, *Until the Last Man,* 28.

25 Sybil Stockdale diary, n.d., 5, box 11, folder 22, SBSP.

26 Debby Burns Henry and Jenny Connell Robertson, in conversation with the author, January 16, 2016.

27 Andrea Rander, in conversation with the author, May 7, 2018.

28 Stockdale and Stockdale, *In Love and War,* 297.

29 Davis, *Long Road Home,* 5–11.

30 Senate Report 2832, "Communist Interrogation, Indoctrination and Exploitation of American Military and Civilian Prisoners," 84th Cong., December 31, 1956, in collection of Max Friedman, 3.

31 Ibid., 2.

32 Ibid., 21.

33 Sybil Stockdale diary, n.d., 5, box 11, folder 22, SBSP.

34 Louise Mulligan, email message to author, November 2017; McDaniel, *After the Hero's Welcome,* 52.

35 Stockdale and Stockdale, *In Love and War,* 299–300.

36 Sybil Stockdale, "1968: What Was Changing," 5, box 3, SBSP.

37 Sybil Stockdale diary, n.d., 101–102, box 11, folder 22, SBSP.

38 "Navy Wife Keeps Vigil for Captive Pilot," *San Diego Union-Tribune,* October 27, 1968, box 5, folder 10, SBSP.

39 Sybil Stockdale, "1968: What Was Changing," 5, box 3, SBSP.

40 Stockdale and Stockdale, *In Love and War,* 303, 305; Sybil Stockdale diary, n.d., 103, box 11, folder 22, SBSP.

41 "An Appeal to the World: POW Wives Break Silence," *San Diego Union-Tribune,* June 4, 1969, collection of Debby Burns Henry.

42 McDaniel, *After The Hero's Welcome,* 53.

43 Denis Collins, "The Deprogramming of a POW," *Washington Post,* August 31, 1981.

44 Louise Mulligan, oral history interview with Heath Hardage Lee, December 10, 2016, REDASC.

Chapter Ten: "Nixon's the One!"

1 Jason L. Riley, "Martin Luther King: 'We Can't Keep Blaming the White Man,'" *Wall Street Journal,* April 4, 2018, A-15.

2 Andrea Rander, in conversation with the author, May 7, 2018.

3 Dr. Frank Ochberg, "There Is Reason in Action," in *Mapping Trauma and Its Wake: Autobiographical Essays by Pioneer Trauma Scholars,* ed. Charles R. Figley (New York: Routledge, 2006), 135; Dr. Frank Ochberg, in conversation with the author, February 28, 2017.

4 Dr. Luke Nichter, in conversation with the author, April 25, 2018.

5 John A. Farrell, *Richard Nixon: The Life* (New York: Doubleday, 2017), 4.

6 Will Swift, *Pat and Dick: The Nixons, an Intimate Portrait of a Marriage* (New York: Simon & Schuster, 2014), 26.

7 Ibid., 12.

8 Farrell, *Richard Nixon,* 1–8; Evan Thomas, *Being Nixon: A Man Divided* (New York: Random House, 2015), 7–14.

9 Richard Nixon, *The Memoirs of Richard Nixon* (New York: Grosset & Dunlap, 1978), 27.

10 Thomas, *Being Nixon,* 28–29.

11 Farrell, *Richard Nixon,* 7.

12 "Selections from the Collection, April 17 to June 7, 2015," Nixon Library and Museum, accessed January 9, 2018, www.nixonlibrary.gov /themuseum/exhibits/2015/specialexhibits_Slections.php.

13 Dr. Irwin Gellman, in conversation with the author, October 17, 2017.

14 Nixon, *The Memoirs,* 30.

15 "Nixon, Richard Milhous," Biographical Directory of the United States Congress online, accessed April 26, 2018, http://bioguide.congress.gov /scripts/biodisplay.pl?index=N000116.

16 Farrell, *Richard Nixon,* 293.

17 Nixon, *The Memoirs,* 224.

18 Ibid., 228.

19 Ibid., 252–55.

20 William Safire, "The Way We Live Now: 5-21-00: On Language; Secret Plan," *New York Times,* May 21, 2000.

21 Nixon, *The Memoirs,* 258.

22 Dr. Luke Nichter, in conversation with the author, April 25, 2018.

23 Thomas, *Being Nixon,* 174.

24 Ibid.

25 Dr. Luke Nichter, in conversation with the author, April 25, 2018.

26 Sybil Stockdale diary, n.d., 103, box 11, folder 22, SBSP.

27 Ibid.

28 Sybil Stockdale diary, n.d., 104, box 11, folder 22, SBSP.

29 Andrea Rander, in conversation with the author, May 7, 2018.

30 Sybil Stockdale, oral history interview with Steven L. Smith, June 8, 2000, 4, in Smith, "Reluctant Sorority"; Sybil Stockdale diary, n.d., 104, box 11, folder 22, SBSP.

31 Richard Nixon, Roger Shields, and Henry Cabot Lodge to Phyllis Eason Galanti, telegrams, January 30, 28, and 29, 1969, folder 7, PEGP.

Chapter Eleven: Go Public

1 Stockdale and Stockdale, *In Love and War,* 306.

2 Sybil Stockdale diary, n.d., 110, box 11, folder 22, SBSP.

3 Frank Sieverts to Brigadier General Leo Benade, February 6, 1969, folder 7, PEGP.

4 Dale Van Atta, *With Honor: Melvin Laird in War, Peace and Politics* (Madison: University of Wisconsin Press, 2008), 207.

5 Richard Capen, untitled autobiography, n.d., collection of Richard Capen.

6 Sybil Stockdale, oral history interview with Steven L. Smith, June 8, 2000, 3, in Smith, "Reluctant Sorority"; Stockdale and Stockdale, *In Love and War,* 307.

7 Stockdale and Stockdale, *In Love and War,* 306–7.

8 Sybil Stockdale diary, n.d., 111, box 11, folder 22, SBSP.

9 Ibid.; Karen Butler, in conversation with the author, January 27, 2017.

10 Richard Capen, in conversation with the author, January 18, 2016.

11 Van Atta, *With Honor,* 207.

12 Ibid.

13 Sybil Stockdale diary, n.d., 113, box 11, folder 22, SBSP.

14 Stockdale and Stockdale, *In Love and War,* 308.

15 Sybil Stockdale diary, n.d., 114, box 11, folder 22, SBSP; Stockdale and Stockdale, *In Love and War,* 308.

16 Van Atta, *With Honor,* 208.

17 Stockdale and Stockdale, *In Love and War,* 308; Sybil Stockdale diary, n.d., 114, box 11, folder 22, SBSP.

18 *Look* covers: John Lennon and Yoko Ono, March 18, 1969; Smothers Brothers, May 27, 1969; Mia Farrow, August 26, 1969.

19 Sybil Stockdale diary, n.d., 115–16, box 11, folder 22, SBSP.

20 Karen Butler to Sybil Stockdale, July 1, 1969, collection of Karen Butler.

21 Sybil Stockdale diary, n.d., 116, box 11, folder 22, SBSP.

22 Sybil Stockdale diary, n.d., 117–23, box 11, folder 22, SBSP; McDaniel, *After the Hero's Welcome,* 63; folders 4–7, PEGP.

23 Judy Klemesrud, "Navy Wives Who Find Comfort in Sharing a Common Bond," *New York Times,* August 25, 1970, collection of Louise Mulligan.

24 Jack Kestner, "POW Mail Less After Bomb Halt," *Ledger-Star* (Norfolk, VA), June 9, 1969, B1, collection of Sean Mulligan.

25 Louise Mulligan to Phyllis Galanti, August 18, 1969, folder 7, PEGP.

26 Rochester and Kiley, *Honor Bound,* 347.

27 Ward and Burns, *Vietnam War,* 423.

28 Ibid.

29 Rochester and Kiley, *Honor Bound,* 373–75.

30 Powell, *Covert Cadre,* 39; "A Chosen Few Tread a Productive Path," *Virginian-Pilot* (Norfolk, VA), June 16, 1970, B7, collection of Max Friedman. Multiple attempts were made to interview Cora Weiss; she refused all requests.

31 "Woman Here Uses Peace Group's Aid," article from unidentified Richmond, VA, newspaper, February 12, 1971, collection of Max Friedman.

32 Cindy Parmenter, "Wives of Missing Military Keep [text missing]," *Denver Post,* September 28, 1969, collection of Helene Knapp.

33 Joan Pollard, in conversation with the author, April 24, 2018.

34 Sybil Stockdale to government officials, n.d., SBSP; Stockdale and Stockdale, *In Love and War,* 318.

35 Rochester and Kiley, *Honor Bound,* 173–76; Ward and Burns, *Vietnam War,* 408–9; Gerald F. Goodwin, "Black and White in Vietnam," *New York Times,* July 18, 2017.

36 Sybil Stockdale diary, n.d., 125, box 11, folder 22, SBSP.

37 Andrea Rander, in conversation with the author, May 7, 2018.

38 Unidentified newspaper article, n.d., collection of Louise Mulligan.

39 Andrea Rander, in conversation with the author, June 29, 2018.

40 Sybil Stockdale diary, n.d., 130, box 11, folder 22, SBSP.

41 Ibid.; Stockdale and Stockdale, *In Love and War,* 322.

42 Andrea Rander, in conversation with the author, June 29, 2018.

43 Sybil Stockdale to Louise Mulligan ("Dear Wives and Families of the MIA and POW, En Route to California"), October 11, 1969, 2, collection of Louise Mulligan.

44 Unidentified newspaper article, n.d., collection of Louise Mulligan.

45 Stockdale and Stockdale, *In Love and War,* 320–23; Sybil Stockdale diary, n.d., 128–31, box 11, folder 22, SBSP.

46 Andrea Rander, in conversation with the author, June 29, 2018.

47 Thomas, *Being Nixon,* 237.

48 Van Atta, *With Honor,* 182–84.

49 Thomas, *Being Nixon,* 240.

50 Ibid., 242.

51 Van Atta, *With Honor,* 230.

52 Sybil Stockdale diary, n.d., 135, box 11, folder 22, SBSP.

53 Joan Pollard, in conversation with the author, April 24, 2018; Gene Birkhead, "90 Words from POW-Husband: Woman Receives Letter," *Colorado Springs Sun,* November 14, 1970, collection of Helene Knapp.

54 Van Atta, *With Honor,* 211.

55 Dr. Luke Nichter, in conversation with the author, April 25, 2018.

56 Sybil Stockdale diary, n.d., 138, box 11, folder 22, SBSP.

57 Richard M. Nixon, "Remarks of the President Following a Meeting with Wives and Mothers of Prisoners of War and of Servicemen Missing in Action," December 12, 1969, SBSP.

58 Stockdale and Stockdale, *In Love and War,* 366.

Chapter Twelve: Don't Mess with Texas

1 "Perot to Fly to Moscow in Attempt to Aid POWs," *Richmond Times-Dispatch,* December 28, 1969, folder 113, PEGP.

2 H. Bruce Franklin, *M.I.A., or Mythmaking in America* (Brooklyn, NY: Lawrence Hill Books, 1992), 50.

3 Van Atta, *With Honor,* 208.

4 "Perot to Fly to Moscow."

5 Sybil Stockdale, oral history interview with Steven L. Smith, June 8, 2000, in Smith, "Reluctant Sorority."

6 Sallie Stratton, email messages to author, May 2, 2018.

7 Franklin, *M.I.A.,* 50.

8 "Perot to Fly to Moscow."

9 Estimate from archivist for Braniff Airlines, March 25, 2018.

10 "The Perot Mission" (January–April 1970), disc 4 of *United We Stand* DVD series, produced by Braniff et al., H. Ross Perot private collection.

11 Ibid.; Braniff Flying Colors (@braniffflyingcolors), "Braniff History Today," Facebook, December 22, 2017, www.facebook.com/braniffflyingcolors/posts/braniff-history-today-on-this/1444737182262249.

"The 'second aircraft' dubbed 'Goodwill Toward Men' never actually existed as far as I can tell. Newspaper articles imply there was a second A/C 'assigned and waiting' but I have never been able to confirm. In fact, more than one person involved has told me that Braniff had yet to assign a second aircraft or charter number as they were waiting for word from abroad and it became clear fairly quickly they were not going to Hanoi! So Perot did not want to needlessly spend the money on a second charter aircraft. I do still wonder about all of this and have not yet ruled out the possibility that an aircraft was at least assigned."

12 Fred Powledchs, "H. Perot Pays His Dues," *New York Times,* February 28, 1971.
13 Libby Craft, Perot historian, email message to author, March 26, 2018.
14 "The Perot Mission," *United We Stand*, disc 4, H. Ross Perot private collection.
15 Grubb and Jose, *You Are Not Forgotten*, 114–15.
16 Richard Capen, email message to author, March 1, 2018.
17 Kathleen Johnson Frisbie, in conversation with the author, October 3, 2017.
18 Bruce Johnson, in conversation with the author, April 5, 2018.
19 Goodwin, "Black and White in Vietnam."
20 Marc Leepson, in conversation with the author, June 15, 2018.
21 Lawrence M. Baskir and William A. Strauss, *Chance and Circumstance: The Draft, the War, and the Vietnam Generation* (New York: Knopf, 1978), 49.
22 Mark Leepson, ed., *Webster's New World Dictionary of the Vietnam War* (New York: Macmillan, 1999), s.v. "African-American," 5.
23 "About the Agency," Selective Service System, accessed August 4, 2018, www.sss.gov/About/History-And-Records/Induction-Statistics.
24 Sarena F. Goodman and Adam M. Isen, "Un-Fortunate Sons: Effects of the Vietnam Draft Lottery on the Next Generation's Labor Market," Finance and Economics Discussion Series 2015-119 (Washington, DC: Board of Governors of the Federal Reserve System, 2015), accessed August 4, 2018, www.federalreserve.gov/econresdata/feds/2015/files/2015119pap.pdf.
25 Moreau, *Waiting Wives*, 151.
26 Kathleen Johnson Frisbie, in conversation with the author, October 3, 2017.
27 Kathleen Johnson Frisbie, in conversation with the author, March 18, 2018.
28 Bruce Johnson, in conversation with the author, April 5, 2018.
29 "Braniff Was Beautiful," 2, in "The B1 B-liner" (January–April 1970), disc 1 of *United We Stand* DVD series, produced by Braniff et al.,

collection of H. Ross Perot; Kathleen Johnson Frisbie, in conversation with the author, March 18, 2018.

30 Kathleen Johnson Frisbie, in conversation with the author, March 18, 2018.

31 Kathleen Johnson Frisbie, in conversation with the author, October 3, 2017.

32 Andrea Rander, in conversation with the author, June 29, 2018.

33 Bruce Johnson, in conversation with the author, April 5, 2018.

34 James Bond Stockdale, *Thoughts of a Philosophical Fighter Pilot* (Stanford, CA: Hoover Institution Press, 2000), 28.

35 Sybil Stockdale diary, n.d., 132, box 11, folder 22, SBSP.

36 Nancy Zaroulis, *Who Spoke Up? American Protest Against the War in Vietnam, 1963–1975* (New York: Henry Holt, 1985), 337.

37 "POW Wives Reply to Von Hoffman," letter to the editor, from Barbara P. Ondrasik, *Washington Post*, May 19, 1970, Cora Weiss Papers (DG 222), SCPC.

38 Clinton, *Loyal Opposition*, 170.

39 Ted Sienicki, in conversation with the author, December 18, 2015.

40 Sybil Stockdale diary, n.d., 133, box 11, folder 22, SBSP.

41 "Greetings from the Committee of Liaison," statement of Ethel Taylor to the Pennsylvania National League of Families, n.d., Cora Weiss Papers (DG 222), SCPC.

42 Clinton, *Loyal Opposition*, 15.

43 Ibid., 167.

44 "Reaction Mixed on Prisoner List," *Evening Tribune* (San Diego), November 27, 1969, box 4, SBSP.

45 Louise Mulligan to Ethel Taylor, November 23, 1969, Cora Weiss Papers (DG 222), SCPC.

46 Sybil Stockdale diary, n.d., 133, box 11, folder 22, SBSP.

47 *Hearings on Restraints to Travel in Hostile Areas, H.R. 1594 (Clean Bill H.R. 8023), H.R. 278, H.R. 297, H.R. 2691, H.R. 3999, H.R. 6047, before the Committee on Internal Security*, 93rd Cong., May 9–10, 1973, 3–4, collection of Max Friedman.

48 Ted Sienicki, email message to author, February 16, 2018.

49 Grubb and Jose, *You Are Not Forgotten*, 117.

50 Sybil Stockdale diary, n.d., 141, box 11, folder 22, SBSP.

51 James T. Yenckel, "335-Name List of POWs Regarded as Incomplete," *Washington Post*, June 27, 1970, collection of Max Friedman.

52 Marie Estocin, email message to author, February 21, 2018; Marie Estocin, in conversation with the author, February 22, 2018.

53 Grubb and Jose, *You Are Not Forgotten*, 117.

54 Ibid., 134.

55 Various references to COLIAFAM in collection of Louise Mulligan; SBSP; PEGP; JJDPC.

56 *Hearings on Restraints to Travel in Hostile Areas, H.R. 1594 (Clean Bill H.R. 8023), H.R. 278, H.R. 297, H.R. 2691, H.R. 3999, H.R. 6047, before the Committee on Internal Security*, 93rd Cong., May 9–10, 1973, 3–4, collection of Max Friedman.

Chapter Thirteen: May Day Debut

1 Shirley Chisholm, *Unbought and Unbossed* (Boston: Houghton Mifflin, 1970), 20.

2 *1969 Time Annual: The Year in Review* (New York: Time-Life Books, 1969), 41.

3 Louise Mulligan oral history interview with Heath Hardage Lee (re-creation of May Day 1970 speech), December 10, 2016, REDASC.

4 Andrea Rander, in conversation with the author, June 29, 2018.

5 Bob Dole, *One Soldier's Story: A Memoir* (New York: Harper, 2005), 41.

6 "Early Life," CNN All Politics, accessed March 5, 2018, www.cnn .com/ALLPOLITICS/1996/candidates/republican/dole/early.life /index.shtml.

7 Dole, *One Soldier's Story*, 73, 146–58, 254, 259–64.

8 "'Close-Up' Interview of Bob Dole on the Nixon Presidency and Vietnam," May 10, 1970, item 72, REDASC.

9 Senator Bob Dole, in conversation with the author, October 13, 2016.

10 Charles A. Moser, press release for Freedom Rally, Washington, DC, February 21, 1970, collection of Louise Mulligan.

11 Louise Mulligan, speech at Freedom Rally, Washington, DC, February 21, 1970, 2, collection of Louise Mulligan.

12 Clara Bingham, *Witness to the Revolution: Radicals, Resisters, Vets, Hippies, and the Year America Lost Its Mind and Found Its Soul* (New York: Random House, 2016), 185–87, 198–99.

13 Press release from the office of Senator Robert Dole, April 19, 1970, REDASC.

14 "'Close-Up' Interview of Bob Dole."

15 Appeal for International Justice for American POWs and MIAs in Southeast Asia, event program, 1970, REDASC.

16 Sybil Stockdale diary, n.d., 150, box 11, folder 22, SBSP.

17 Press release from the office of Senator Robert Dole, March 20, 1970, 30, collection of Louise Mulligan.

18 Allen, *Until the Last Man*, 38.

19 Sybil Stockdale diary, n.d., 151, box 11, folder 22, SBSP.

20 Sandy McElhanon, in conversation with the author, March 10, 2018; "Olin E. Teague; Texan in House Over 3 Decades," *New York Times,* January 24, 1981.

21 Senator Bob Dole, in conversation with the author, October 13, 2016.

22 Susan Stamberg, "Denied a Stage, She Sang for a Nation," *Morning Edition,* NPR, April 9, 2014, accessed March 12, 2018, www.npr.org/2014/04/09/298760473/denied-a-stage-she-sang-for-a-nation.

23 Tom Boroughs, in conversation with the author, December 4, 2016.

24 Remarks of Honorable Bob Dole, "Appeal for International Justice," Constitution Hall, Washington, DC, May 1, 1970, 1, REDASC.

25 Ibid., 2.

26 Sybil Stockdale, address to Appeal for International Justice, Constitution Hall, Washington, DC, May 1, 1970, 2–3, REDASC.

27 Ibid., 3.

28 Kathleen Johnson Frisbie, in conversation with the author, March 21, 2018; Moreau, *Waiting Wives,* 196–203.

29 Louise Mulligan, address to Appeal for International Justice, Constitution Hall, Washington, DC, May 1, 1970, collection of Louise Mulligan.

30 Sybil Stockdale diary, n.d., 151, box 11, folder 22, SBSP; Stockdale and Stockdale, *In Love and War,* 374.

31 Stockdale and Stockdale, *In Love and War,* 374.

32 National League of Families newsletter, August 1970, collection of Madeleine Denton Doak.

33 "'Close-Up' Interview of Bob Dole."

34 Ross and Ginni Mackenzie, in conversation with the author, September 10, 2016.

35 Phyllis Galanti to Ross Mackenzie, November 12, 1970, collection of Ross Mackenzie.

36 Ross Mackenzie retirement scrapbook, December 11, 2006, collection of Ross Mackenzie.

37 Ross and Ginni Mackenzie, in conversation with the author, September 10, 2016; Ross Mackenzie, letter to author, June 10, 2018; Ross Mackenzie, email messages to author, June 11 and 14, 2018; "1971 Mrs. Paul Galanti, Wife of Prisoner of War, Pleads for Prisoner Release," YouTube, video, 1:33, from a news report broadcast by WSLS TV on February 9, 1971, uploaded by nutty.archives, September 27, 2016, accessed June 16, 2018, www.youtube.com/watch?v=id6h-ikbQA.

38 Allen, *Until the Last Man,* 57–58.

39 McDaniel, *After the Hero's Welcome,* 72.

40 Allen, *Until the Last Man,* 58.

41 Ibid.

42 Franklin, *M.I.A.*, 57.

43 Phyllis Galanti, VIVA scrapbook, PPGPC; Grubb and Jose, *You Are Not Forgotten*, 190–91.

44 Carol Bates Brown, "History of the POW/MIA Bracelet," The Wall USA, accessed March 15, 2018, http://thewall-usa.com/bracelet.asp.

45 Porter and Marty Halyburton POW bracelet chandelier, on loan to *League of Wives* exhibit; Marty and Porter Halyburton, in conversation with the author, May 7, 2015.

46 Dr. Henry Kissinger, in conversation with the author, October 15, 2015.

47 Sybil Stockdale diary, n.d., 150, box 11, folder 22, SBSP.

48 Jack Kestner, "POW Wife Couldn't Remain Silent," *Ledger-Star* (Norfolk, VA), August 14, 1970, collection of Louise Mulligan.

Chapter Fourteen: Here Comes Your Nineteenth Nervous Breakdown

1 "Wives of Missing Men in SEA Open Office Here, Set Objectives," *Commander's Digest* 8, no. 15 (July 11, 1970): 1, 5–7, Jeremiah Denton CACO file, collection of Mike Denton.

2 Franklin, *M.I.A.*, 53.

3 Dr. Henry Kissinger, in conversation with the author, October 15, 2015.

4 "National League of Families Summary: Articles of Incorporation and By-Laws," 1–2, REDASC.

5 McDaniel, *After the Hero's Welcome*, 73.

6 Sybil Stockdale diary, n.d., 153–54, box 11, folder 22, SBSP.

7 List of regions served by National League of Families, n.d., box 4, SBSP; National League of Families materials, July 6, 1972, collection of Sallie Stratton.

8 Sybil Stockdale diary, n.d., 155, box 11, folder 22, SBSP.

9 Ibid.

10 Sybil Stockdale, oral history interview with Steven L. Smith, June 17, 2000, 4, in Smith, "Reluctant Sorority."

11 James R. McGovern, *Black Eagle* (Tuscaloosa: University of Alabama Press, 1985), by 125–36.

12 Ralph Novak, "General 'Chappie' James Is the Boss of America's 'Defense Business' and Its Four-Star Salesman," *People*, July 18, 1977.

13 McGovern, *Black Eagle*, 125.

14 Sybil Stockdale, oral history interview with Steven L. Smith, June 8, 2000, 2, in Smith, "Reluctant Sorority."

15 Sallie Stratton, in conversation with the author, September 7, 2017.

16 McGovern, *Black Eagle*, 137; interview with MIA wife who wishes to remain anonymous.

17 Franklin, *M.I.A.*, 54.

18 "Write Hanoi Group Gets 100,000 Letters May Extend Drive," "Bring Paul Home" scrapbook, PEGP; McDaniel, *After the Hero's Welcome,* 72.

19 "Holland, Jerome Heartwell (1916–1985)," BlackPast.org, accessed February 10, 2017, http://www.blackpast.org/aah/holland-jerome-heartwell -1916-1985; Joan Cook, "Jerome Holland, Former U.S. Envoy," obituary, *New York Times,* January 14, 1985.

20 Senator Robert Dole to Olof Palme, telegram, June 5, 1970, folder 11, Section 1, PEGP.

21 Sybil Stockdale diary, n.d., 156, box 11, folder 22, SBSP.

22 Phyllis Galanti to Senator Robert Dole, June 18, 1970, REDASC.

23 *Richmond News Leader* article, n.d. (June 1970?), collection of Judi Clifford.

24 Judi Clifford, in conversation with the author, September 19–20, 2016.

25 McDaniel, *After the Hero's Welcome,* 71.

26 Jane Maury Denton diary, September 17, 1970, JJDPC.

27 Ibid., October 26, 1970.

28 Vice Admiral Charles K. Duncan, Chief of Naval Personnel, to POW wives, April 6, 1970, Jeremiah Denton CACO file, collection of Mike Denton.

29 *Jeremiah,* directed by Mark Fastoso (Birmingham: Alabama Public Television, 2015).

30 Admiral E. R. Zumwalt Jr., Chief of Naval Operations, to Jane Denton, October 12, 1970, Jeremiah Denton CACO file, collection of Mike Denton.

31 Jane Maury Denton diary, October 7 and 13, 1970, JJDPC.

32 Ibid., October 22, 1970.

33 Sybil Stockdale diary, n.d., 157, box 11, folder 22, SBSP.

34 Patsy Crayton, in conversation with the author, July 22, 2016.

35 Sybil Stockdale diary, n.d., 157, box 11, folder 22, SBSP.

36 Patsy Crayton, in conversation with the author, July 22, 2016.

37 Sybil Stockdale diary, n.d., 172–73, box 11, folder 22, SBSP; Stockdale and Stockdale, *In Love and War,* 386.

38 Patsy Crayton, in conversation with the author, July 22, 2016; unidentified *Colorado Springs Advertiser and News* article, A-19, collection of Helene Knapp.

39 Sybil Stockdale diary, n.d., 161, box 11, folder 22, SBSP.

40 Ibid., 162; Stockdale and Stockdale, *In Love and War,* 377–8.

41 Emails with Karen Butler, March 28–29, 2018.

42 Sybil Stockdale diary, n.d., 162, box 11, folder 22, SBSP.

43 Jane Maury Denton Diary, November 14, 1970.

44 Sybil Stockdale, oral history interview with Steven L. Smith, June 17, 2000, 6, in Smith, "Reluctant Sorority."

45 Sybil Stockdale diary, n.d., 163, box 11, folder 22, SBSP.

46 Townley, *Defiant,* 303–4, 321.

47 Sybil Stockdale diary, n.d., 167, box 11, folder 22, SBSP.

48 Stockdale and Stockdale, *In Love and War,* 382; Sybil Stockdale diary, n.d., 175, box 11, folder 22, SBSP.

49 "A Tradition of Service," exhibit panel in *The League of Wives: Vietnam's POW/MIA Allies & Advocates* exhibit, Colorado Springs Pioneers Museum, March 23–December 9, 2018.

50 John Herzog, comments at panel discussion, Colorado Springs Pioneers Museum, opening event for *The League of Wives* exhibition, March 24, 2018.

51 Sybil Stockdale diary, n.d., 173, box 11, folder 22, SBSP; Stockdale and Stockdale, *In Love and War,* 386.

52 Dr. Henry Kissinger, in conversation with the author, October 15, 2015.

53 Sybil Stockdale diary, n.d., 172–73, box 11, folder 22, SBSP; Stockdale and Stockdale, *In Love and War,* 384–86.

Chapter Fifteen: Write Hanoi and Silent Nights

1 "Apollo 14: Shepard Back in Space . . ." NASA website, July 8, 2009, accessed May 1, 2018, www.nasa.gov/mission_pages/apollo/missions/apollo14.html.

2 Judi Clifford, in conversation with the author, September 19–20, 2016.

3 Ibid.

4 "This Week Richmond," local events guide, February 6–13, 1971, collection of Judi Clifford.

5 "1971 Mrs. Paul Galanti, Wife of Prisoner of War, Pleads for Prisoner Release," YouTube video, 1:33, from a news report broadcast by WSLS TV on February 9, 1971, uploaded by nutty.archives, September 27, 2016, accessed June 16, 2018, www.youtube.com/watch?v=id6h-ik-bQA.

6 Brian Kelly, "A Fantastic Response: Richmond Citizens Write for POWs," *Sunday Star* (Washington, DC), February 14, 1971, collection of Judi Clifford.

7 "Woman Here Uses Peace Group's Aid," article from unidentified Richmond, VA, newspaper, February 12, 1971, collection of Max Friedman.

8 Phyllis Galanti, report on Sweden trip, n.d., 2, folder 32, section 2, PEGP.

9 Judi Clifford, in conversation with the author, September 19, 2016.

10 Ibid.

11 Nick Thimmesch, "Sweden and the POWs," *Colorado Springs Sun,* June 24, 1971 (reprinted from *Newsday,* June 23, 1971), collection of Helene Knapp.

12 Judi Clifford, in conversation with the author, September 19, 2016.

13 Phyllis Galanti to Frank Sieverts, March 21, 1971, folder 31 or 34, PEGP.

14 Ibid.

15 Judi Clifford, in conversation with the author, January 5, 2016.

16 Phyllis Galanti, "Richmond Write Hanoi Delegation," n.d., folder 32, section 2, PEGP.

17 Judi Clifford, in conversation with the author, January 5, 2016.

18 Judi Clifford, in conversation with the author, September 19, 2016.

19 Judi Clifford, in conversation with the author, January 5, 2016; Phyllis Galanti, report on Sweden trip, n.d., 2, folder 32, section 2, PEGP.

20 Judi Clifford, email message to author, January 29, 2018.

21 Richard Capen, email message to author, October 11, 2016.

22 Phyllis Galanti to Ross Perot, April 6, 1971, 2, folder 31, section 2, PEGP.

23 "May 27, 1971: Sweden Announces Support to Viet Cong," *This Day in History*, History.com, accessed July 28, 2016, www.history.com/this-day-in-history/sweden-announces-support-to-viet-cong.

24 Nick Thimmesch, "Sweden and the POWs," *Colorado Springs Sun*, June 24, 1971 (reprinted from *Newsday*, June 23, 1971), collection of Helene Knapp.

25 General James D. Hughes to Honorable Robert Dole, U.S. Senate, May 19, 1971, Robert J. Dole Senate Papers, Constituent Relations 1969–1996, box 293, folder 18, REDASC.

26 Bob Dole to General James Hughes, May 21, 1971, Robert J. Dole Senate Papers, Constituent Relations 1969–1996, box 293, folder 18, REDASC.

27 Philip Galanti to Bob Dole, June 15, 1971, REDASC.

28 Sybil Stockdale diary, n.d., 176, SBSP.

29 *Colorado Springs Advertiser and News* article, August, 18, 1971, A-19, collection of Helene Knapp.

30 "Colorado Wives of U.S. Military POW's-MIA's Leave for Geneva-Paris Conventions," clipping from unidentified newspaper, May 1971, collection of Helene Knapp.

31 *Colorado Springs Advertiser and News* article, August, 18, 1971, A-19, collection of Helene Knapp.

32 Helene Knapp, in conversation with the author, March 16, 2015.

33 *Colorado Springs Advertiser and News* article, August, 18, 1971, A-19, collection of Helene Knapp; Helene Knapp to Philip Habib, July 16, 1971, collection of Helene Knapp.

34 *Rocky Mountain News* (Denver) article, June 5, 1971, collection of Helene Knapp.

35 Sybil Stockdale diary, n.d., 180, SBSP; Stockdale and Stockdale, *In Love and War,* 388–89.

36 Katharine Graham, *Personal History* (New York: Vintage, 1998), 456–58; McNamara, *In Retrospect,* 280–82; "Pentagon Papers," History .com, accessed April 1, 2018, www.history.com/topics/vietnam-war/pe ntagon-papers.

37 Jordan Moran, "Nixon and the Pentagon Papers," Miller Center, University of Virginia, accessed June 15, 2018, https://millercenter.org/the -presidency/educational-resources/first-domino-nixon-and-the-pentagon -papers.

38 Helene Knapp, in conversation with the author, 2015–2018.

39 "POW Group Head Sees Hope for End to War," *Colorado Springs Sun,* January 27, 1972, collection of Helene Knapp.

40 Sybil Stockdale diary, n.d., 180, SBSP.

41 Ibid., 181.

42 Ibid.

43 Carole Hanson Hickerson, in conversation with the author, April 11, 2018.

44 Carole Hanson Hickerson, email message to author, April 11, 2018.

45 Helene Knapp, "Helene's Memoire from the Years 1946–1978" (unpublished memoir, n.d.), 10.

46 "Christmas Seals Tell World Story of Silent Nights," *Colorado Springs Gazette-Telegraph,* December 5, 1971, collection of Helene Knapp; "30,000 from Seals Presented," *Colorado Springs Gazette-Telegraph,* January 1972, collection of Helene Knapp.

47 Stockdale and Stockdale, *In Love and War,* 390.

48 Jane Denton to Phyllis Galanti, November 23, 1971, folder 32, section 2, PEGP.

Chapter Sixteen: Is Peace at Hand?

1 Sybil Stockdale diary, n.d., 184, SBSP.

2 Ibid.

3 Sallie Stratton, "Losing Chuck, Finding Sallie: Odyssey of an MIA Wife" (unpublished memoir, 2016), chap. 4, 2.

4 Sallie Stratton, in conversation with the author, September 7, 2017.

5 Jack Anderson, "The Washington Merry Go-Round," *Washington Post,* February 3, 1972, C23, collection of Sallie Stratton.

6 Franklin, *M.I.A.,* 61; Allen, *Until the Last Man,* 53; Karen Thorsen, "A P.O.W. Wife Turns Political" *Life,* September 29, 1972, 32–42.

7 Thorsen, "P.O.W. Wife Turns Political," 32–42.

8 Kathleen Johnson Frisbie, in conversation with the author, April 20, 2018.

9 Allen, *Until the Last Man,* 53; Louise Mulligan, email message to author, April 23, 2018; Franklin, *M.I.A.,* 61; Don Hill, "Many POW Families, Changing Attitudes," *Virginian-Pilot* (Norfolk, VA), July 1971, REDASC.

10 Louise Mulligan, in conversation with the author, August 14, 2015.

11 Louise Mulligan, email message to author, April 24, 2018.

12 Phyllis Galanti, "Report on Paris Trip," February 10–19, 1972, folder 60, section 3, PEGP.

13 Ibid.

14 "Paris P.O. Swamped with POW Letters," *Richmond News Leader,* April 28, 1971, section 5, PEGP.

15 Phyllis Galanti, "Report on Paris Trip," February 10–19, 1972, 1–2, folder 60, section 3, PEGP.

16 Moreau, *Waiting Wives,* 276; Kathleen Johnson Frisbie, in conversation with the author, April 20, 2018.

17 Phyllis Galanti, "Report on Paris Trip," February 10–19, 1972, 1–2, folder 60, section 3, PEGP.

18 Phyllis Galanti to the North Vietnamese Delegate General, February 1972, folder 60, section 3, PEGP (translation mine).

19 Phyllis Galanti diary, "Report on Paris Trip," February 18, 1972, folder 60, section 3, PEGP. Photograph by Kathleen Johnson.

20 Phyllis Galanti, "Report on Paris Trip," February 10–19, 1972, 1–2, folder 60, section 3, PEGP.

21 Judi Clifford, in conversation with the author, September 16, 2016.

22 Phyllis Galanti, "Report on Paris Trip," February 10–19, 1972, 3, folder 60, section 3, PEGP.

23 Ibid., 4.

24 National Week of Concern for Americans Who Are Prisoners of War or Missing in Action, proclamation 4115, National Security Council, March 26–April 1, 1972.

25 Sybil Stockdale diary, n.d., 185, SBSP.

26 Ibid.

27 Stratton, "Losing Chuck," chaps. 4, 5.

28 Sybil Stockdale diary, n.d., 186, SBSP.

29 "POW Wife Accuses Republicans of False Claims," news release, Virginia Beach, VA, n.d., JJDPC; Ethel A. Steadman, "Fund-Raising Letter: POW's Wife Cites False Nixon Claims," *Virginian-Pilot* (Norfolk, VA), n.d.

30 Steadman, "Fund-Raising Letter."

31 Sybil Stockdale diary, n.d., 185–86, SBSP.

32 Stratton, "Losing Chuck," chaps. 4, 7.

33 Admiral Elmo Zumwalt, cassette tape, labeled tape 2, side A, parts 1–2, JJDPC.

34 Sybil Stockdale diary, n.d., 186–87, SBSP.

35 Wiest and McNab, *Illustrated History,* 208.

36 Louise Mulligan, email message to author, April 24, 2018.

37 Dr. Roger Shields, in conversation with the author, April 23, 2018.

38 Phyllis Galanti, index card speech, n.d., card 7, PPGPC; Phyllis Galanti to "Dear Delegate," June 14, 1972, PPGPC.

39 Stratton, "Losing Chuck," chaps. 4, 9.

40 Sybil Stockdale diary, n.d., 186, SBSP.

41 Press release, Office of the White House Press Secretary, May 15, 1972, 2.

42 Ibid., 4; Phyllis Galanti to Richard Nixon, May 19, 1972, folder 18, section 1, PEGP.

43 Melissa B. Robinson and Maureen Dunn, *The Search for Canasta 404: Love, Loss and the POW/MIA Movement* (Boston: Northeastern University Press, 2006), 127–28.

44 Press release, Office of the White House Press Secretary, May 15, 1972, 6; Sybil Stockdale diary, n.d., 190, box 11, folder 22, SBSP.

45 Sybil Stockdale diary, n.d., 189, SBSP.

46 Ibid.

47 Henry Mark Holzer and Erika Holzer, *Aid and Comfort: Jane Fonda in North Vietnam* (Jefferson, NC: McFarland, 1990), 59–76.

48 Sybil Stockdale diary, n.d., 210, SBSP.

49 Henry Kissinger, *Ending the Vietnam War: A History of America's Involvement in and Extrication from the Vietnam War* (New York: Simon & Schuster, 2003), 375–77.

50 National League of Families convention minutes, October 1972, Cora Weiss Papers (DG 222), SCPC.

51 Kissinger, *Ending the Vietnam War,* 340–45.

52 National League of Families board election document, October 1972, Cora Weiss Papers (DG 222), SCPC.

53 National League of Families convention minutes, October 1972, folder 47, section 3, PEGP; National League of Families convention minutes, October 14–16, 1972, collection of Sallie Stratton.

54 Helene Knapp, "Helene's Memoire from the Years 1946–1978" (unpublished memoir, 1978), 9; Helene Knapp to author, May 30, 2019.

55 Kissinger, *Ending the Vietnam War,* 375.

56 Sybil Stockdale diary, n.d., 211, SBSP.

57 Stratton, "Losing Chuck," chap. 4, 31–32.

58 National League of Families voter appeal, 1972, PPGPC.

59 Van Atta, *With Honor,* 422.

60 Sybil Stockdale diary, n.d., 211–12, SBSP.

61 Ward and Burns, *Vietnam War,* 511.

62 John McCain, *Faith of My Fathers,* 337.

63 Jack Taylor, "Risner, POW Leader, Says Protestors Prolonged War," *Washington Post,* 1973 (specific date unknown), collection of Max Friedman.

64 Dr. Henry Kissinger, in conversation with the author, October 15, 2015.

Chapter Seventeen: "We Chose to Be Together"

1 Sybil Stockdale diary, n.d., 213, SBSP.

2 Ibid.

3 Louise Mulligan to Helene Knapp and Phyllis Galanti, January 9, 1973, folder 49, section 3, PEGP.

4 Ward and Burns, *Vietnam War,* 512

5 Richard M. Nixon, "Address to the Nation Announcing Conclusion of an Agreement on Ending the War and Restoring Peace in Vietnam," January 23, 1973, American Presidency Project, accessed August 6, 2018, www.presidency.ucsb.edu/ws/?pid=3808.

6 Donald P. Baker, "We Chose to Be Together," *Washington Post,* folder 118, section 4, PEGP.

7 Helene Knapp, email message to author, May 8, 2018.

8 Sybil Stockdale diary, n.d., 216, SBSP.

9 Phyllis Galanti diary, January 24, 1973, PPGPC.

10 Phyllis Galanti, gift list from Paul's return home, PPGPC.

11 Loudon Wainwright, "When Johnny Comes Marching Home Again— or Doesn't," *Life,* November 10, 1972, 37.

12 Louise Mulligan, email message to author, May 4, 2018.

13 Wainwright, "When Johnny Comes," 37.

14 Ibid.

15 Andrea Rander, email to the author, August 8, 2018.

16 Kathleen Johnson Frisbie, in conversation with the author, October 3, 2017.

17 Patsy Crayton and Karen Butler, in conversation with the author, January, 17, 2015; Stockdale and Stockdale, *In Love and War,* 439; "Home At Last!" *Newsweek,* February 26, 1973, folder 34, section 2, PEGP.

18 Jane Griffin, "POW Husband Due Back. For Mrs Galanti: Excitement," unidentified publication, n.d., folder 34, section 2, PEGP.

19 G. Warren Nutter, Assistant Secretary of Defense, "When They Return: Plans for PW/MIA Repatriation Detailed," May 11, 1972, 3, collection of Debby Burns Henry.

20 Wainwright, "When Johnny Comes," 34.

21 Davis, *Long Road Home,* 491.

22 Wainwright, "When Johnny Comes," 34.

23 Van Atta, *With Honor,* 235.

24 Dr. Roger Shields, email message to author, May 1, 2018.

25 Davis, *Long Road Home,* 494.

26 Rochester and Kiley, *Honor Bound,* 587–89.

27 Phyllis E. Galanti, Chairman of the Board, National League of Families (and wife of POW Paul E. Galanti), to Roger Shields, Assistant to the Assistant Secretary of Defense, Washington, DC, December 20, 1972, record group 59, National Archives at College Park, College Park, MD.

28 Davis, *Long Road Home,* 493.

29 Alvin Townley, "Jerry Denton: POW, Admiral, Senator, Hero," *USA Today,* March 29, 2014; Denton, *When Hell Was in Session,* 235.

30 Davis, *Long Road Home,* 528–29.

31 *Jeremiah,* directed by Mark Fastoso (Birmingham: Alabama Public Television, 2015).

32 Denton, *When Hell Was in Session,* 236–37.

33 Griffin, "POW Husband Due Back."

34 "Home At Last!" *Newsweek,* February 26, 1973, folder 34, section 2, PEGP; various newspaper clippings, collection of Judi Clifford.

35 "The Shift to Freedom Brings Happiest Week," *Virginian-Pilot* (Norfolk, VA), February 1, 1973, Merriann Boroughs scrapbook, Boroughs family private collection.

36 Ibid.

37 "Mr. POW" award, Boroughs family private collection, on loan to *League of Wives* exhibit, REDASC.

38 Jim Mulligan to Merriann Boroughs, February 17, 1973, Merriann Boroughs scrapbook, Boroughs family private collection.

39 Jim Stockdale to Merriann Boroughs, March 6, 1973, Merriann Boroughs scrapbook, Boroughs family private collection.

40 Andrea Rander, in conversation with the author, May 8, 2018.

41 Townley, *Defiant,* 348–49.

42 Stockdale and Stockdale, *In Love and War,* 440–41.

43 Ibid., 441–43.

44 David Brown, "POW Aftereffects in McCain Unlikely," *Washington Post,* May 23, 2008.

45 David J. Morris, *The Evil Hours* (New York: Houghton Mifflin Harcourt, 2015), 48–49.

46 Ibid., 49.

47 Ibid.

48 Andrea Rander, email messages to author, August 3 and 8, 2018.

49 Morris, *Evil Hours,* 49.

50 Helene Knapp, in conversation with the author, March 18, 2015.

51 Ibid.

52 *Hearing on American Prisoners of War and Missing in Action in Southeast Asia, 1973, before the House Subcommittee on National Security Policy*

and Scientific Developments, Committee on Foreign Affairs, 93rd Cong., May 23, 30, and 31, 1973, 33, collection of Helene Knapp.

53 Ibid, 37, collection of Helene Knapp.

54 Kathleen Johnson Frisbie, in conversation with the author, March 1, 2018.

55 Andrea Rander, email message to author, August 8, 2018.

56 Memorandum of conversation between President Nixon and Dr. Roger E. Shields, April 11, 1973, National Security Adviser, Memoranda of Conversations, Gerald R. Ford Presidential Library, www .fordlibrarymuseum.gov/library/dmemcons.asp.

57 Graham, *Personal History,* 503–4.

58 Thomas, *Being Nixon,* 486.

59 Nixon, *Memoirs,* 867.

60 Various POW wives and spouses, in conversation with the author, 2015–2018.

61 Wiest and McNab, *Illustrated History,* 233.

62 Ibid., 236.

63 Karnow, *Vietnam,* 665–69; Burns and C. Ward, *Vietnam,* 555–562.

64 "Vietnam War Accounting," Department of Defense POW/MIA Accounting Agency, accessed May 10, 2018, www.dpaa.mil/Our-Missing /Vietnam-War.

65 James Rosenthal, "The Myth of the Lost POWs," *The New Republic,* July 1, 1985, accessed April 23, 2018.

66 Helene Knapp, in conversation with the author, March 15, 2015; Kathleen Johnson Frisbie, in conversation with the author, May 15, 2018; Bruce Johnson Jr., email message to author, May 15, 2018.

67 Vietnam War POW/MIA List, Defense POW/MIA Accounting Agency, accessed May 10, 2018, www.dpaa.mil/Our-Missing/Vietnam -War/Vietnam-War-POW-MIA-List.

68 Helene Knapp, in conversation with the author, March 18, 2015; Helene Knapp to the author, May 30, 2019.

69 Kathleen Johnson Frisbie, in conversation with the author, October 3, 2017.

Chapter Eighteen: To the First Ladies of America!

1 Ross H. Perot, interview with the author, March 15, 2015.

2 Senator John McCain, in conversation with the author, March 10, 2016.

3 H. Ross Perot, in conversation with the author, March 15, 2015.

4 Ibid.

5 Carole Hanson Hickerson, email message to author, April 11, 2018.

6 Ibid.

7 Carole Hanson Hickerson, in conversation with the author, July 10, 2015.

8 Carole Hanson Hickerson, email message to author, May 12, 2018.

9 "President Nixon's Toast to Returned Prisoners of the Vietnam War, May 24, 1973," C-SPAN, accessed August 6, 2018, www.c-span.org/video/?313093-1/president-nixons-toast-returned-prisoners-vietnam-war.

10 Paul Galanti, in conversation with the author, December 15, 2016.

11 Ken Khachigian, in conversation with the author, March 12, 2017.

12 Dr. Roger Shields, in conversation with the author, April 23, 2018.

13 "President Nixon's Toast to Returned Prisoners," C-SPAN; Senator John McCain, in conversation with the author, March 10, 2016.

14 Dr. Henry Kissinger, in conversation with the author, October 15, 2015.

15 "Revised Schedule of Events for Navy Returnees and Their Guests," U.S. Department of State, May 23–25, 1973, 4, PPGPC.

16 White House Gala menu, White House Social Secretary, collection of Ted Sienicki.

17 Nixon Gala footage, Nixon Library and Archive.

18 Ken Khachigian, in conversation with the author, March 3, 2017.

19 Ellen Robertson and Jeremy Slayton, "Jane Maury Denton Dies at 81," *Richmond Times-Dispatch,* December 3, 2007.

20 Phyllis Galanti, index card speech, n.d., card 12, PPGPC.

21 Various papers, PPGPC.

22 Ross Mackenzie, eulogy at Phyllis Galanti Memorial Service, First Presbyterian Church, Richmond, VA, April 29, 2014.

23 Andrea Rander, email to the author, August 8, 2018.

24 Andrea Rander, in conversation with the author, June 29, 2018.

25 Patricia Sullivan, "Donald J. Rander Dies; Was POW in Vietnam for 5 Years," *Washington Post,* May 1, 2005.

26 Andrea Rander, in conversation with the author, May 7, 2018.

27 Cheryl J. Cease, "The Mulligans: Life After Hanoi," *Tidewater Virginian: Business Magazine of Southeastern Virginia,* August 1986, 45.

28 Louise Mulligan, email message to author, May 14, 2018.

29 Lynn Boroughs Amwake, in conversation with the author, February 27, 2017; Merriann Boroughs Lynch, in conversation with the author, July 20, 2017.

30 Stockdale and Stockdale, *In Love and War,* 448.

31 Sybil Stockdale, "Reflections of a POW Wife" speech, JSSP.

Epilogue: "That Other Stockdale Naval Hero(ine)"

1 Stockdale and Stockdale, *In Love and War,* 451.

2 "Sybil Bailey Stockdale," obituary, *Coronado Eagle & Journal,* October 14, 2015.

3 Jim, Taylor, and Sid Stockdale, eulogies at Sybil Bailey Stockdale memorial service, U.S. Naval Academy, Annapolis, MD, November 6, 2015.

4 Stockdale and Stockdale, *In Love and War,* 491.
5 Jeremiah Denton III, Q&A with unidentified interviewer, no. 2-101, collection of Madeleine Denton Doak.
6 Cease, "The Mulligans," 42.
7 Senator John McCain, in conversation with the author, March 10, 2016.
8 Richard Capen, in conversation with the author, March 4, 2016.
9 Sybil Stockdale, oral history interview with Steven L. Smith, n.d., 8, in Smith, "Reluctant Sorority."
10 Allen, *Until the Last Man,* 29.

SELECTED BIBLIOGRAPHY

Archives and Special Collections
Note: The abbreviations used in the notes for archival sources, both public and private, are listed below.

JJDPC   Jane and Jeremiah Denton family private collection
JSSP   James and Sybil Stockdale Papers, Collection of the Coronado Historical Association, Coronado, CA
JSSPC   James and Sybil Stockdale family private collection
PEGP   Phyllis Eason Galanti Papers, Virginia Museum of History and Culture, Richmond, VA
PPGPC   Paul and Phyllis Galanti family private collection
REDASC   Robert and Elizabeth Dole Archive and Special Collections, Dole Institute of Politics, University of Kansas, Lawrence, KS
SBSP   Sybil Bailey Stockdale Papers, Hoover Institution Archives, Stanford, CA
SCPC   Swarthmore College Peace Collection, Swarthmore, PA

Author Interviews
Amwake, Lynn Boroughs. February 27, 2017.
Boroughs, Tom. December 4, 2016.
Butler, Karen. January 17, 2015, and January 27, 2017.
Capen, Richard. January 18 and March 4, 2016; March 30, 2017.
Clifford, Judi. January 5 and September 16, 19, and 20, 2016; various dates, May 2016–December 2017.

Crayton, Patsy. January 17, 2015; July 22, 2016; January 27, 2017; and February 16, 2018.

Dennison, Sandy. March 9, 2016.

Denton, Jeremiah, III. May 7 and 8, 2016.

Dole, Senator Bob. October 13, 2016.

Estocin, Marie. February 22, 2018.

Frisbie, Kathleen Johnson. October 3, 2017; March 1, 18, and 21, April 20, and May 15, 2018.

Galanti, Paul. December 15, 2016; various dates, May 2016–December 2017.

Gellman, Dr. Irwin. October 17, 2017.

Halyburton, Marty. May 7, 2015.

Halyburton, Porter. May 7, 2015.

Henry, Debby Burns. January 16 and May 2, 2016

Hickerson, Carole Hanson. July 10, 2015, and April 11, 2018.

Johnson, Bruce. April 5, 2018

Khachigian, Ken. March 3 and 12, 2017.

Kissinger, Dr. Henry. October 15, 2015.

Knapp, Helene. March 15–18, 2015; various dates, 2015–2018.

Leepson, Marc. June 15, 2018; various dates, 2016–2018.

Lynch, Bernard. July 20, 2017.

Lynch, Merriann Boroughs. February 8 and July 20, 2017.

Mackenzie, Ginni. September 10, 2016.

Mackenzie, Ross. September 10, 2016.

Martin, Sherry. January 30, 2016.

McCain, Senator John. March 10, 2016.

McDaniel, Dorothy. January 16 and 18, 2018.

McDaniel, Red. January 16, 2018.

McElhanon, Sandy. March 10, 2018.

Mulligan, Louise. August 14, 2015.

Nichter, Dr. Luke. April 25, 2018.

Ochberg, Dr. Frank. February 28, 2017.

Perot, H. Ross. March 15, 2015.

Pollard, Joan. April 24, 2018.

Rander, Andrea. May 7 and 8 and June 29, 2018.

Robertson, Jenny Connell. January 16, 2016.

Shields, Dr. Roger. April 23, 2018.

Sienicki, Ted. December 18, 2015.

Stockdale, Sid. June 8 and 17, 2015.

Stratton, Sallie. September 7, 2017.

Tschudy, Bill. April 11, 2017.

Tschudy, Janie. December 17, 2015, and March 21, 2017.

Twinem, Pat. June 6 and 7, 2017.

Woolfolk, Bebe. November 27, 2015.

Selected Articles

A, Dr. Ganesh, and Dr. Catherine Joseph. "Personality Studies in Aircrew: An Overview." *Indian Journal of Aerospace Medicine* 49, no. 1 (2005).

Cease, Cheryl J. "The Mulligans: Life After Hanoi." *Tidewater Virginian: Business Magazine of Southeastern Virginia,* August 1986.

Collins, Denis. "The Deprogramming of a POW." *Washington Post,* August 31, 1981.

Denton, James S. "Editor's Introduction: In Hanoi, Going Forward and Backward." World Affairs Institute, January/February 2014. http://worldaffairsjournal.org/article/editor's-introduction-hanoi-going-forward-and-backward.

Goodwin, Gerald F. "Black and White in Vietnam." *New York Times,* July 18, 2017.

Luti, William J. "Did Fake News Lose the Vietnam War?" *Wall Street Journal,* January 20, 2018.

Moran, Jordan. "Nixon and the Pentagon Papers." Miller Center, University of Virginia. https://millercenter.org/the-presidency/educational-resources/first-domino-nixon-and-the-pentagon-papers.

Peterson, Captain Gordon I., USN (Ret.), and David C. Taylor. "A Shield and a Sword: Intelligence Support to Communications with US POWs in Vietnam." *Studies in Intelligence* 60, no. 1 (March 2016).

Powledchs, Fred. "H. Perot Pays His Dues." *New York Times,* February 28, 1971.

Riley, Jason L. "Martin Luther King: 'We Can't Keep Blaming the White Man.'" *Wall Street Journal,* April 4, 2018.

Stockdale, Jim, II. "My Father, the Spy in the Hanoi Hilton." *Daily Beast,* April 27, 2015. www.thedailybeast.com/my-father-the-spy-in-the-hanoi-hilton.

Thorsen, Karen. "A P.O.W. Wife Turns Political." *Life,* September 29, 1972.

Wainwright, Loudon. "When Johnny Comes Marching Home Again—or Doesn't." *Life,* November 10, 1972.

Weller, Sheila. "It Happened in 1967." *Vanity Fair,* March 2017.

Websites

BlackPast.org. http://www.blackpast.org.

Defense POW/MIA Accounting Agency. www.dpaa.mil.

History.com. "Operation Rolling Thunder." www.history.com/topics/vietnam-war/operation-rolling-thunder.

Richard M. Nixon Presidential Library and Museum. www.nixonlibrary.gov.

Selective Service System. "About the Agency." www.sss.gov/About/History-And-Records/Induction-Statistics.

Senator Bob Dole Official Website. www.bobdole.org.

Vietnam Veterans Memorial Wall Page/The Wall USA. www.thewall-usa
.com.

Film, Video, and Television Programs
"1971 Mrs. Paul Galanti, Wife of Prisoner of War, Pleads for Prisoner Release." YouTube video, 1:33, from a news report broadcast by WSLS TV
on February 9, 1971. Uploaded by nutty.archives, September 27, 2016.
www.youtube.com/watch?v=id6h-ik-bQA
American Experience. "Return with Honor." PBS, 2000. www.pbs.org/wgbh
/amex/honor/filmmore/ps-geneva.html (webpage discontinued).
Fastoso, Mark, dir. *Jeremiah.* Birmingham: Alabama Public Television, 2015,
57 mins.

Unpublished Works
Boroughs, Merriann. Scrapbook. February–March 1973. Boroughs family
private collection.
Capen, Richard. Untitled autobiography, n.d. Collection of Richard Capen.
Denton, Jeremiah, III. Unpublished memoir, 2017. Collection of Jeremiah
Denton III.
Knapp, Helene. "Helene's Memoire from the Years 1946–1978." Unpub-
lished memoir, 1978.
Mackenzie, Ross. Retirement scrapbook. December 11, 2006.
Smith, Steven L. "The Reluctant Sorority: Stories of American Wives of Pris-
oners of War and Missing in Action, 1965–1973; Lessons in Exercising
Leadership in the Absence of Power." PhD diss., University of San Diego,
April 2006.
Stratton, Sallie. "Losing Chuck, Finding Sallie: Odyssey of an MIA Wife."
Unpublished memoir, 2016.

Books
Abramson, Rudy. *Spanning the Century: The Life of W. Averell Harriman,
1891–1986.* New York: William Morrow, 1992.
Allen, Michael J. *Until the Last Man Comes Home: POWs, MIAs and the Un-
ending Vietnam War.* Chapel Hill: University of North Carolina Press,
2009.
Berrigan, Daniel. *Night Flight to Hanoi: War Diary with 11 Poems.* New York:
Harper & Row, 1968.
Clinton, James W. *The Loyal Opposition.* Niwot: University Press of Colo-
rado, 1995.
Collins, Gail. *When Everything Changed: The Amazing Journey of American
Women from 1960 to the Present.* New York: Little, Brown, 2009.
Cronkite, Walter. *A Reporter's Life.* New York: Knopf, 1996.

Davis, Vernon E. *The Long Road Home: U.S. Prisoner of War Policy and Planning in Southeast Asia*. Washington, DC: Historical Office of the Office of the Secretary of Defense, 2000.

Denton, Jeremiah A., Jr., with Ed Brandt. *When Hell Was in Session*. Clover, SC: Commission Press, 1976.

Dole, Bob. *One Soldier's Story: A Memoir*. New York: Harper, 2005.

Farrell, John A. *Richard Nixon: The Life*. New York: Doubleday, 2017.

Ferguson, Niall. *Kissinger, 1923–1968: The Idealist*. New York: Penguin Press, 2015.

Franklin, H. Bruce. *M.I.A., or Mythmaking in America*. Brooklyn: Lawrence Hill Books, 1992.

Grubb, Evelyn, and Carol Jose. *You Are Not Forgotten*. St. Petersburg, FL: Vandamere Press, 2008.

Halberstam, David. *The Best and the Brightest*. New York: Random House, 1992.

Howes, Craig. *Voices of the Vietnam POWs: Witnesses to Their Flight*. New York: Oxford University Press, 1993.

Karnow, Stanley. *Vietnam: A History—The First Complete Account of Vietnam at War*. New York: Penguin, 1984.

Kissinger, Henry. *Ending the Vietnam War: A History of America's Involvement in and Extrication from the Vietnam War*. New York: Simon & Schuster, 2003.

McCain, John, with Mark Salter. *Faith of My Fathers*. New York: Random House, 1999.

McGovern, James R. *Black Eagle*. Tuscaloosa: University of Alabama Press, 1985.

McMaster, H. R. *Dereliction of Duty: Lyndon Johnson, Robert McNamara, the Joint Chiefs of Staff, and the Lies That Led to Vietnam*. New York: Harper Perennial, 1997.

Moreau, Donna. *Waiting Wives: The Story of Schilling Manor, Home Front to the Vietnam War*. New York: Atria, 2005.

Morris, David J. *The Evil Hours*. New York: Houghton Mifflin Harcourt, 2015.

Nixon, Richard. *The Memoirs of Richard Nixon*. New York: Grosset & Dunlap, 1978.

Olson, Lynne. *Citizens of London: The Americans Who Stood with Britain in Its Darkest, Finest Hour*. New York: Random House, 2010.

Powell, S. Steven. *Covert Cadre: Inside the Institute for Policy Studies*. Ottawa, IL: Green Hill, 1988.

Pye, Anne Briscoe, and Nancy Shea. *The Navy Wife*. New York: Harper & Row, 1965.

Rochester, Stuart I., and Frederick Kiley. *Honor Bound: The History of*

American Prisoners of War in Southeast Asia, 1961–1973. Washington, DC: Historical Office of the Office of the Secretary of Defense, 1998.

Stockdale, Jim and Sybil. *In Love and War: The Story of a Family's Ordeal and Sacrifice During the Vietnam Year*. Annapolis, MD: Naval Institute Press, 1990.

Swerdlow, Amy. *Women Strike for Peace: Traditional Motherhood and Radical Politics in the 1960s*. Chicago: University of Chicago Press, 1993.

Swift, Will. *Pat and Dick: The Nixons, an Intimate Portrait of a Marriage*. New York: Simon & Schuster, 2014.

Thomas, Evan. *Being Nixon: A Man Divided*. New York: Random House, 2015.

Tierney, Helen, ed. *Women's Studies Encyclopedia*. Santa Barbara, CA: Greenwood Press, 2002.

Townley, Alvin. *Defiant: The POWs Who Endured Vietnam's Most Infamous Prison, the Women Who Fought for Them, and the One Who Never Returned*. New York: Thomas Dunne, 2014.

Updegrove, Mark K. *Indomitable Will: LBJ in the Presidency*. New York: Skyhorse, 2012.

Van Atta, Dale. *With Honor: Melvin Laird in War, Peace, and Politics*. Madison: University of Wisconsin Press, 2008.

Ward, Geoffrey C., and Ken Burns. *The Vietnam War: An Intimate History*. New York: Knopf, 2017.

INDEX

ABOUT THE LEAGUE OF WIVES EXHIBIT

In her role as the 2017 Dole Archives Curatorial Fellow, Heath Hardage Lee conceived of and curated a museum exhibit titled *The League of Wives. Vietnam's POW/MIA Allies & Advocates,* based on her research for *The League of Wives: The Untold Story of the Women Who Took On the U.S. Government to Bring Their Husbands Home from Vietnam.* The Dole Institute's assistant director and senior archivist, Audrey McKanna Coleman, led the exhibit team, which also included assistant curator Minda Stockdale and filmmaker Kristine Bartley. The exhibit premiered at the Robert and Elizabeth Dole Institute of Politics, University of Kansas, on May 7, 2017, and ran through December 31 of that year.

Further venues include but are not limited to:

Colorado Springs Pioneers Museum, Colorado Springs, Colorado, March 24–December 29, 2018

Virginia Museum of History and Culture, Richmond, Virginia, March 2, 2019–September 3, 2019

Coronado Historical Association, Coronado, California, October 1, 2019–March 31, 2020

The Richard Nixon Presidential Library and Museum (RNPLM): June 1, 2020–August 31, 2020